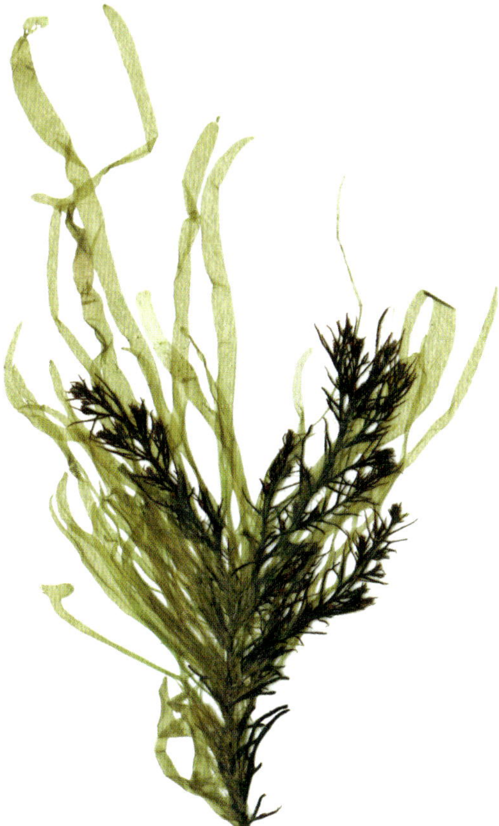

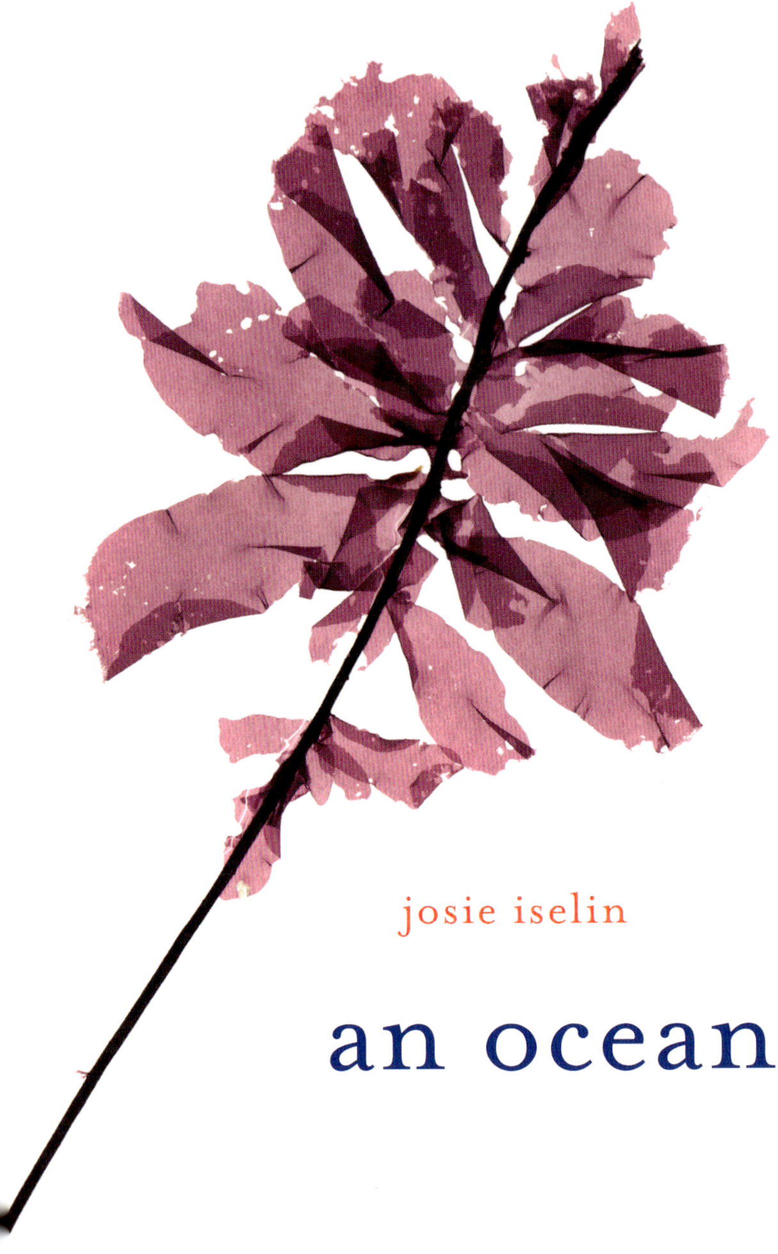

josie iselin

an ocean garden

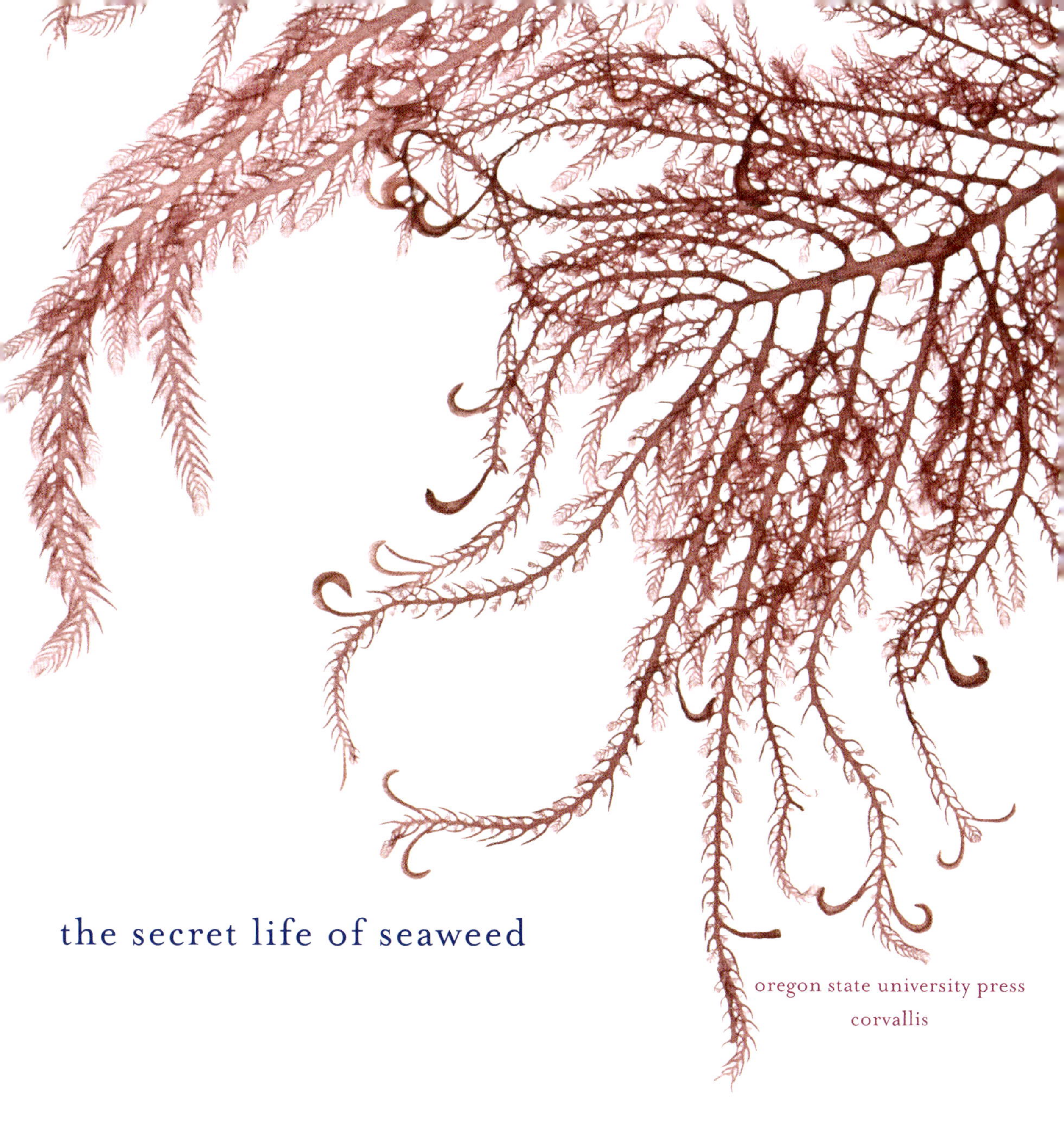

the secret life of seaweed

oregon state university press
corvallis

The Phycological Society of America (www. psaalgae.org) and the John and Shirley Byrne Fund for Books on Nature and the Environment provided generous support that helped make publication of this book possible.

First edition published 2014.
Oregon State University Press edition 2023.
Printed in the United States of America

Library of Congress Cataloging-in-Publication Data
Names: Iselin, Josie, author.
Title: An ocean garden : the secret life of seaweed / Josie Iselin.
Description: First edition. | Corvallis : Oregon State University Press, 2023. | Includes bibliographical references and index.
Identifiers: LCCN 2023003749 | ISBN 9780870712395 (trade paperback) | ISBN 9780870712401 (ebook)
Subjects: LCSH: Marine algae—California—Pictorial works. | Marine algae—Maine—Pictorial works.
Classification: LCC QK571.5.C2 I84 2023 | DDC 579.8/809741—dc23/eng/20230323
LC record available at https://lccn.loc.gov/2023003749

♾ This paper meets the requirements of ANSI/NISO Z39.48-1992 (Permanence of Paper).

Oregon State University
OSU Press

Oregon State University Press
121 The Valley Library
Corvallis OR 97331
www.osupress.oregonstate.edu

Book Design: Josie Iselin

Oregon State University Press in Corvallis, Oregon, is located within the traditional homelands of the Mary's River or Ampinefu Band of Kalapuya. Following the Willamette Valley Treaty of 1855, Kalapuya people were forcibly removed to reservations in Western Oregon. Today, living descendants of these people are a part of the Confederated Tribes of Grand Ronde Community of Oregon (grandronde.org) and the Confederated Tribes of the Siletz Indians (ctsi.nsn.us).

cover:
Ocean's Edge #2
Josie Iselin, 2020

page 1:
Ulva linza on *Odonthalia floccosa*
Pillar Point, Moss Beach, CA
May 2, 1977
Collection: California Academy of Sciences
San Francisco, CA

page 2:
Smithora naiadum
Outlet Cove, Bodega Head, CA
July 5, 2008

page 3:
Bonnemaisonia californica
Pacific Grove, CA
c. 1880
Collection: University Herbarium
UC Berkeley, CA

opposite:
Egregia menziesii
Stone Beach, San Mateo, CA
February 25, 2010

This book is dedicated to
KATHY ANN MILLER,
who finds so much joy among the weeds.

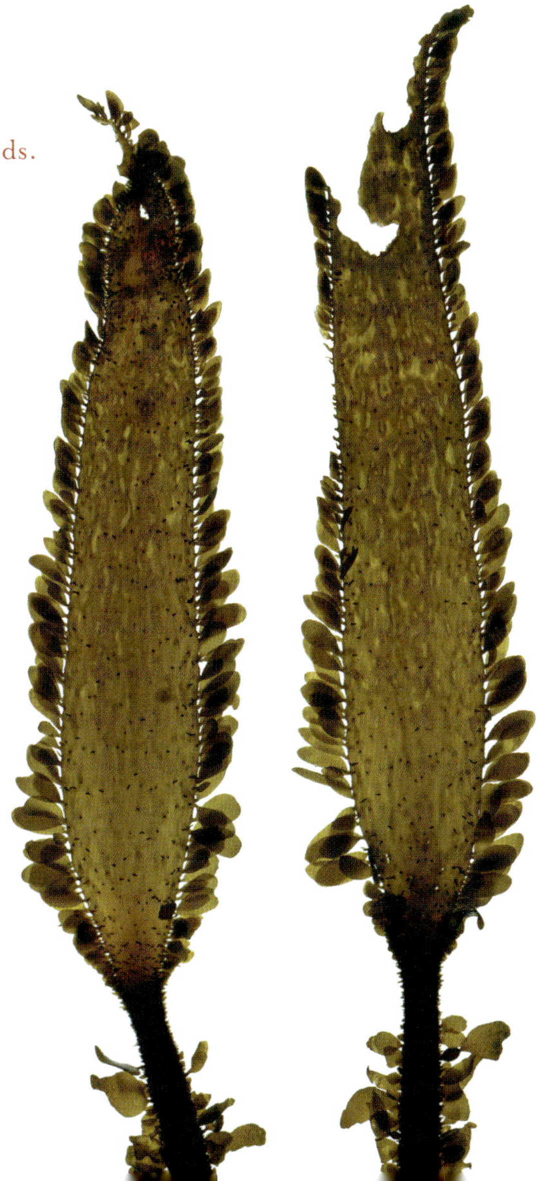

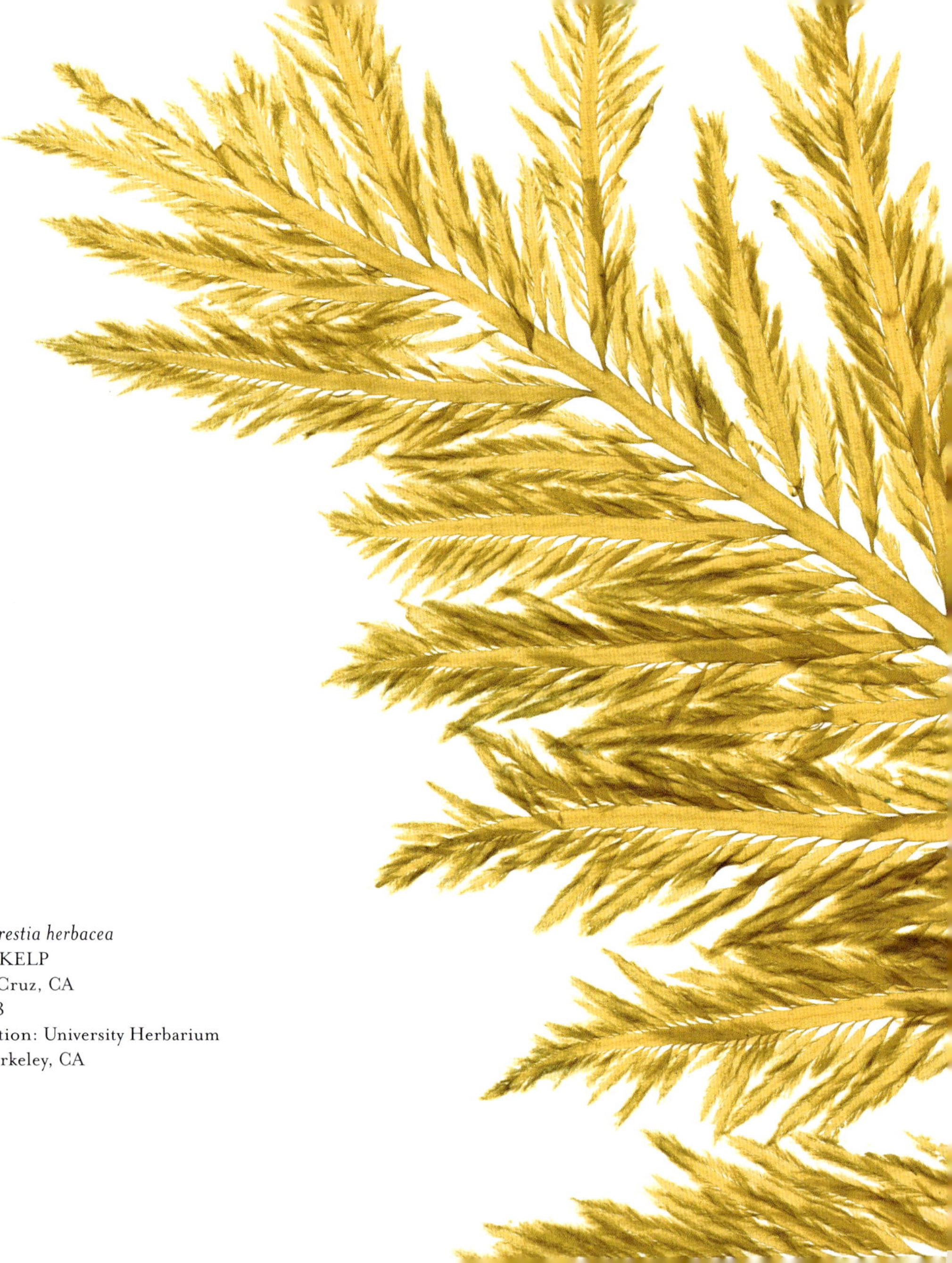

Desmarestia herbacea
ACID KELP
Santa Cruz, CA
c. 1898
Collection: University Herbarium
UC Berkeley, CA

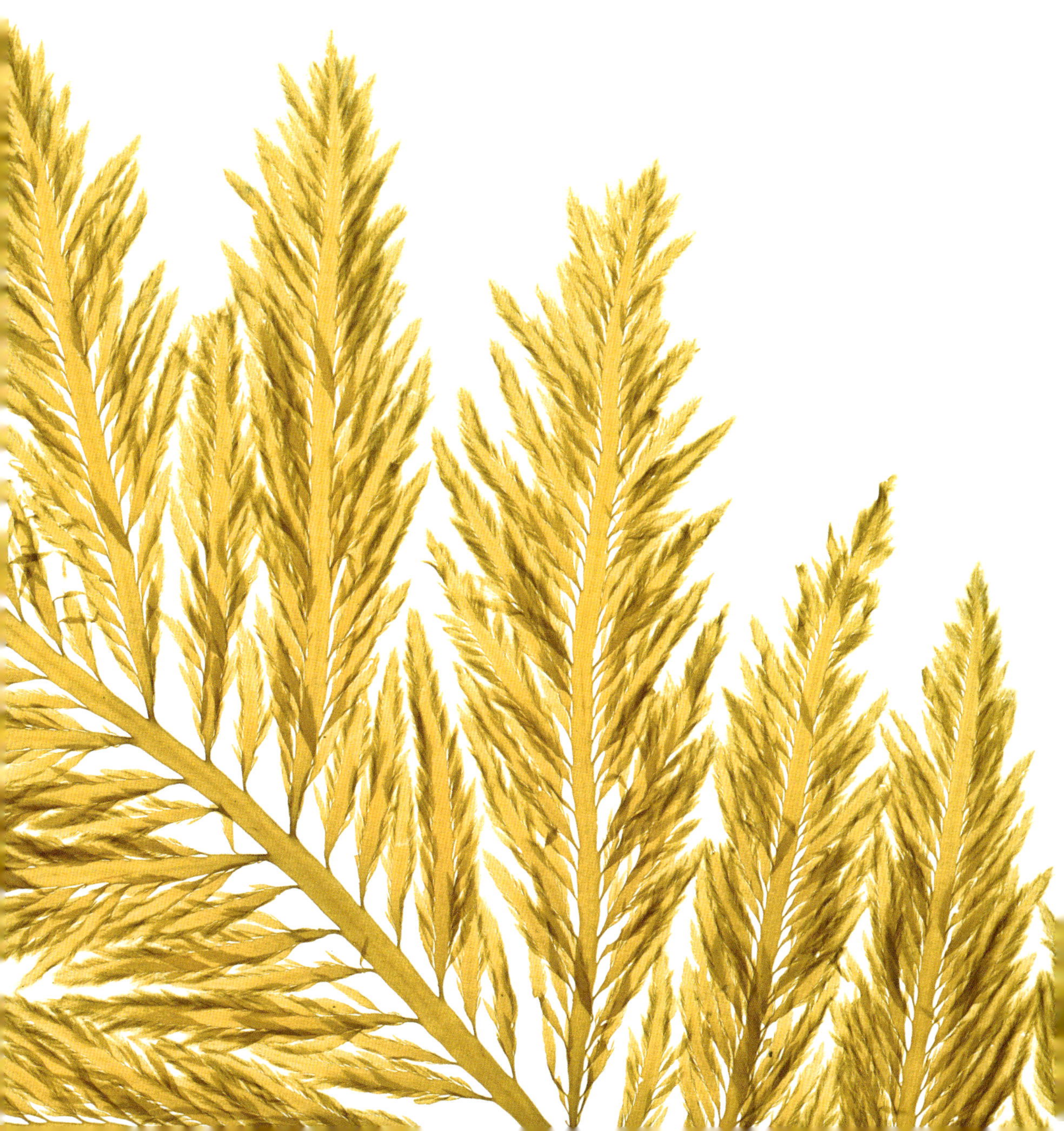

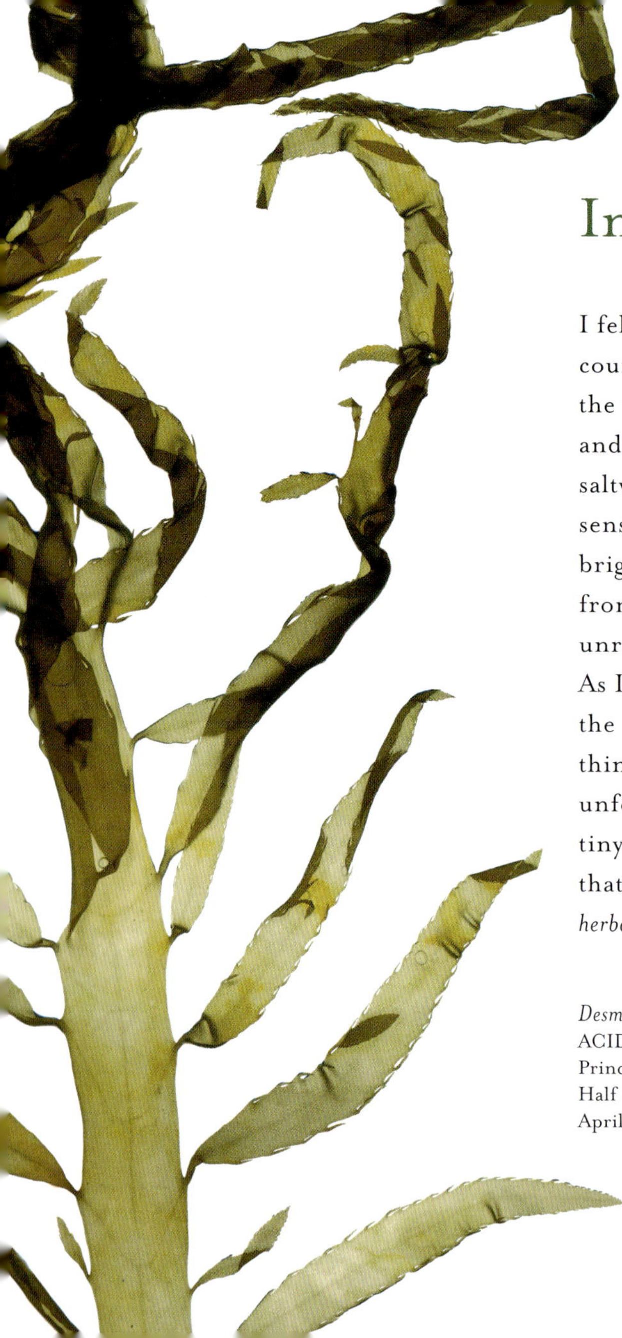

Introduction

I fell in love with seaweed at the kitchen counter. I had returned with a sack full from the windswept beach at Princeton-by-the-Sea, and as I dropped each specimen into a tub of saltwater, its form and color and translucent sensuality awakened. Pale pinks mingled with bright greens and yellow oranges. Rounded fronds, bumpy textures, and slender tendrils unraveled. I focused on one green algal mass. As I teased apart the pale fronds, I noticed the delicate connections between the razor-thin blades were surprisingly strong, and as I unfolded them, one by one, I could see their tiny serrated edges. I was discovering a secret that few have seen, the secret of *Desmarestia herbacea*, or acid kelp.

Desmarestia herbacea
ACID KELP
Princeton-by-the-Sea,
Half Moon Bay, CA
April 21, 2010

That was over ten years ago. I am still falling in love with seaweed, over and over again. How can it be helped? In 2009, I held a scrap of red algae up to the sky and was smitten by color and form and, using my flatbed scanner and learning from the master algal taxonomist, Kathy Ann Miller, made this book, originally published in 2014. In 2016, I discovered the visual artistry of the historical record—magnificent lithographs accompanying the naming and describing of seaweeds. In 2018, to honor Anna Atkins, I began making cyanotypes of my seaweed specimens, using the sunlight of my backyard to make their white algal shadows on the deep Prussian blue ground. In 2019, *The Curious World of Seaweed* was published, and in 2020, I snorkeled for the first time in the bull kelp forest of the northern California coast. The two-inch difference from above the waterline to below reveals the ocean world of filtered sunlight and the gestural motion of the seaweeds and kelps. I was enraptured!

But I come back again and again to the simple portraits and names of the seaweeds in this book. The explanations of algal color and architecture, seaweed community and life cycles are as important to understand and honor as ever. And interest is burgeoning!

In 1955 Rachel Carson published *The Edge of the Sea*, a lyrical and intimate prose portrait of the intertidal world—that universe of life that resides just below and between the tides. In describing the complexities of existence wherein the basic fabric of life, the ocean itself, is wrenched away and comes flooding back twice a day, her intense love and care for the seashore is palpable in every word. The rockweeds and kelps are an

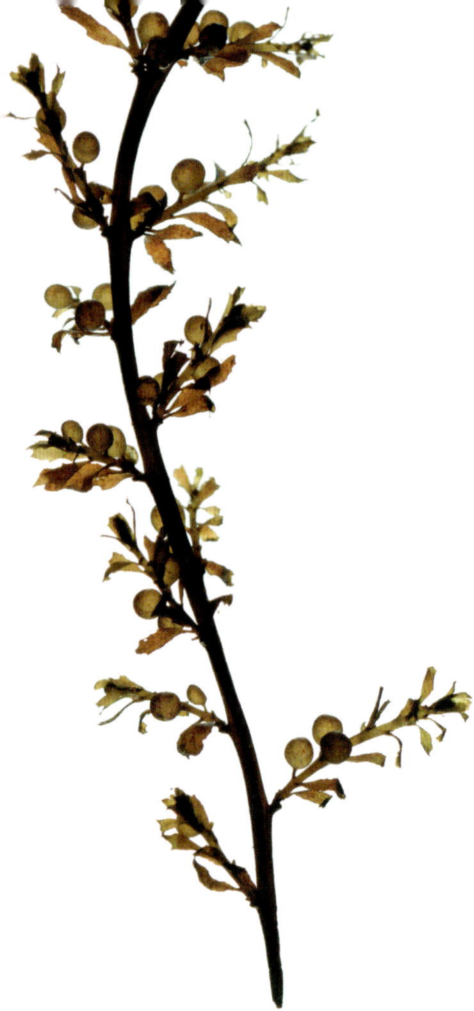

Sargassum muticum
Crissy Field, San Francisco, CA
April 26, 2012

integral part of her explanations of the rocky intertidal zone; her home base was the seaweed-strewn rocks and beaches of southern Maine, and so how could it be otherwise? Yet it is astonishing how often the seaweeds are overlooked when describing life in the sea. In John Steinbeck's famous *The Log from the Sea of Cortez* and in the first edition of Ed Ricketts's *Between Pacific Tides*, seaweeds are ignored. Carson, however, saw the integral nature of all organisms living at the seashore. Her ecological view remains a contemporary one, and she celebrates seaweed as one of the great ecosystem engineers of our planet. It fixes carbon, generating the base of the food chain, and creates habitat; it is fundamental not only to life in the sea but to all life on earth.

What if Rachel Carson had been able to observe firsthand the intense diversity of the tide pools of the wild California coast? Marine algae alone number more than seven hundred species on the Pacific coast. Compared to the monochrome presence of knotweed (*Ascophyllum*) and bladderwrack (*Fucus*) on the Maine coast, a California shoreline can seem like a wonderland. The wrack line of its beaches is full of washed-up kelps, including the feather boa, bull kelp, and giant kelp. The tide pools of the Pacific reefs are crowded with smaller and more delicate seaweeds (and yet they can withstand the punishing surf) that range in color from reds and magentas to iridescent blues.

I am lucky to have a foot on both the East and West Coasts, and to be deeply involved in communicating the world of the seaweeds to as wide an audience as possible. The plight of the kelp forests across the globe is a major concern and deserves all the attention we can give it. And while I am still passionately in love with the seaweeds and kelps, I am not making as many images these days. My role as an artist has shifted to creating networks of knowledge as much as algal portraits. A broader audience has discovered the world of marine algae, inspiring new attention, innovative research, and intensive restoration projects. I find myself poring over seafloor maps, and keeping tabs on scientific papers, symposium speakers, webinars and extensive restoration efforts as well as snorkeling in as many far-flung kelp beds as I can. As the stakes in our ocean are increasingly understood to be high, I am committed to discerning the

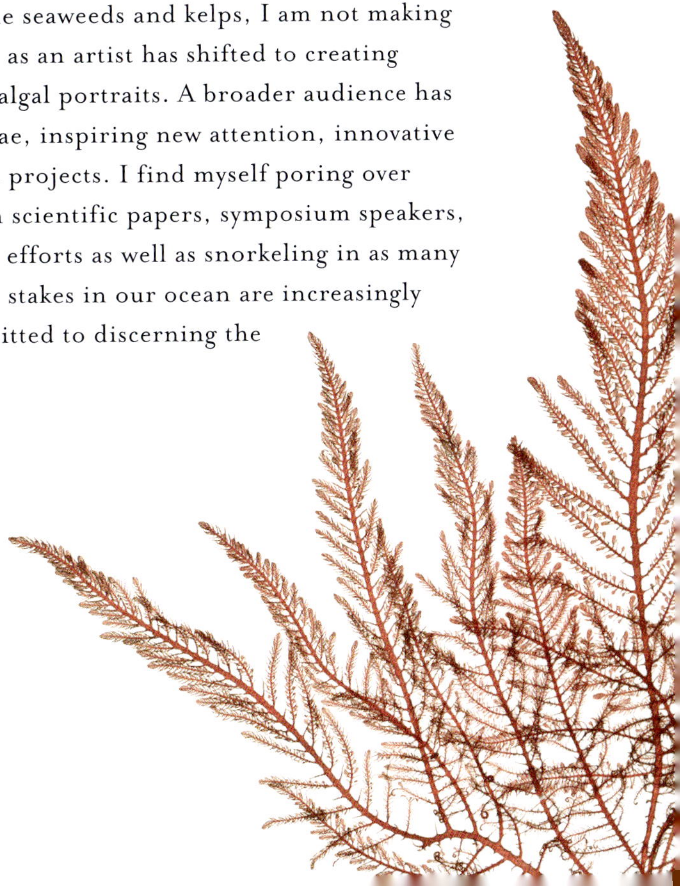

Bonnemaisonia californica
Mar Vista, San Juan Island, WA
April 17, 1983
Collection: University Herbarium
UC Berkeley, CA

myths from the reality, to parsing the science with responsible storytelling, and to connecting centers of kelp knowledge with algal elements of delight and joy.

With all the added attention, I come back to the specimens in my studio, plucked from the wrack line on my beach walks. Scuba divers and snorkelers know what a treasure these seaweeds are; they experience, in situ, the underwater kelp forests and ocean prairies of algae that gracefully ride the currents and provide shelter and sustenance to all manner of fish and other species. They know it's amazing resilience and beauty underwater in the face of strong physical forces. The Victorian amateur naturalists knew this, as they assiduously collected "ocean flowers" from the rugged coastlines of Britain. But how do we present-day shore huggers know this? While the tide pools offer fascinating anemones and crabs and the occasional nudibranch, the seaweeds there most often drape unceremoniously over the rocks, sticky and dark. They do not present themselves like the flowers in a garden. But by looking with focused intent and with a scrupulous eye—and using the scanner in the tradition of the photograms, sun prints, and pressings of artists and naturalists past—this little book reveals the largely unseen forms of ocean flora as a nexus where art and science converge. For the shore lovers and inveterate beachcombers among us, this book will be our seaweed garden.

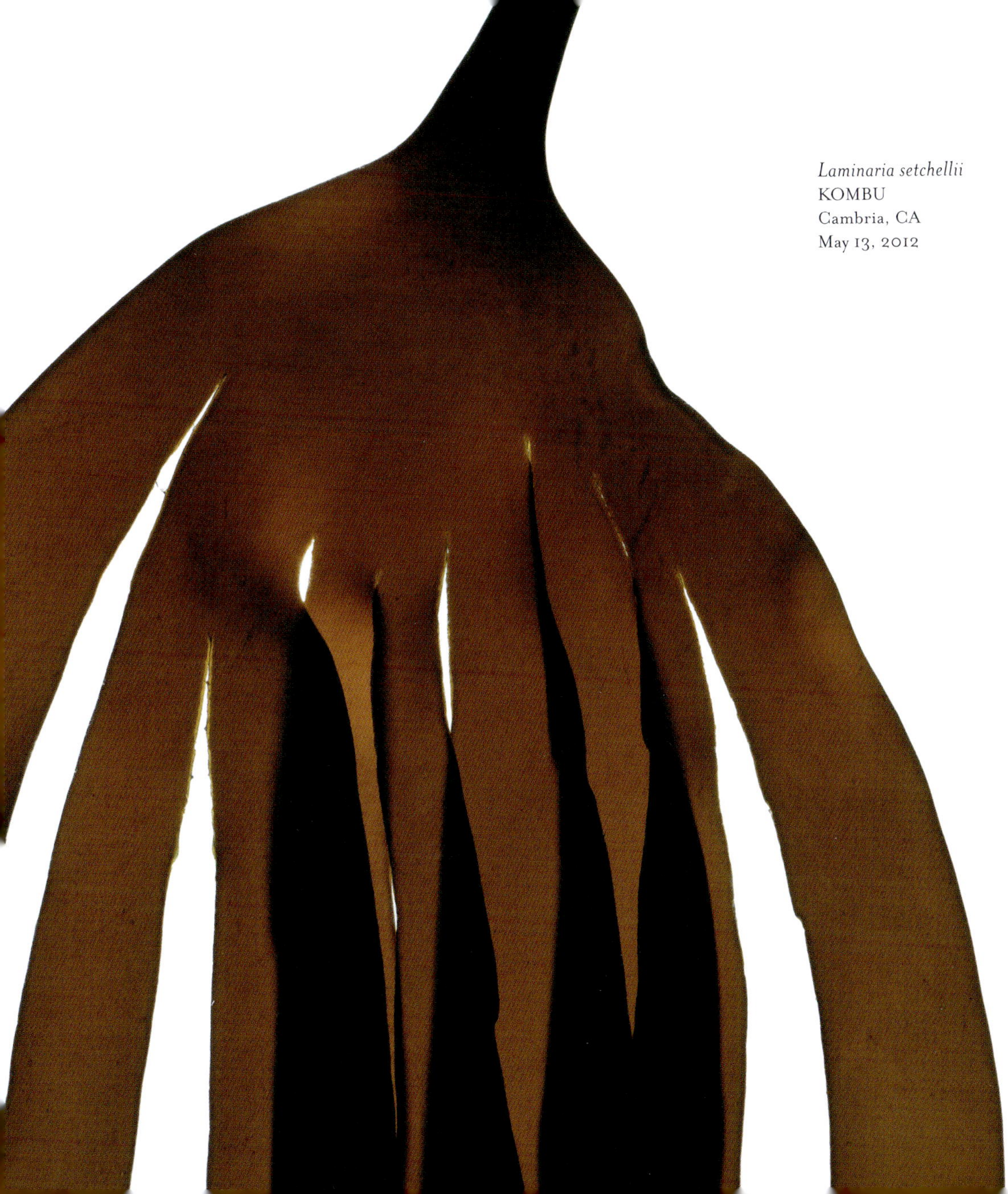

Laminaria setchellii
KOMBU
Cambria, CA
May 13, 2012

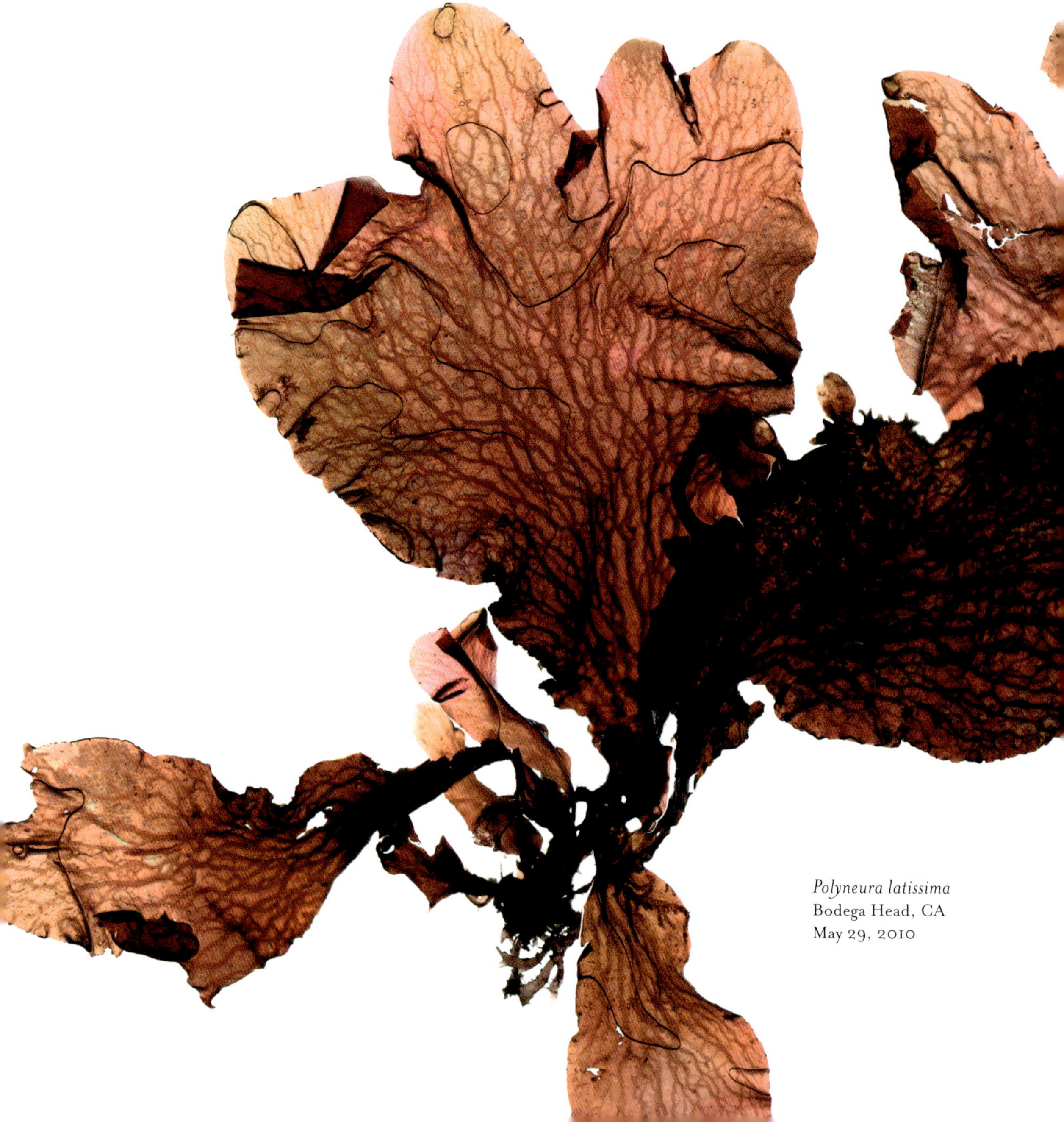

Polyneura latissima
Bodega Head, CA
May 29, 2010

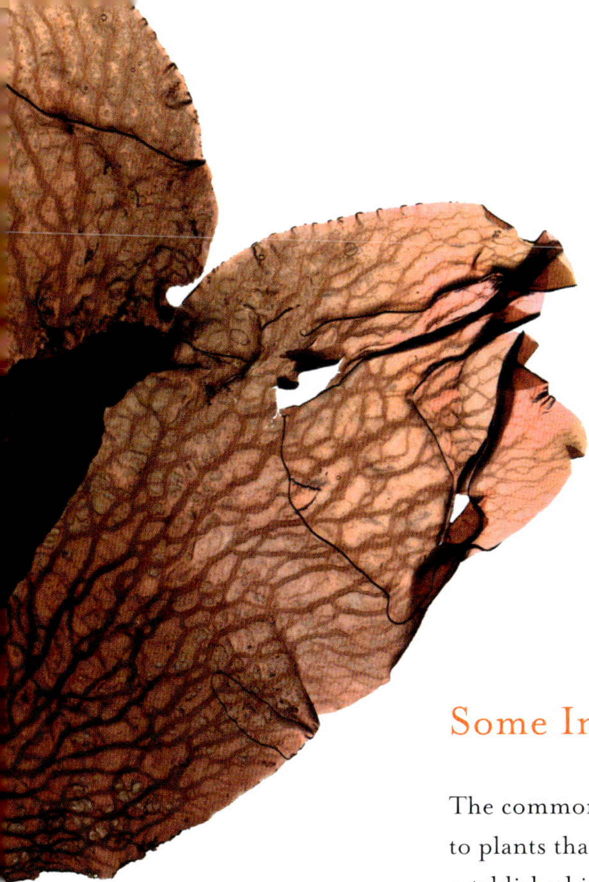

Some Initial Basics

The common name "seaweed" implies a kinship to plants that is misleading. Algae of all sorts were established in the oceans well before the arrival of vascular plants on land, which resulted from the migration of a few ancestral green algae from the top of the surf zone up onto terra firma. Vascular plants inherit their chlorophyll (and thus their green color) from these ancient algal migrants, but the relationship ends there.

The term "algae" covers the domains of *microalgae* as well as *marine algae*, *multicellular algae*, or *macroalgae*, all three of which are synonyms for "seaweed." *Microalgae* are the invisible, single-celled organisms that populate our oceans and waterways, and produce more than half the oxygen in our atmosphere. *Macroalgae*, or seaweed, produce another 20 percent. All of this oxygen is generated as a by-product of photosynthesis, and seaweeds and kelps are astoundingly good at this life-giving process. Both land-based plants and oceanic flora use the energy of sunlight to split water molecules and transform (or fix) carbon dioxide into organic matter. But seaweeds do not expend precious resources fighting gravity—the buoyancy of the ocean pulls them upward—and, as a result, they are masters of efficiency when it comes to converting light energy into chemical energy, and from there, into metabolic energy, or growth. Giant kelp can fix from 1 to 4.8 kilograms of carbon per square meter of plant per year, growing almost 2 feet a day. Other species display even higher productivities. The kelp forests of the oceans rival the rainforests of the continents in terms of photosynthetic production.

Macrocystis pyrifera
GIANT KELP
(sporophyll blades)
Cambria, CA
May 12, 2012

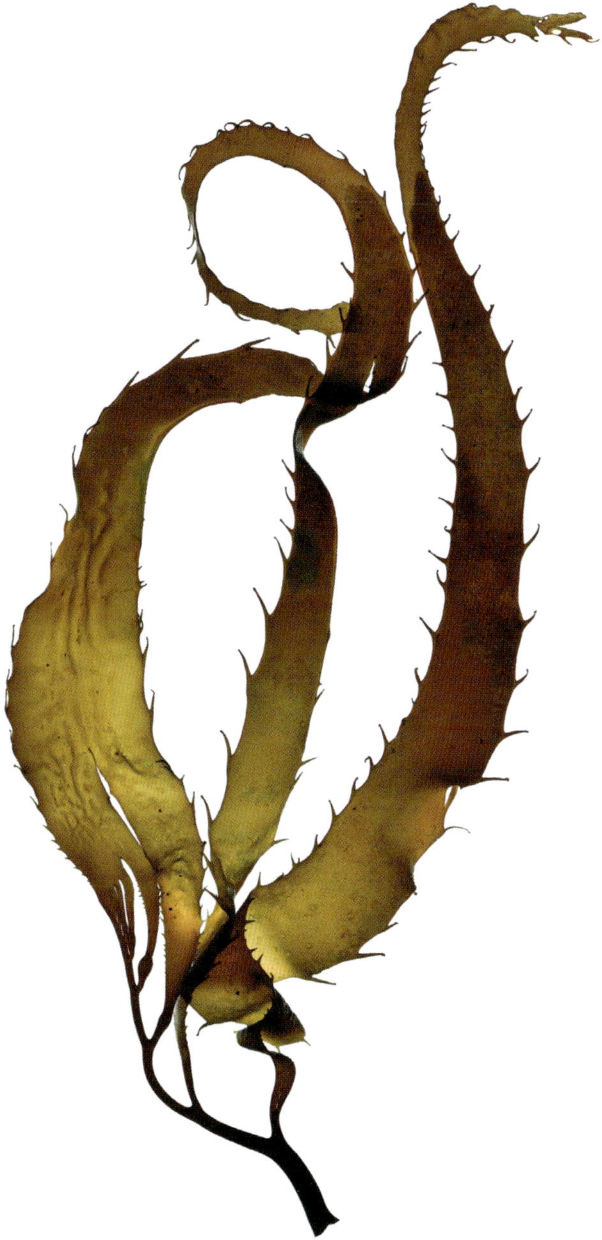

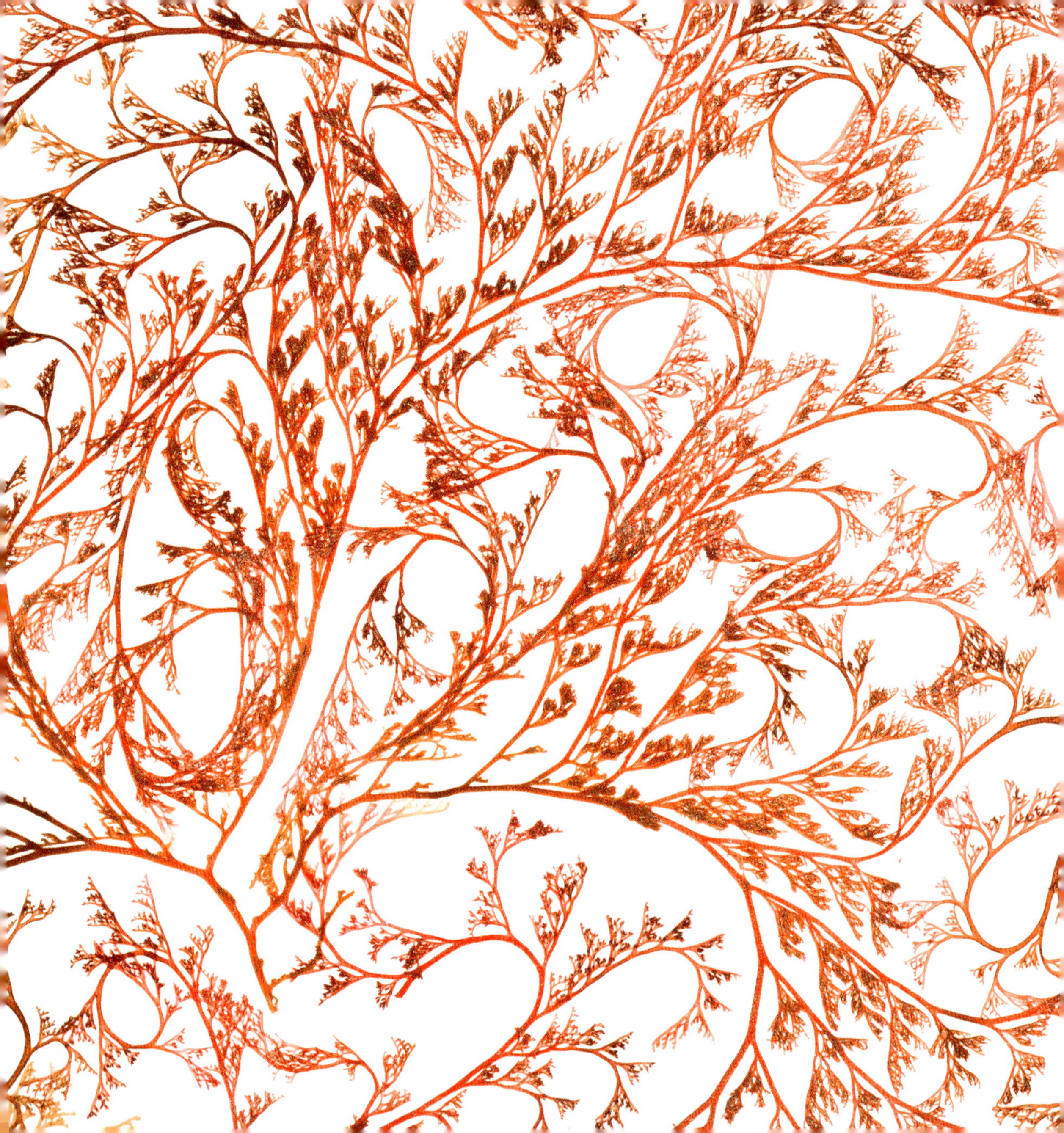

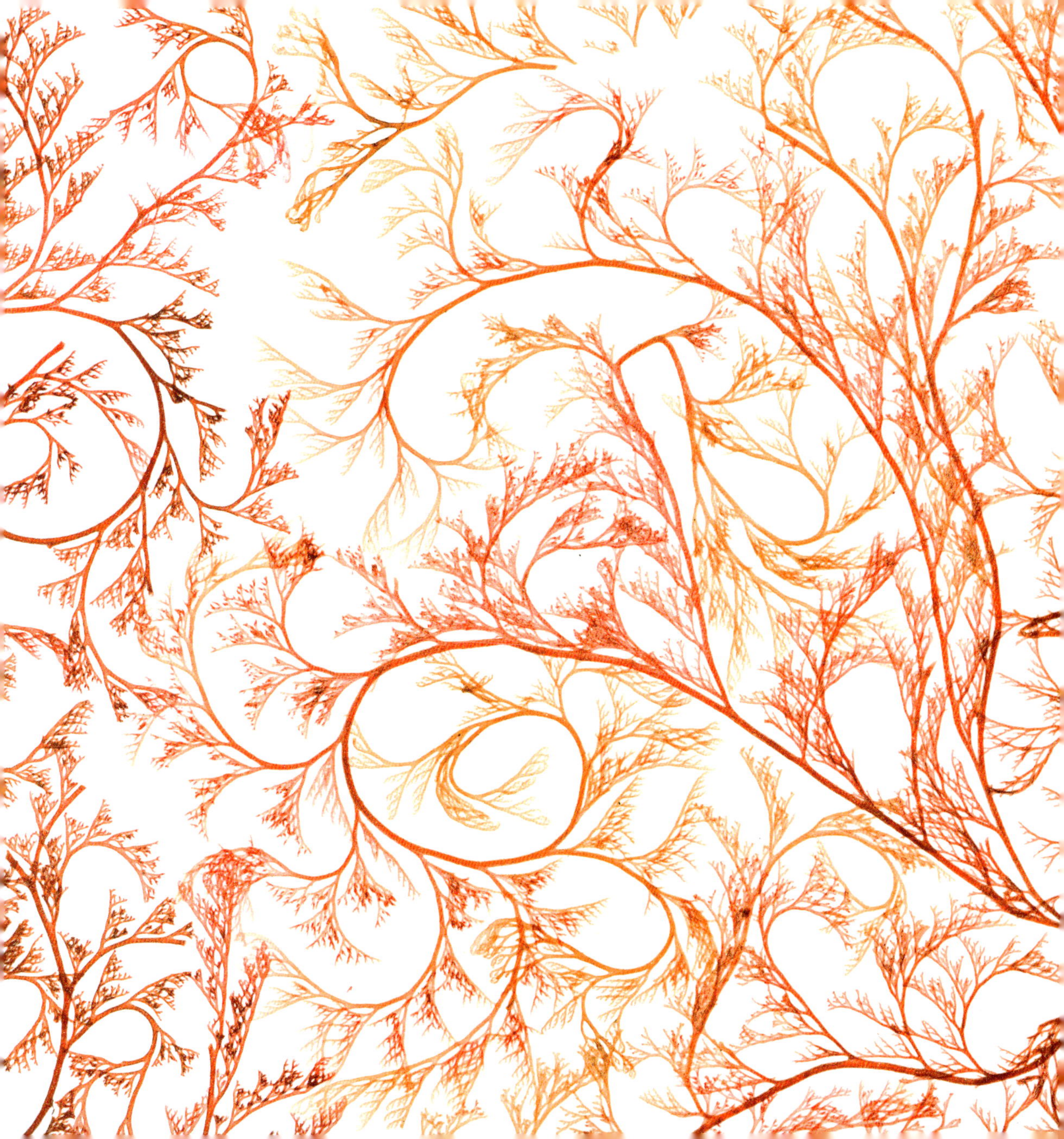

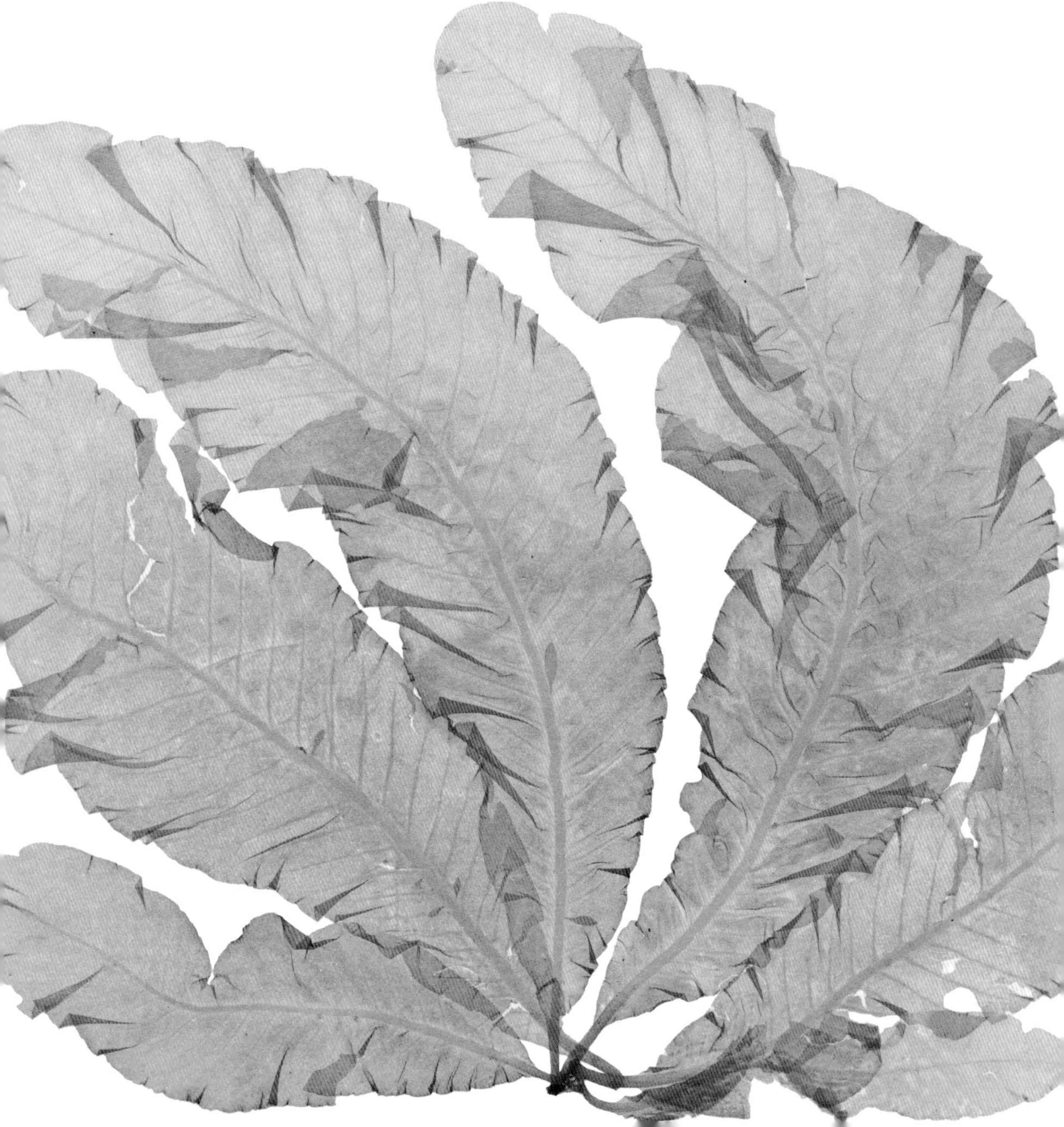

previous spread:
Microcladia borealis
no date
Collection: University Herbarium
UC Berkeley, CA

left:
Delesseria sanguinea
Britain
c. 1880
Collection: University Herbarium
UC Berkeley, CA

What Color Is Your Seaweed: Green, Brown, or Red?

Color is perhaps a seaweed's most striking characteristic. When held up to the light, the intensity of its magenta, the subtlety of its golden brown, or the clarity of its kelly green can take your breath away. William Henry Harvey, a colorful Irishman who traveled the nineteenth-century world collecting specimens, became the father of modern-day phycology, that arm of botany that studies marine flora. Harvey was the first to use color as the basis for identifying seaweeds. While his specimens had infinite variations of color, their spores, clearly visible under his primitive microscope, were definitive circles of super color: vibrantly green, vividly pink, or intensely olive brown. In 1839 Harvey segregated algae into the three taxonomic groups of green, brown, and red that we still use today to classify seaweed.

A seaweed's color is determined by the combination of pigments housed in its chloroplasts or plastids (a specialized substructure within its cells). Green algae (phylum Chlorophyta), like plants, have chlorophyll *a* and *b* in their chloroplasts. They are, in fact, typically green. Brown algae (class Phaeophyceae), which include kelps and rockweeds, have a third, brown accessory pigment that, when combined in different amounts with the green chlorophyll, creates their array of colors. Browns can range from olive green to golden brown to yellow orange. The six thousand or so species of red algae (phylum Rhodophyta) have red and blue accessory pigments that overshadow the single chlorophyll *a* pigment. When these pigments combine, the color can be dazzling: striking scarlet, maroon, pale pink, or deep purple.

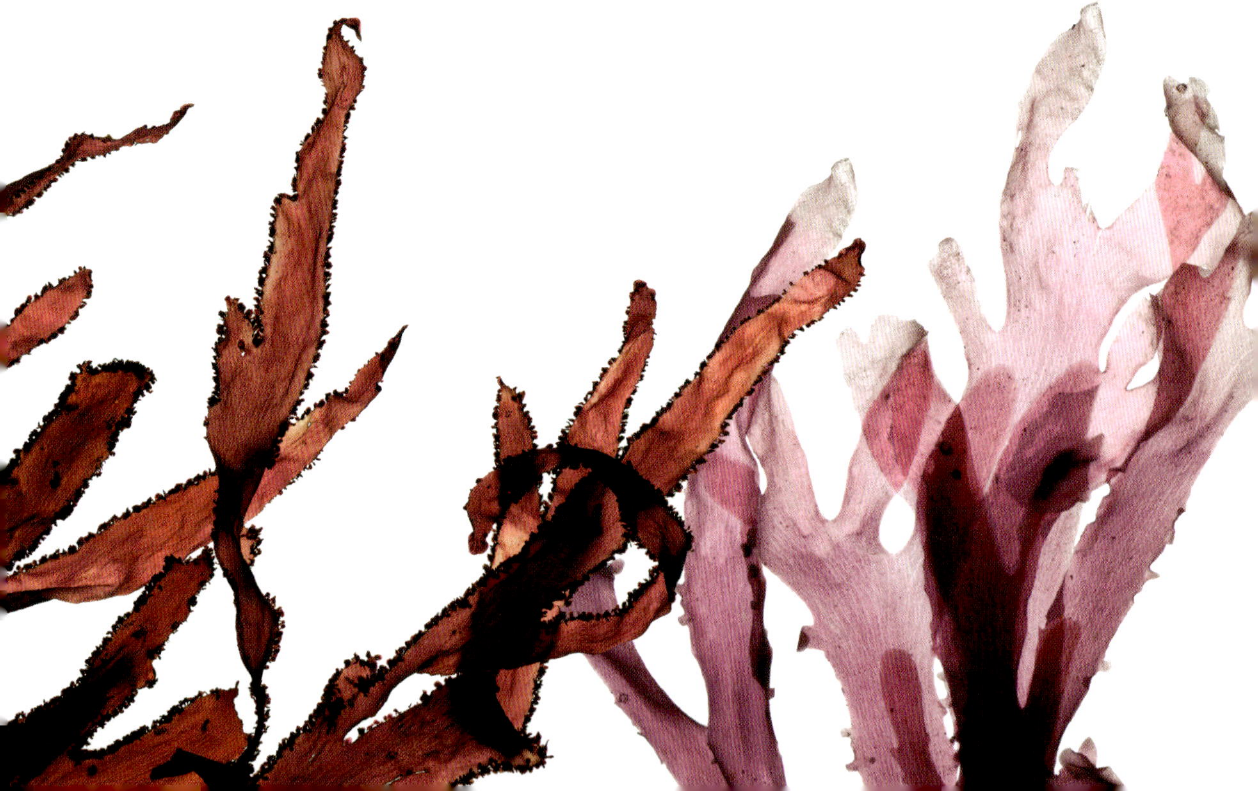

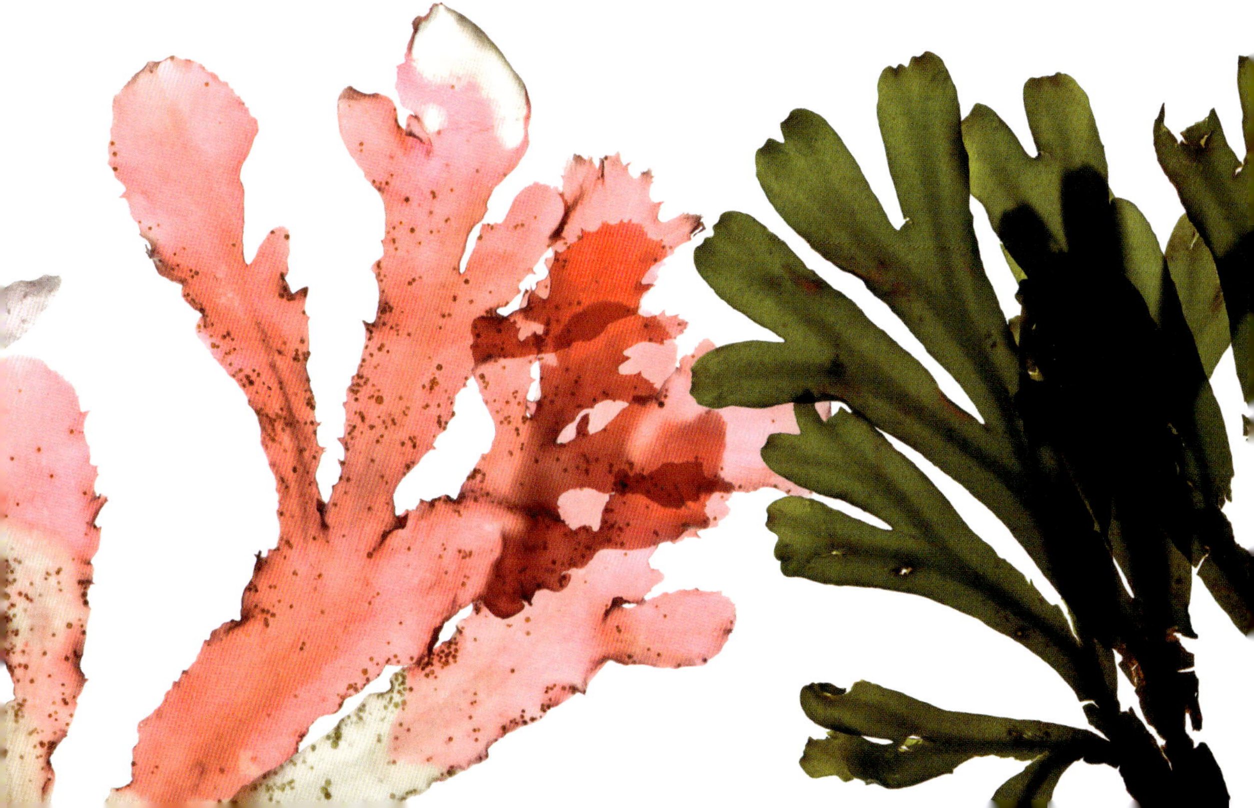

Cryptopleura ruprechtiana,
Cryptopleura violacea,
Hymenena flabelligera, and
Fucus distichus
Duxbury Reef, Bolinas, CA
May 8, 2009

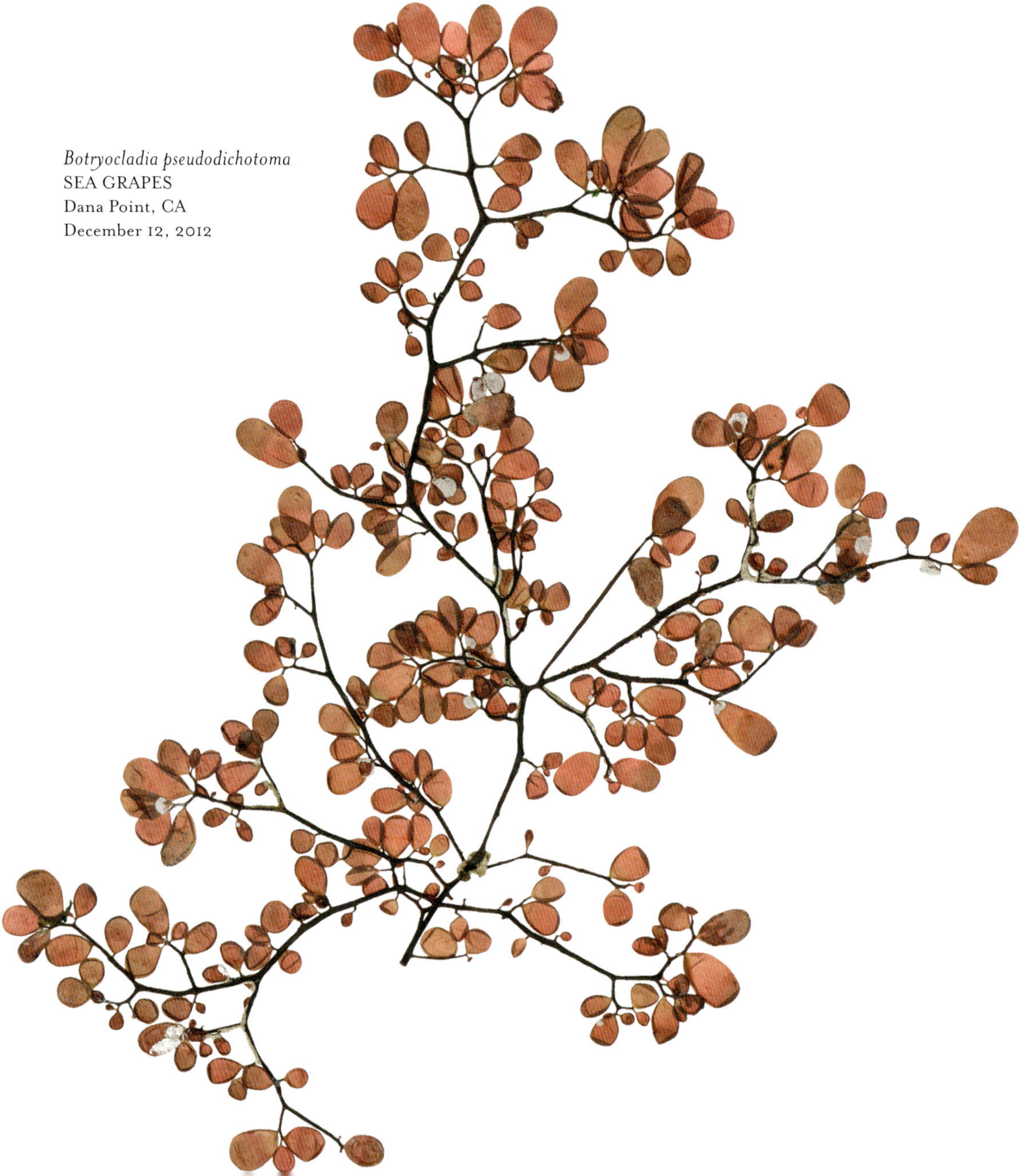

Botryocladia pseudodichotoma
SEA GRAPES
Dana Point, CA
December 12, 2012

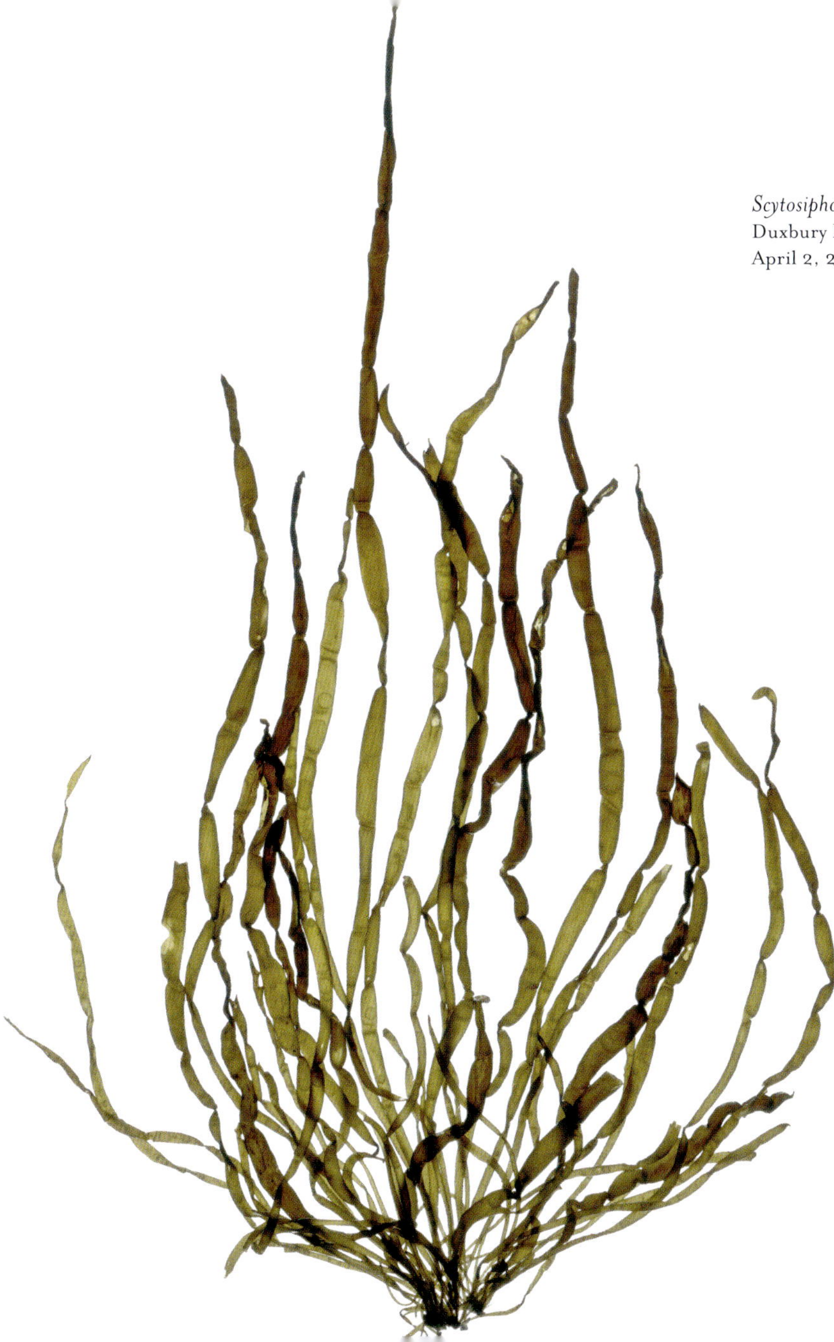

Scytosiphon lomentaria
Duxbury Reef, Bolinas, CA
April 2, 2013

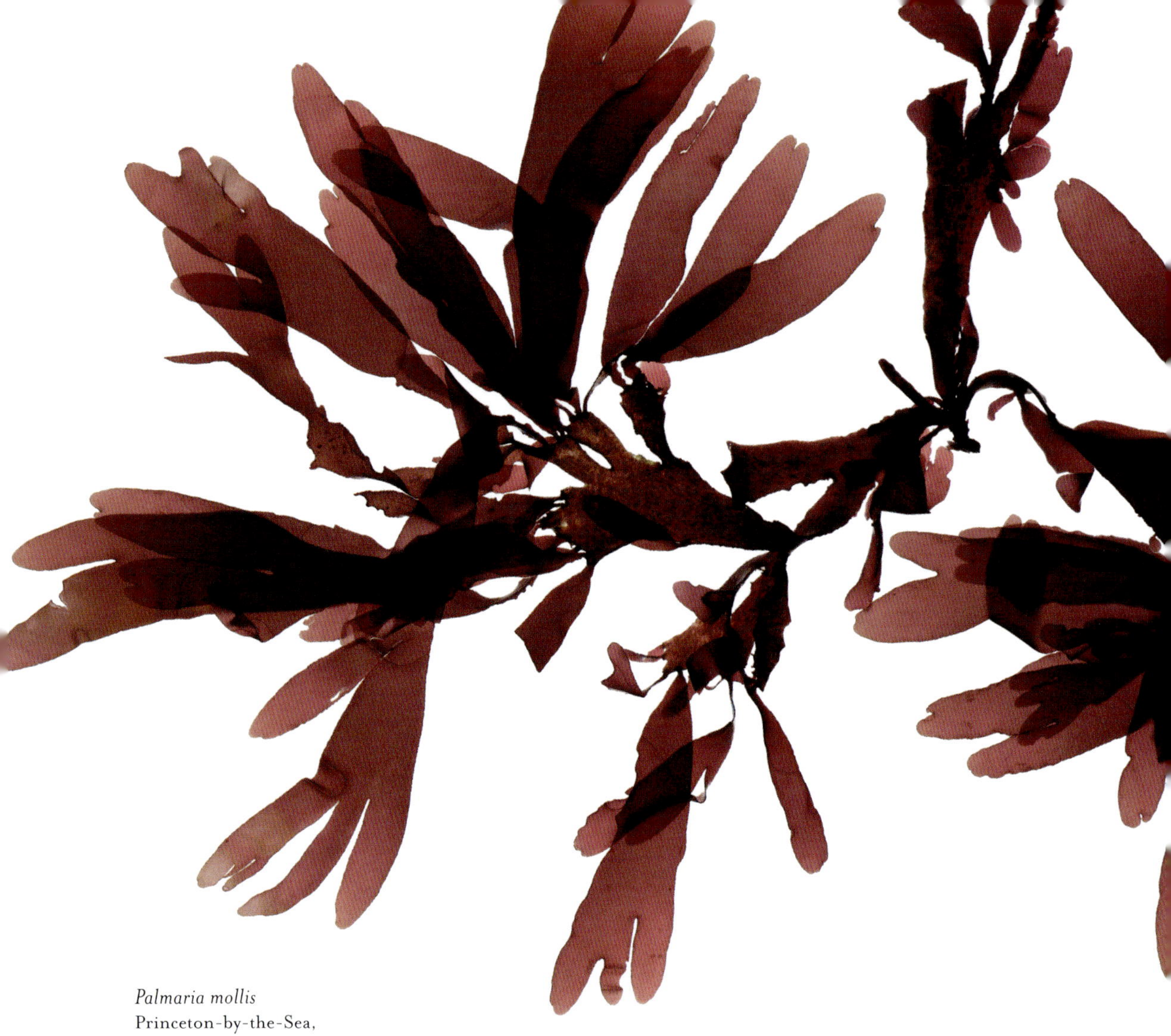

Palmaria mollis
Princeton-by-the-Sea,
Half Moon Bay, CA
April 21, 2010

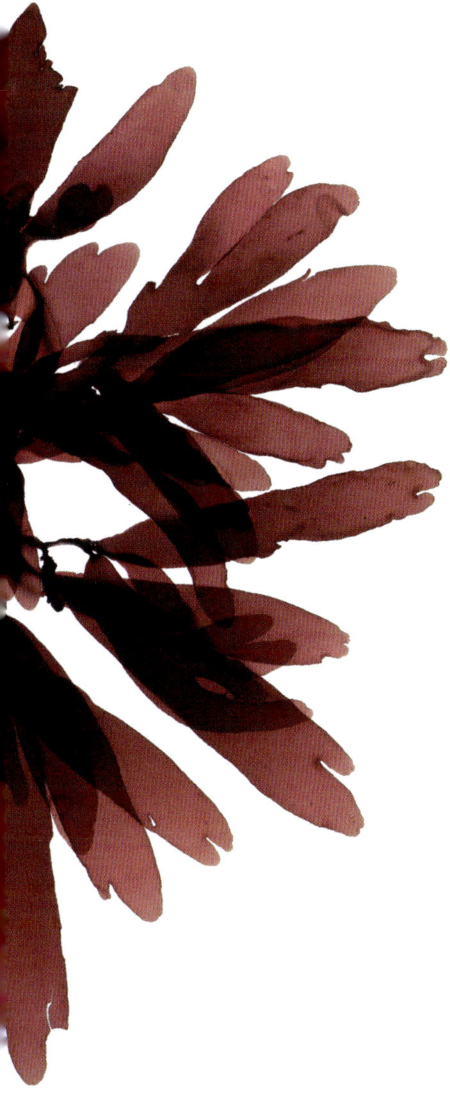

It is within the chloroplasts of the cell, where pigments gather specific spectra of light, that the mystical process of photosynthesis occurs. While plants on land have the full spectrum of daylight available to them, seaweeds must be resourceful with whatever light filters through the dense ocean waters—some reds and browns live at depths of 100 to 200 feet. Chlorophyll *a* is the powerhouse activator for photosynthesis and efficiently collects the longer red wavelengths available in the surface waters and on shore, reflecting the greens back to our eyes. It is present in all seaweeds, but brown, red, and blue pigments have evolved alongside it to capture the shorter wavelengths of blue and green light that penetrate the deeper waters where the red and brown seaweeds find their space. Each algal species has a unique combination of pigments, and thus the range of colors is astounding.

The Evolution of Color

Color has been the center of algal life since the very beginning. In fact, seaweed evolution, which is the story of acquiring the ability to capture the energy of sunlight for self-generation, starts with the color blue-green, or cyan. Cyanobacteria—tiny, unicellular organisms without nuclei (prokaryotes)—have, since the beginning of time, used a bluish pigment called phycocyanin and the green chlorophyll *a* enfolded in its cell membrane

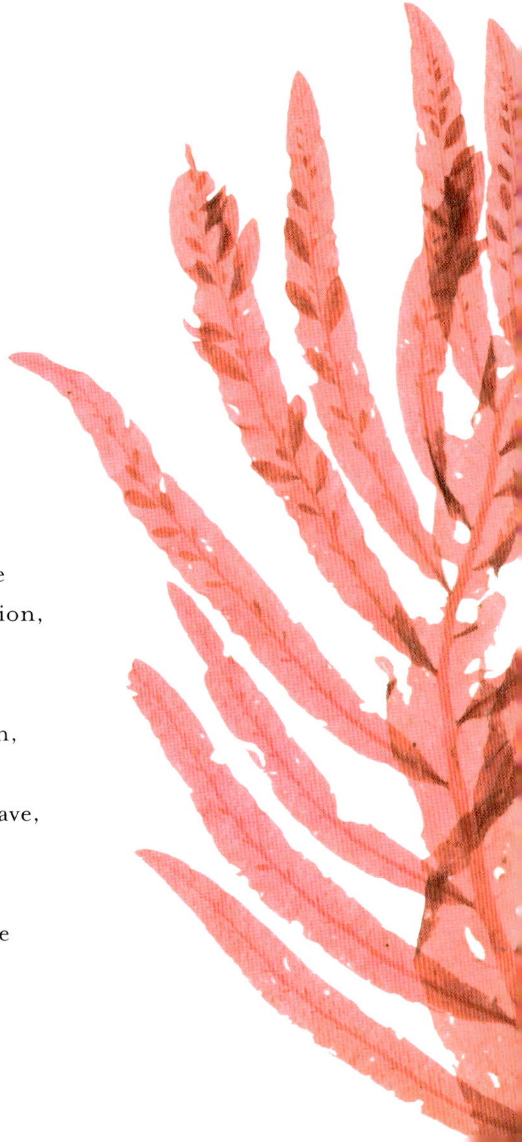

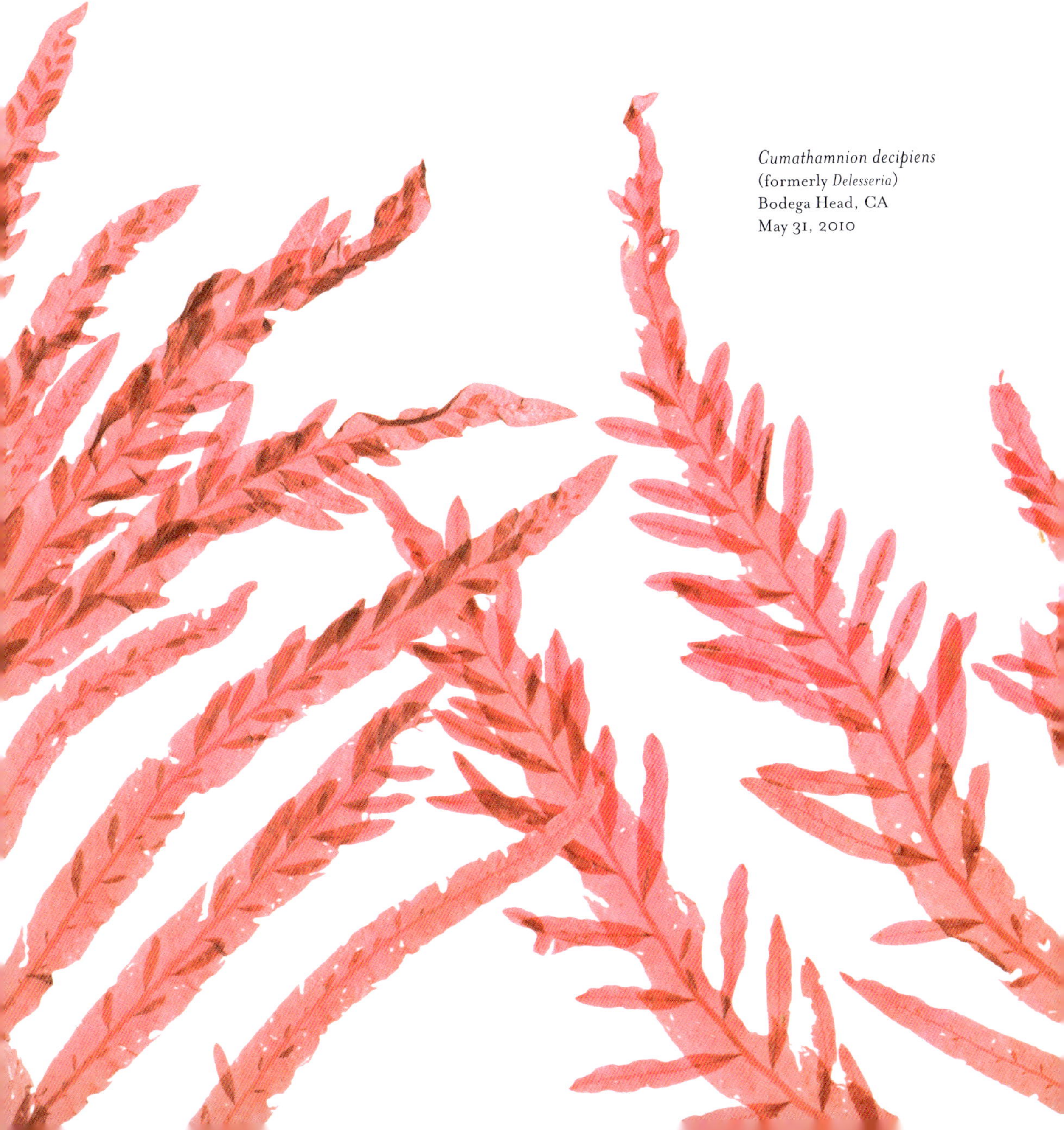

Cumathamnion decipiens
(formerly *Delesseria*)
Bodega Head, CA
May 31, 2010

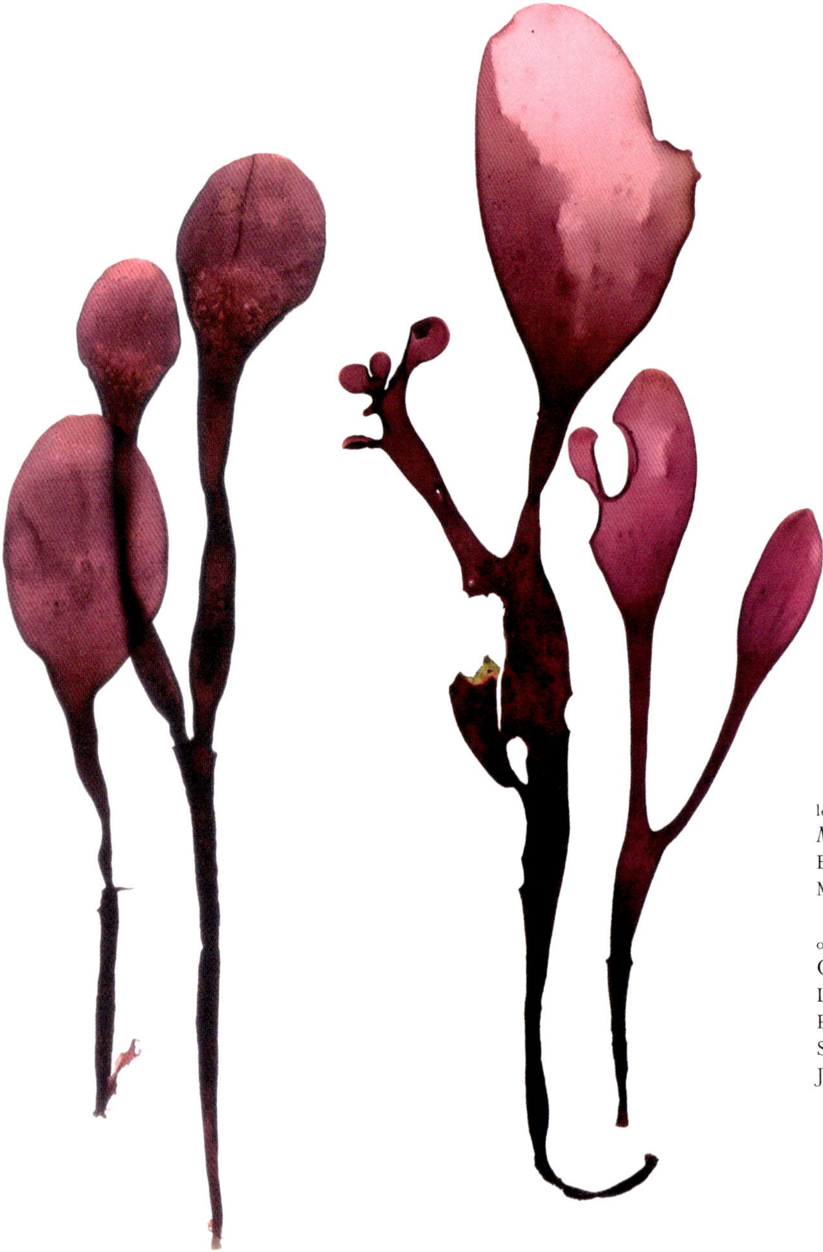

left:
Mazzaella volans
Bodega Head, CA
May 30, 2010

opposite:
Green scrap
Limantour Beach,
Point Reyes National
Seashore, CA
January 1, 2011

to translate sunlight into metabolic energy. At some point in the primordial stew, an ancestral cyanobacterium was engulfed by a higher-level organism (eukaryote). The once free-living bacterium was transformed into an organelle, the chloroplast, in which the chlorophyll and other light-grabbing pigments driving photosynthesis in green algae and red algae are found. Green and red multicellular algae evolved separately from this time onward, with only the ancient cyanobacterium as a common connection. Later, a second round of enslavement occurred. A single-cell red alga was similarly engulfed by a eukaryote, its genes similarly hijacked by the host's nucleus, its own nucleus reduced, and the whole alga converted into the chloroplast found in brown algae, which includes the kelps. It can be seen through a high-powered electron microscope that these chloroplasts have multiple membranes surrounding them, holdovers from the various stages of engulfment.

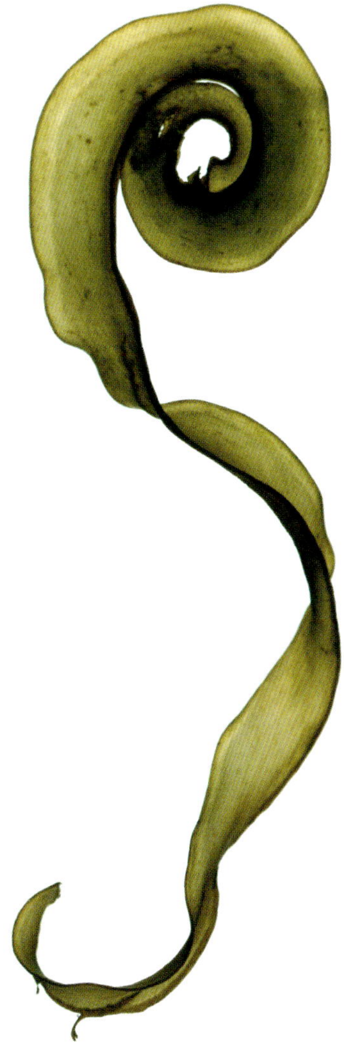

Ulva spp.

Sea Lettuce

AUGUST 10, PENOBSCOT BAY, ME. As I picked my way down the stony beach to plunge into the frigid ocean—a beloved ritual—I was reassured by the patches of sea lettuce plastered to the rocks at intervals along the way. There was just a hint of their brilliant color at this low tide, but they reminded me how rejuvenating the saltwater would be once I was in it. *Ulva*, found in all the oceans, is the signature species of phylum Chlorophyta, the greens. The transparent blades are only two cells thick—so thin that they cannot hold themselves upright without the buoyancy of seawater. When lifted and spread by the rising tide, however, these blades of green present an expansive array of identical cells, each with a chloroplast ready to be ignited by a photon. *Ulva*, like many seaweeds, behaves as if it is all skin, or like a pliant, self-supporting solar panel. *Codium*, another common green, takes a different tack, aggregating its chloroplasts into dense collections (thus its dark color) and funneling light down tubes to strike these loads of pigment. Most seaweeds have evolved highly personalized strategies for grabbing photons, but they all maximize their surface area relative to their volume. On this surface, each cell acts like every other cell. Unlike plants on land, in which a cell specializes to become bark or root or green leaf and the organism relies on a vascular system of internal canals to provide it with water and nutrients, each surface cell of the sea lettuce is exposed to sunlight and seawater; every cell of all seaweeds can both photosynthesize and access the vast resources dissolved in the shallow ocean waters.

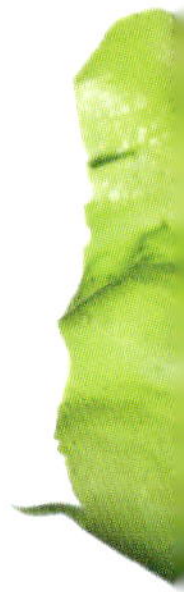

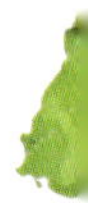

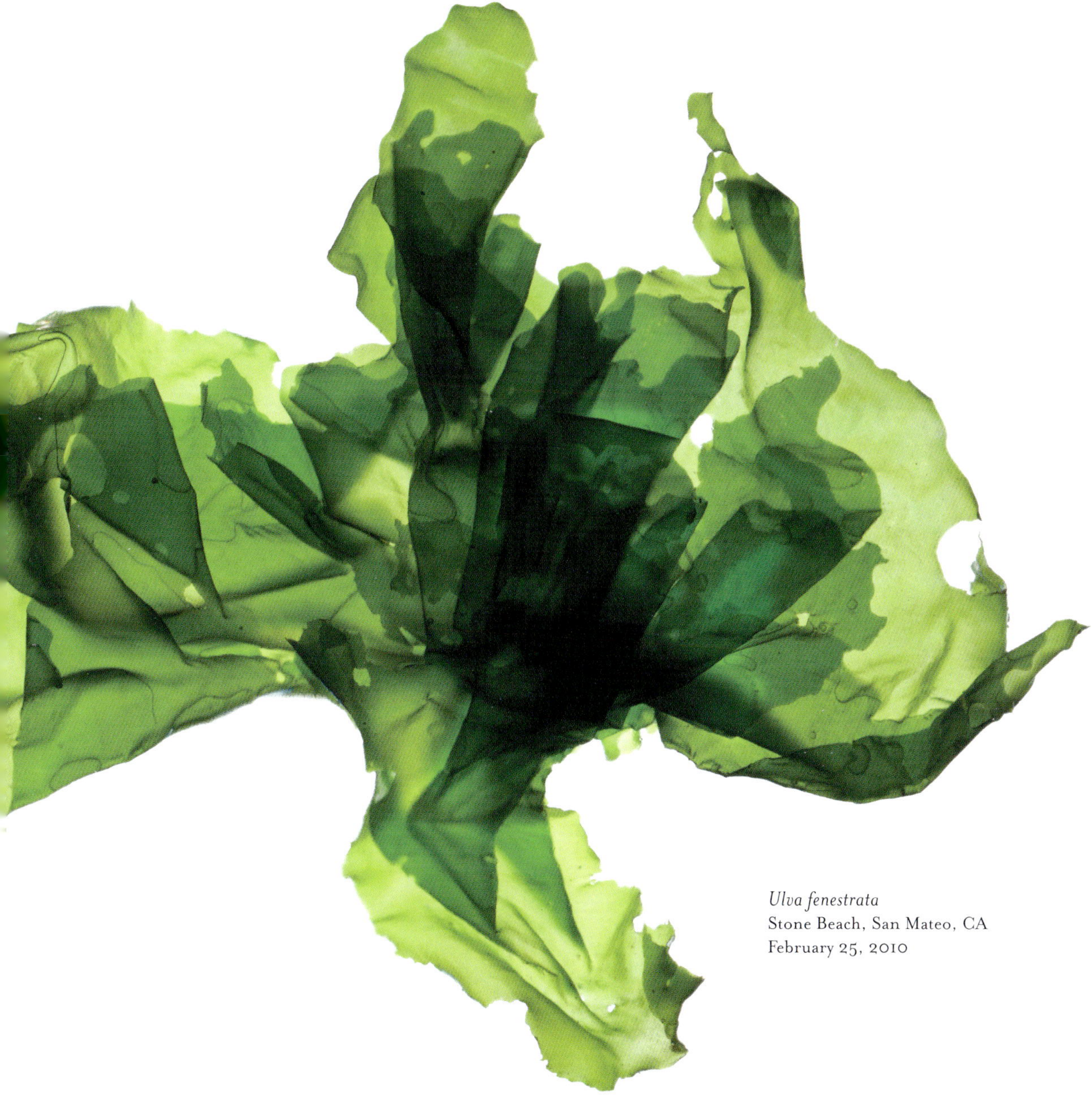

Ulva fenestrata
Stone Beach, San Mateo, CA
February 25, 2010

Calliarthron and others

Red Coralline Algae

Plucked by algae researchers from the rocks of the remote Farallon Islands, 30 miles west of the Golden Gate, this tiny coralline algae plays an outsize role in the diverse marine ecology that surrounds the islands. In fact, coralline algae make an enormous impact on intertidal environments all over the globe. They thrive in both deep (that is, as deep as light will penetrate, up to 500 feet) and shallow environments as well as cold or warm waters. A coralline grows as either a branching (articulated) or encrusting form (see the encrusted limpet on pages 36–37). When the articulated coralline breaks loose and washes up onto the beach, it loses its rosy hue and becomes the bleached white of bones. It is tiny and fragile and often overlooked by beachcombers, but it is a fantastic example of seaweed resourcefulness and worth our careful regard.

Cell walls are a seaweed's only structural support, and while many seaweeds fill their cell walls with flexible, water-retaining phycocolloids (what makes a seaweed goopy), the coralline does something different: It mineralizes calcium carbonate in its cell walls, making a stiff skeletal armor much like a shell. Making a shell, however, is hard work and takes time. An articulated coralline might take five years to grow 5 inches.

Calliarthron tuberculosum
South Farallon Island, CA
c. 1990
Collection: University Herbarium
UC Berkeley, CA

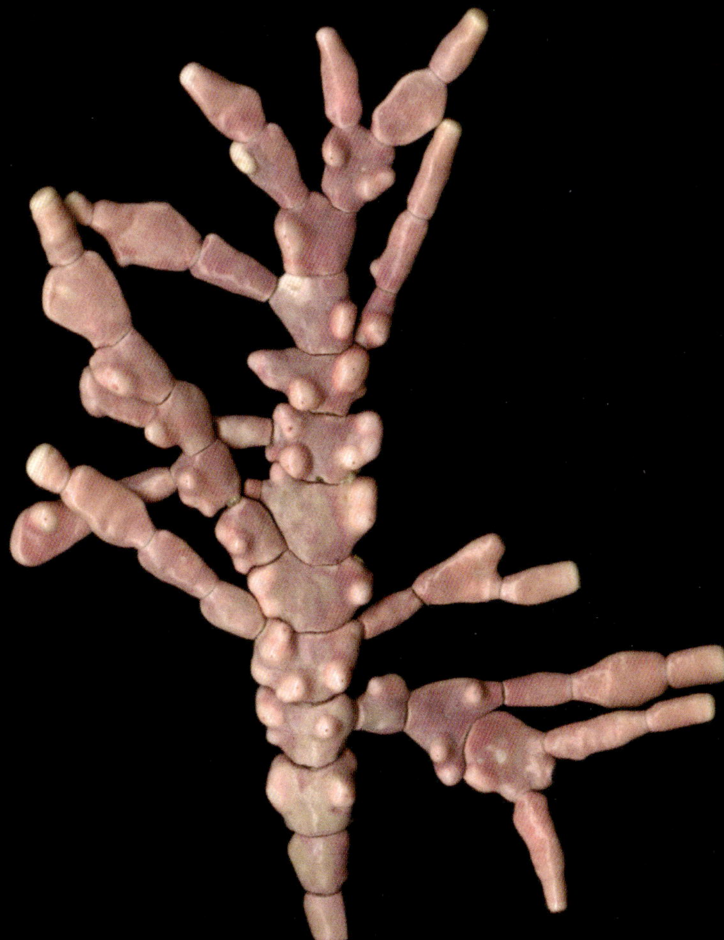

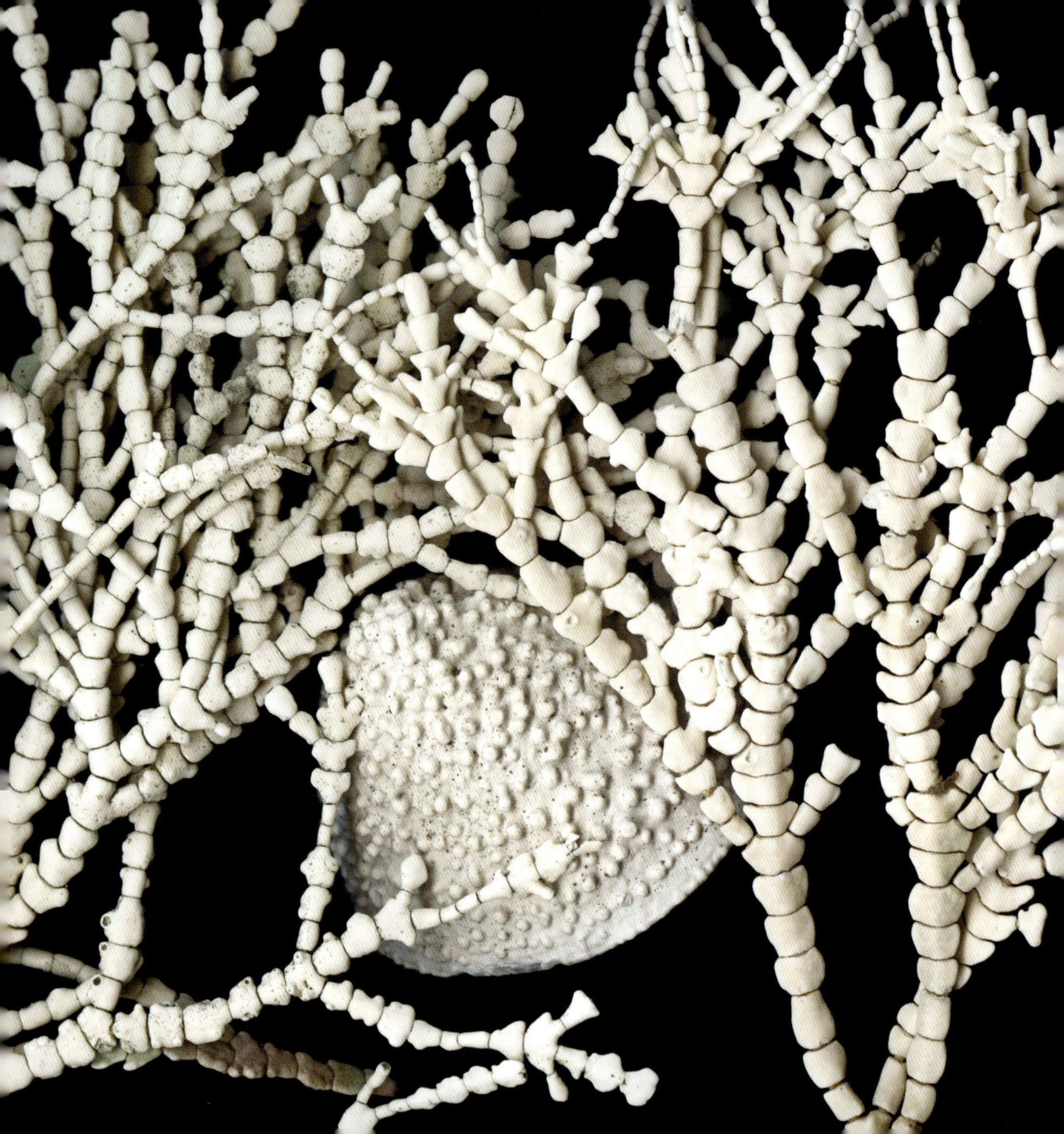

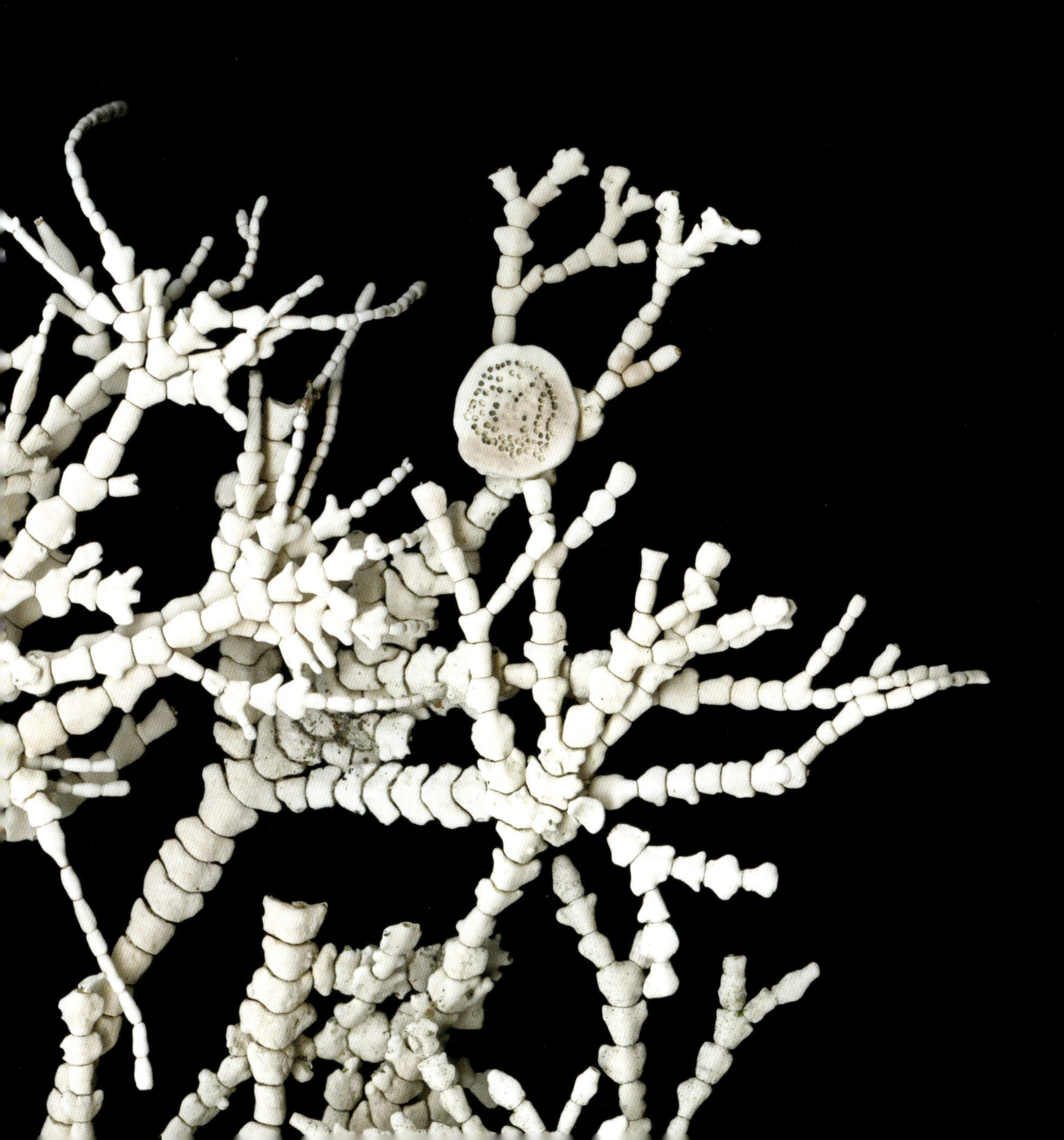

The Holdfast, the Stipe, and the Blade: Seaweed Architecture

From tiny and intricate to enormous and singular, the diverse shapes found among the tangle of seaweed at the ocean shore are all strategies to confront the three tasks essential for success in the intertidal zone: holding on, gathering light and nutrients, and defending against being eaten. A scientist would refer to a seaweed's *morphology* while a designer would use the term *form*, but in either case, the complex and varied shapes that exist across all seaweeds derive from some basic building blocks. The overall body of a seaweed is called the "thallus." What glues the thallus to the benthos, or sea bottom, which is usually a rocky substrate, is a holdfast. Some holdfasts become large and ancient structures in and of themselves. Others are round and flat and remarkably small given the task at hand.

Emerging above the holdfast is the stipe, a "stem" that supports branches and the blades, or "fronds." A blade might be as thin as a single cell or as stretchy and tough as contemporary denim, and closer inspection may offer clues to its identity: There might be a distinct midrib, or a network of slender veins. The branching patterns can be as simple as a single stipe reaching to a single blade, a bifurcation (splitting in two), or an enormously complex system that looks like a lifeless tangle when draped over a rock at low tide but reveals a specific growth pattern when floating in water. The repetition of branching can

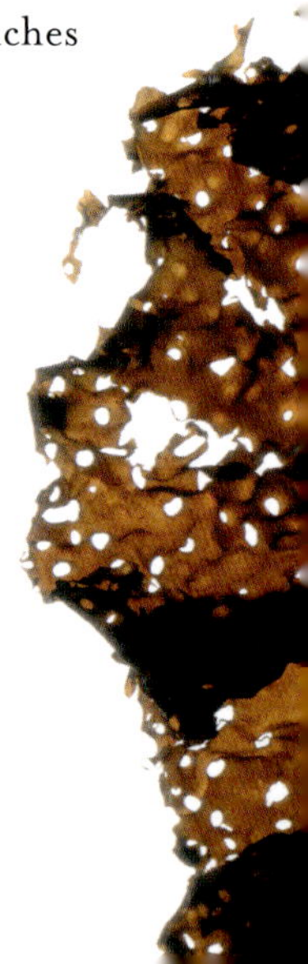

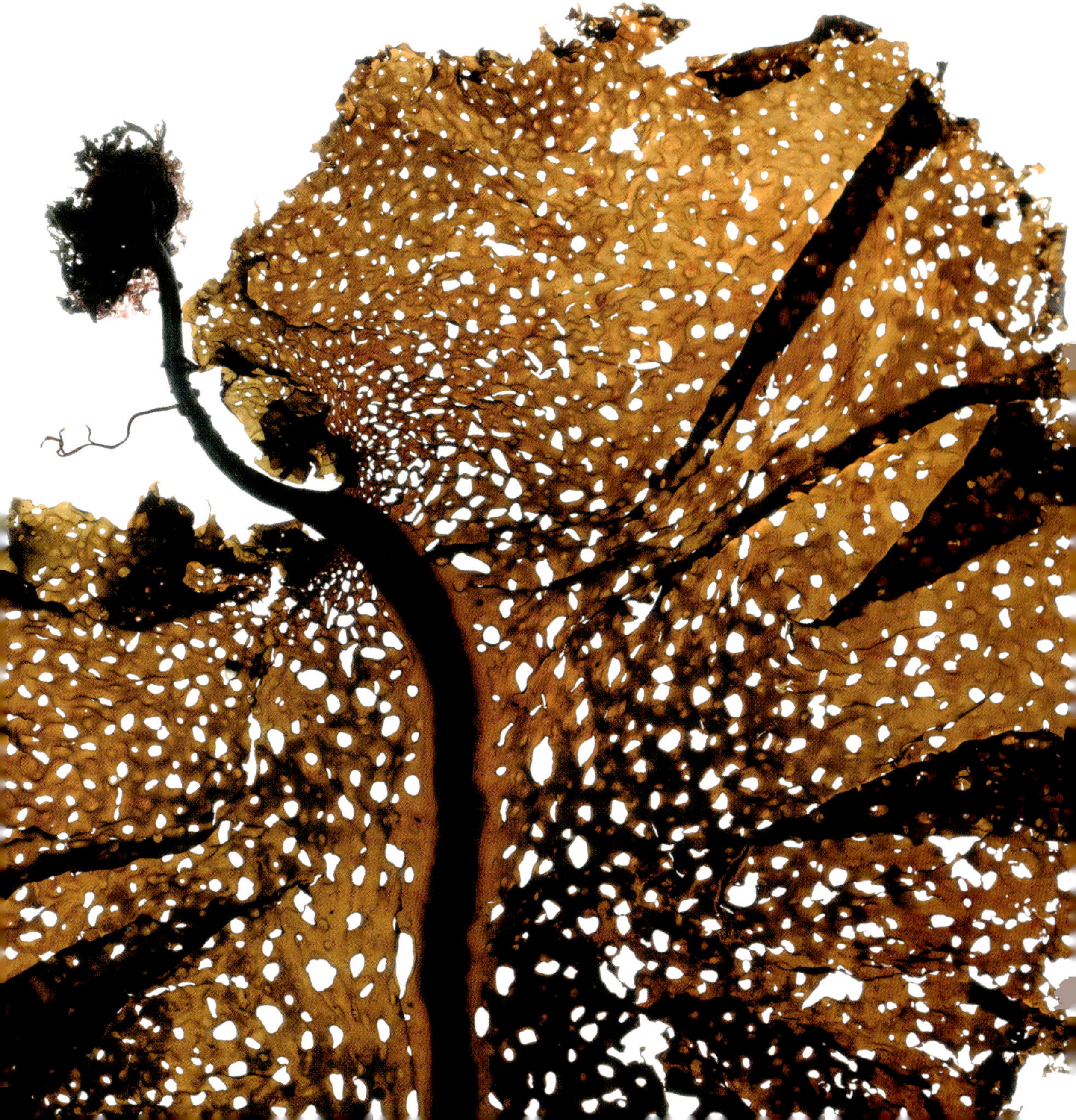

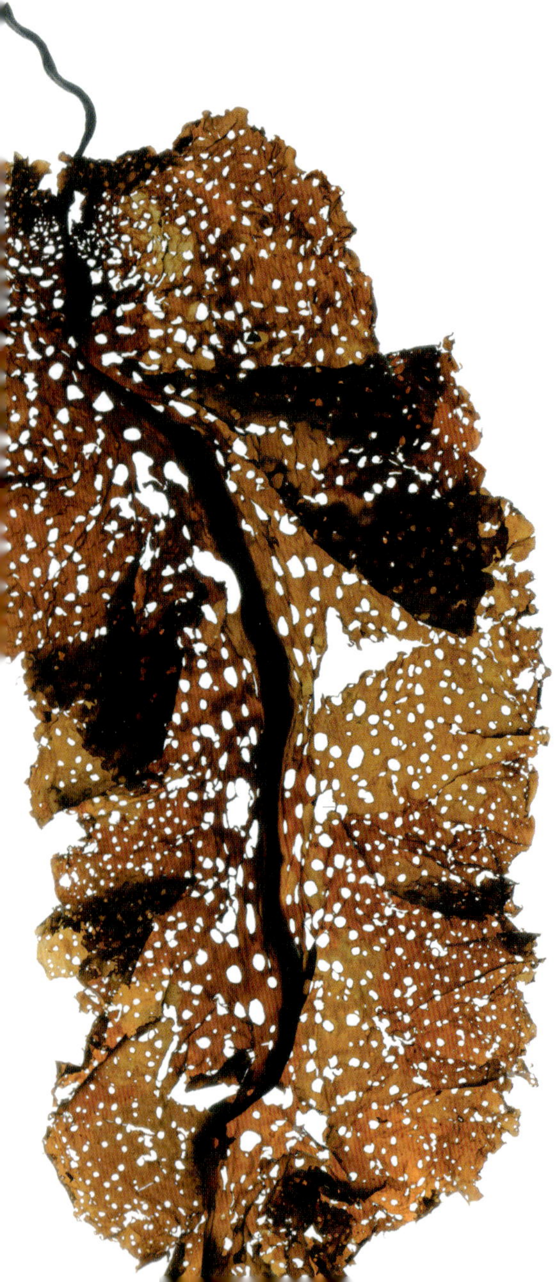

result in self-similar fractal-like patterns, amazing to see under a magnifying lens. Many brown seaweeds have gas-filled bladders (pneumatocysts) that float the blades upward, toward the ocean surface and light. Given the range of environments the intertidal zone offers—more or less protected, rocky or sandy, windblown or not, near a freshwater outlet or in a salty, evaporating tide pool—the morphology of a given algal species can vary tremendously, making identification a tricky business.

pages 36–37:
Various coralline algae

previous spread:
Agarum clathratum
COLANDER KELP
Fox Island Thoroughfare,
Penobscot Bay, ME
July 15, 2011

left and opposite:
Neoagarum fimbriatum
COLANDER KELP
Mendocino, CA
August 12, 2007

Agarum spp.

Colander Kelp

The two specimens of *Agarum* that hang under my studio window are particularly treasured. I found one floating in the Atlantic Ocean, off the Maine coast, while I came upon the other washed ashore near Mendocino in Northern California. Species of *Agarum* are found on both coasts: They flourish in the cold waters of the Arctic and have migrated southward on both sides of North America. When I look carefully at my two perforated treasures, I feel deep appreciation for this kelp's ability to degenerate and regenerate at the same time. The ends of the single blades look ragged and torn—older kelp tissue is sloughing away—but the area where the stipe meets the blade, known as the "meristem," is generating fold after fold of newly minted, magically holey, fresh kelp tissue. To survive, this kelp must grow and die simultaneously. Mightn't this be a refreshing alternative to the wilting blossom as a metaphor for our journey through life?

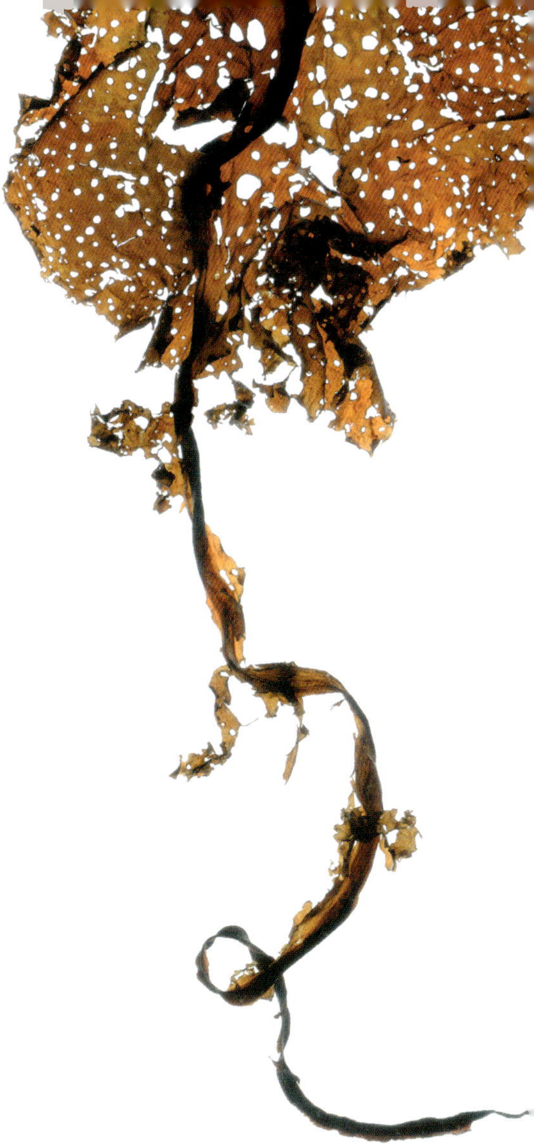

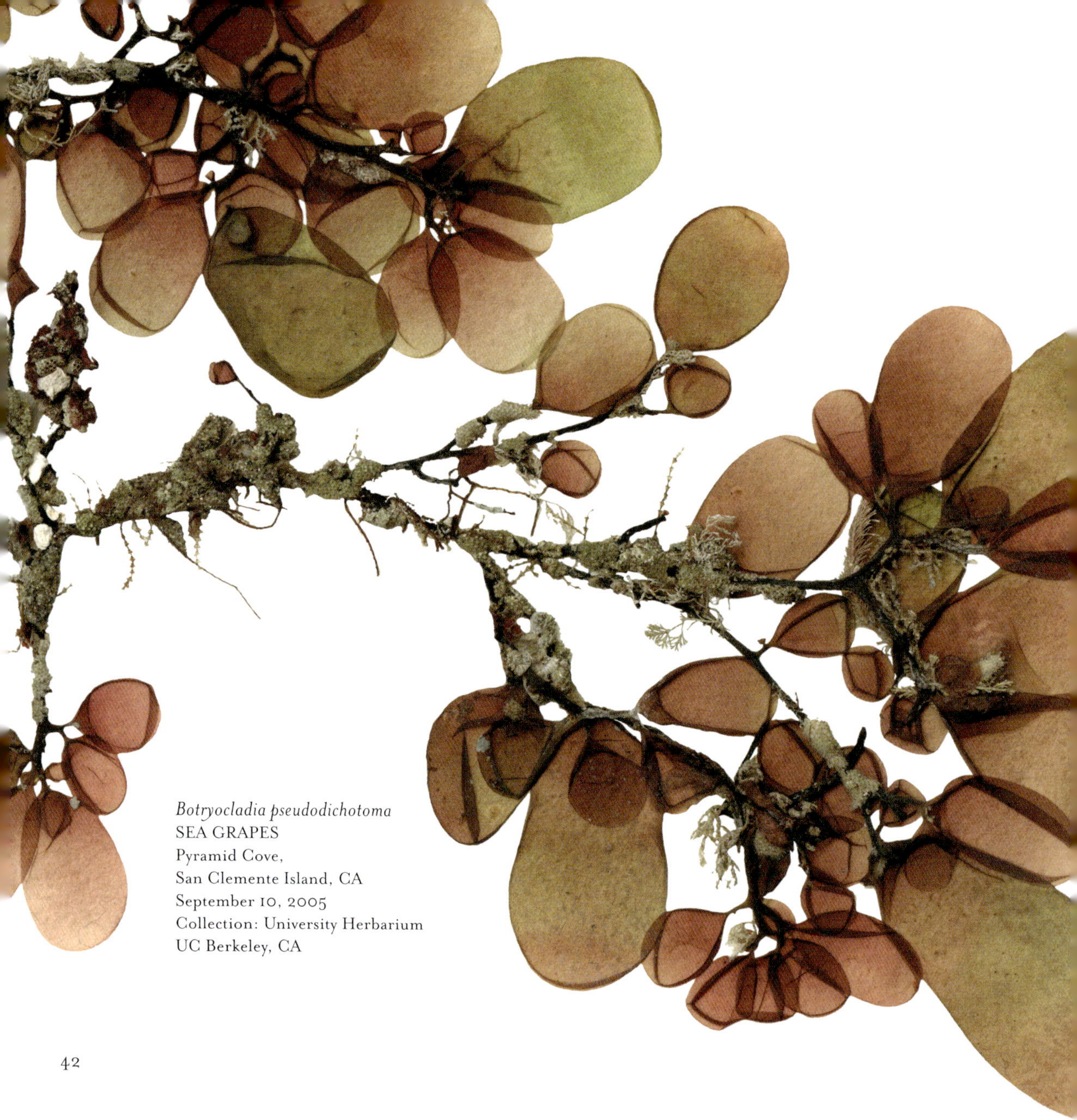

Botryocladia pseudodichotoma
SEA GRAPES
Pyramid Cove,
San Clemente Island, CA
September 10, 2005
Collection: University Herbarium
UC Berkeley, CA

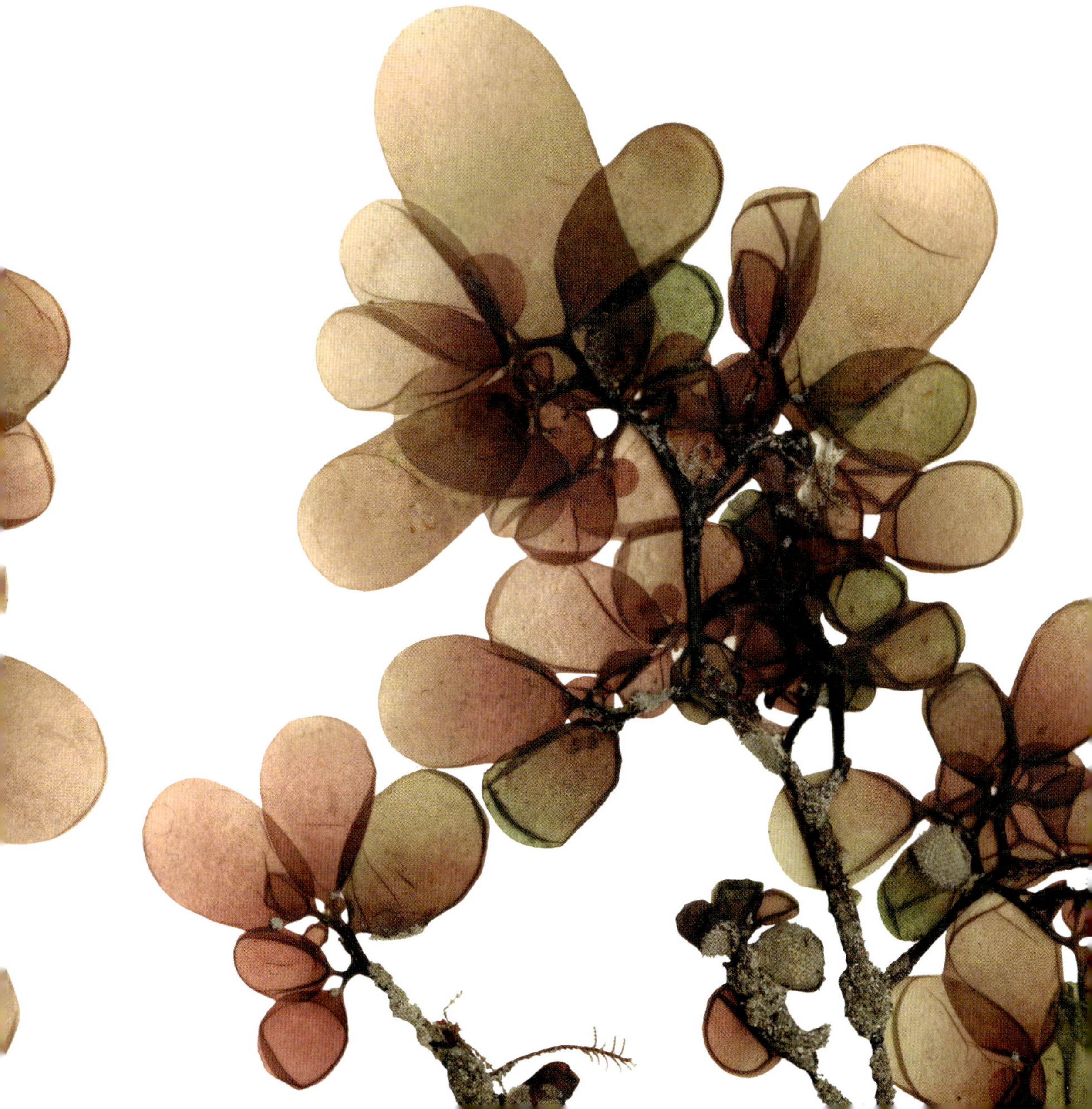

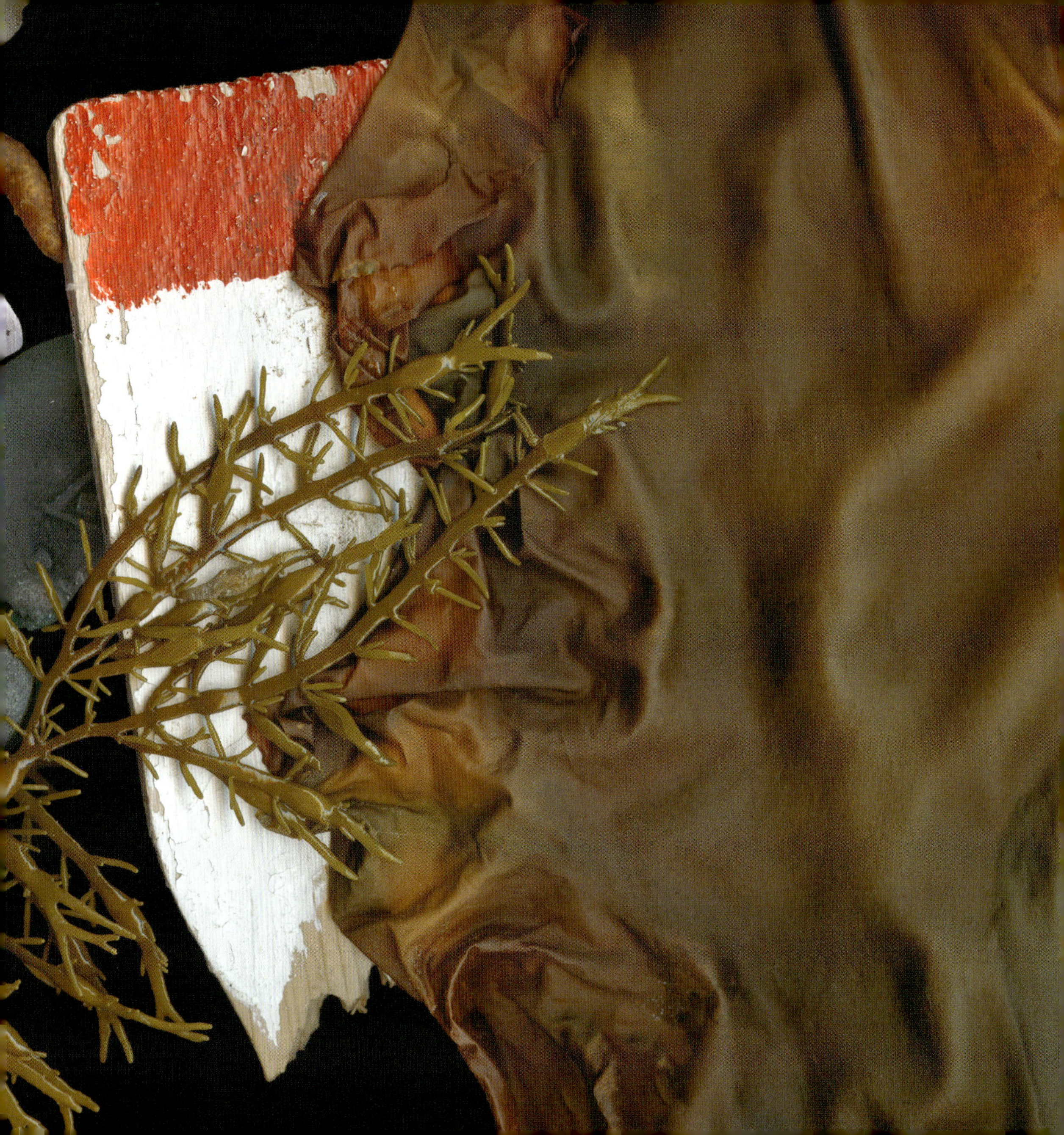

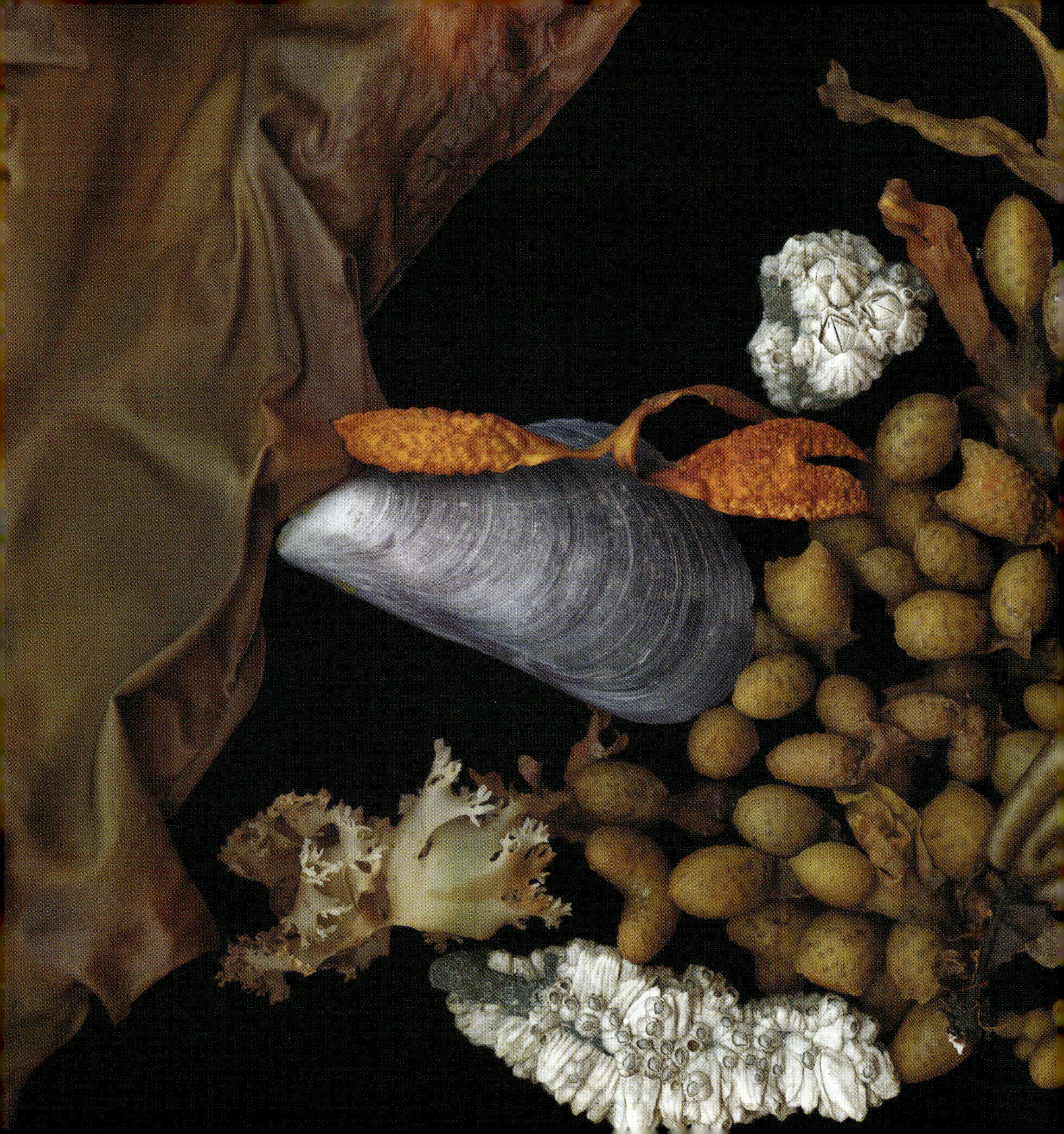

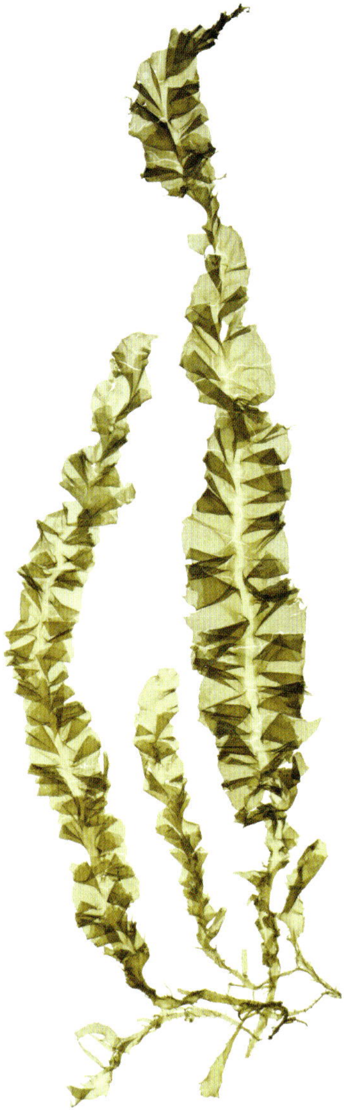

The Tide

JULY 14, FOX ISLAND THOROUGHFARE, PENOBSCOT BAY, ME. I was out on one of the Dumpling Islands early this morning at the turn of the tide. The moment hung in the raking light, the waters of the Thoroughfare neither coming nor going. The mudflats hissed; ducks gaggled on their exposed rocks. The wind tried to fill in from the bay, but the tide said, "Let's wait just a bit." The water was flat as steel, and the knotweed, or *Ascophyllum*, silently draped. I walked around the tiny island, almost holding my breath. It was a spring tide (also called a "minus" tide) and so particularly low, the pull of the new moon a bit stronger on the waters of the ocean. When I returned to where I had begun, my little boat was just as I had left it on the muddy shore, half in the water and half on the beach. I rowed back to the dock, and by the time I got there, the tide had turned and the day had begun. The wind filled in, a whaler buzzed, and the ferry went by.

When the tide comes in, as it does twice a day (it takes about six hours to drain out, or ebb, and another six hours to fill again, or flood), water levels rise throughout the basin of the bay, and the muddy shore is transformed into an underwater world. The flats of prostrate *Ascophyllum* (see page 50) float upward into an erect, rubbery forest undulating under the calm and cold waters of the northern Atlantic. But the tide draws a lid over this other life of the seaweed. The ripples of the wind and reflection of the sky keep this world beyond my consciousness. Under the surface, the *Ascophyllum* jungle, the mainstay to intertidal life on the Maine coast, is madly alive, sheltering fish, crabs, lobsters, and snails. As the tide retreats, the jungle is brought to its knees, again prostrating itself on the shore or hanging in curtains from steep rock walls or pilings. But it keeps the sea with it and protects the multitude of creatures under its heavy blanket from the drying sun.

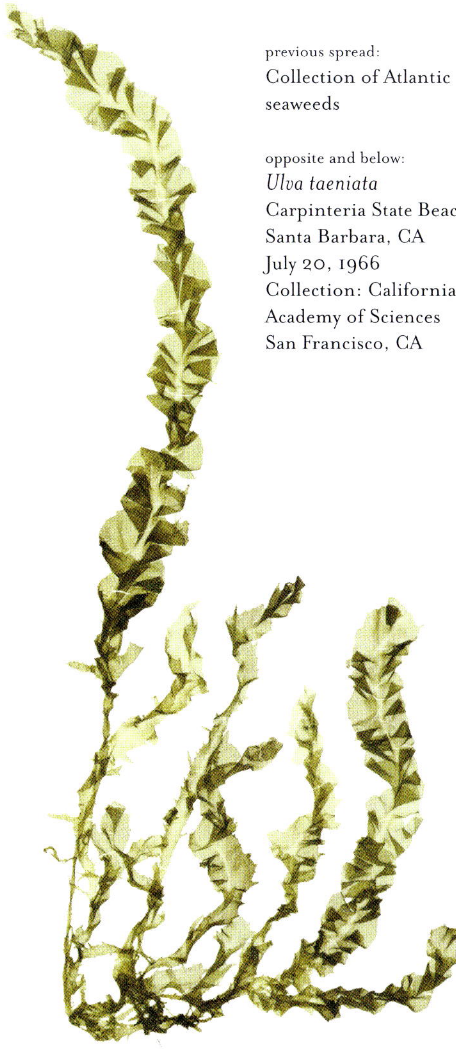

previous spread:
Collection of Atlantic seaweeds

opposite and below:
Ulva taeniata
Carpinteria State Beach, Santa Barbara, CA
July 20, 1966
Collection: California Academy of Sciences
San Francisco, CA

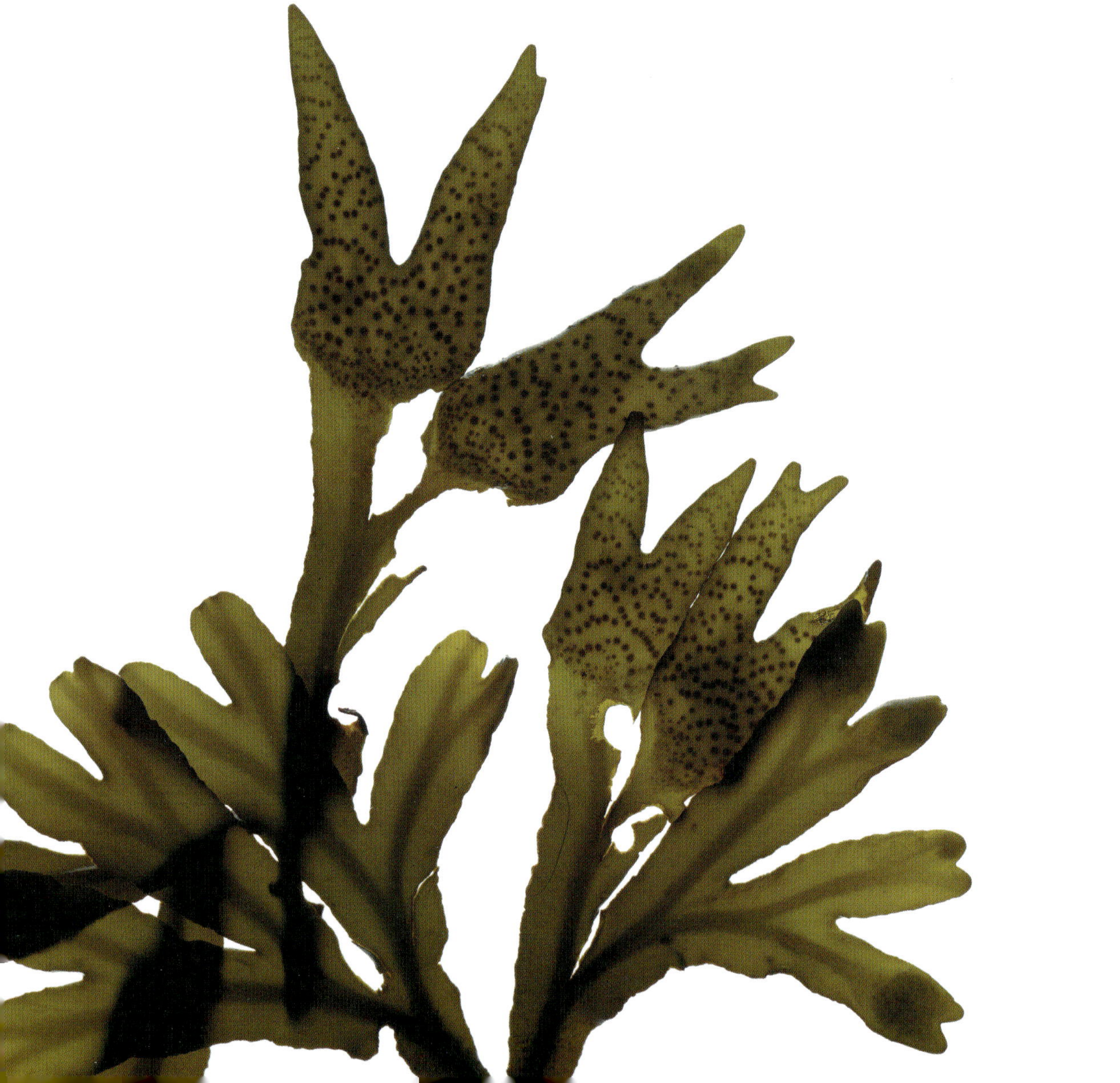

Fucus distichus

Bladderwrack

Ascophyllum and *Fucus*, knotweed and bladderwrack, are good examples of dichotomous growth, where each stipe splits in two. *Ascophyllum* (see page 50) cannot survive rough wave action and will not be found where there is active surf, but the protected bays and coves of North America's northeast coast are ideal. Its slippery composure dominates the beach there, keeping even the most sure-footed beach lovers tentative in their exploration.

Despite the constant drying and wetting, desiccation and rehydration, individual organisms of knotweed can be ten to fifteen years old, the new growth a brilliant olive at the tips of older, darker fronds. Its age can be counted by the bladders it has produced: one per year (plus two—for the first two, bladderless years of its growth). And while these old ladies hold their territory well, producing new blades from existing holdfasts, they do not reproduce efficiently. Finding little ones under the skirts of the established mamas makes for an extended treasure hunt.

opposite:
Fucus distichus
Fort Funston,
San Francisco, CA
April 17, 2012

overleaf left:
Ascophyllum nodosum
KNOTWEED
Fox Island Thoroughfare,
Penobscot Bay, ME
August 8, 2012

overleaf right:
Fucus vesiculosus
BLADDERWRACK
Fox Island Thoroughfare,
Penobscot Bay, ME
August 8, 2012

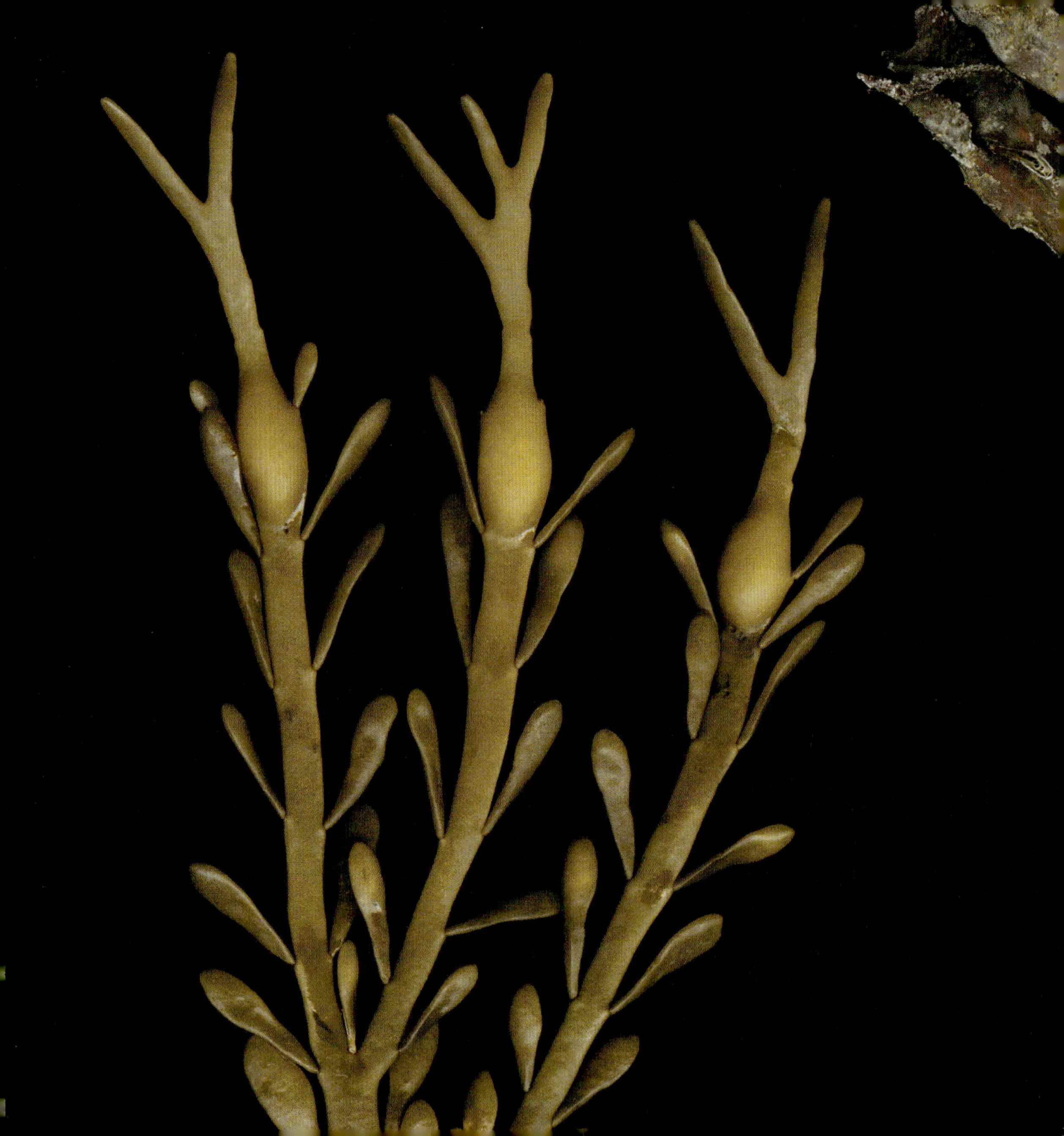

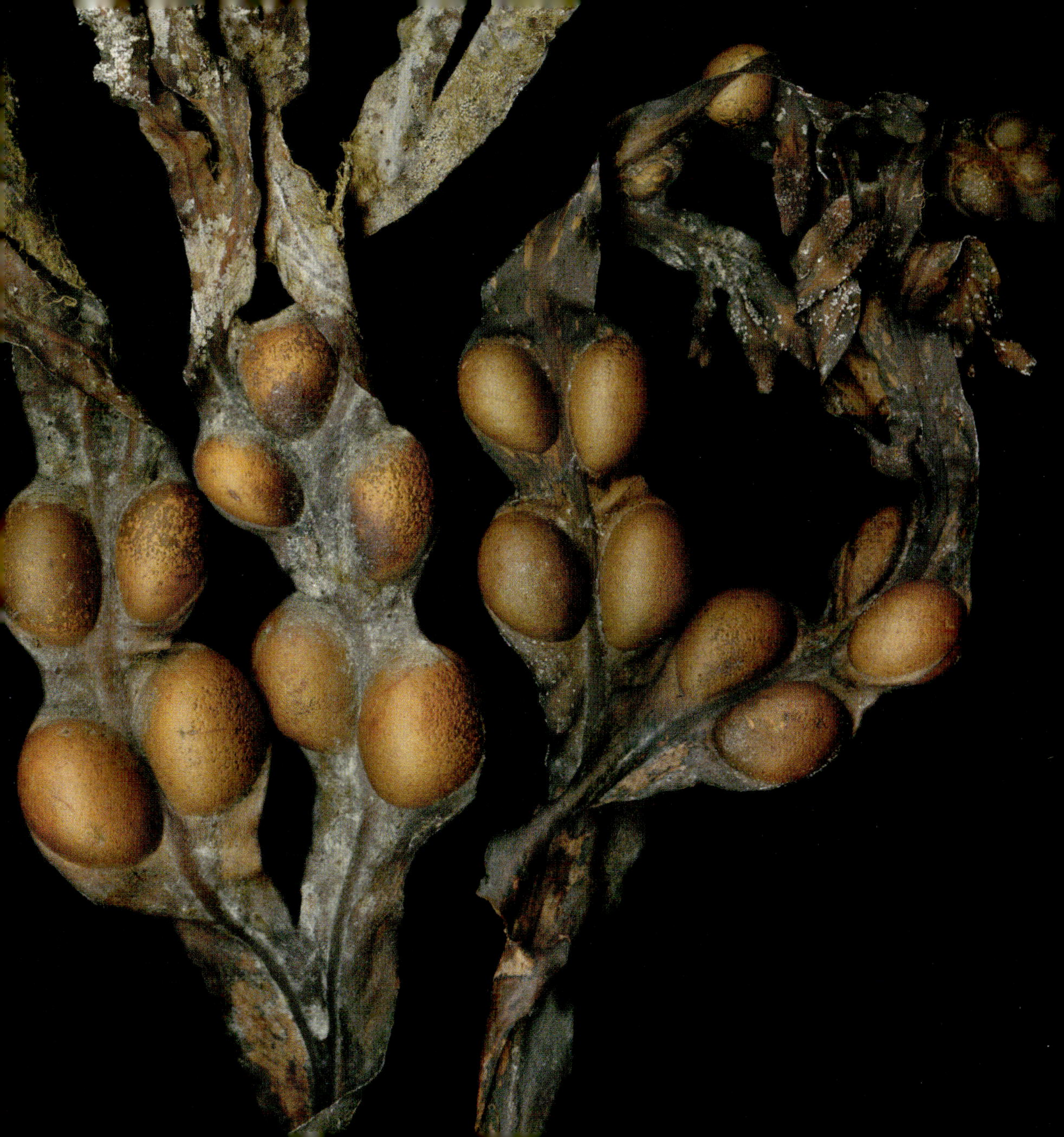

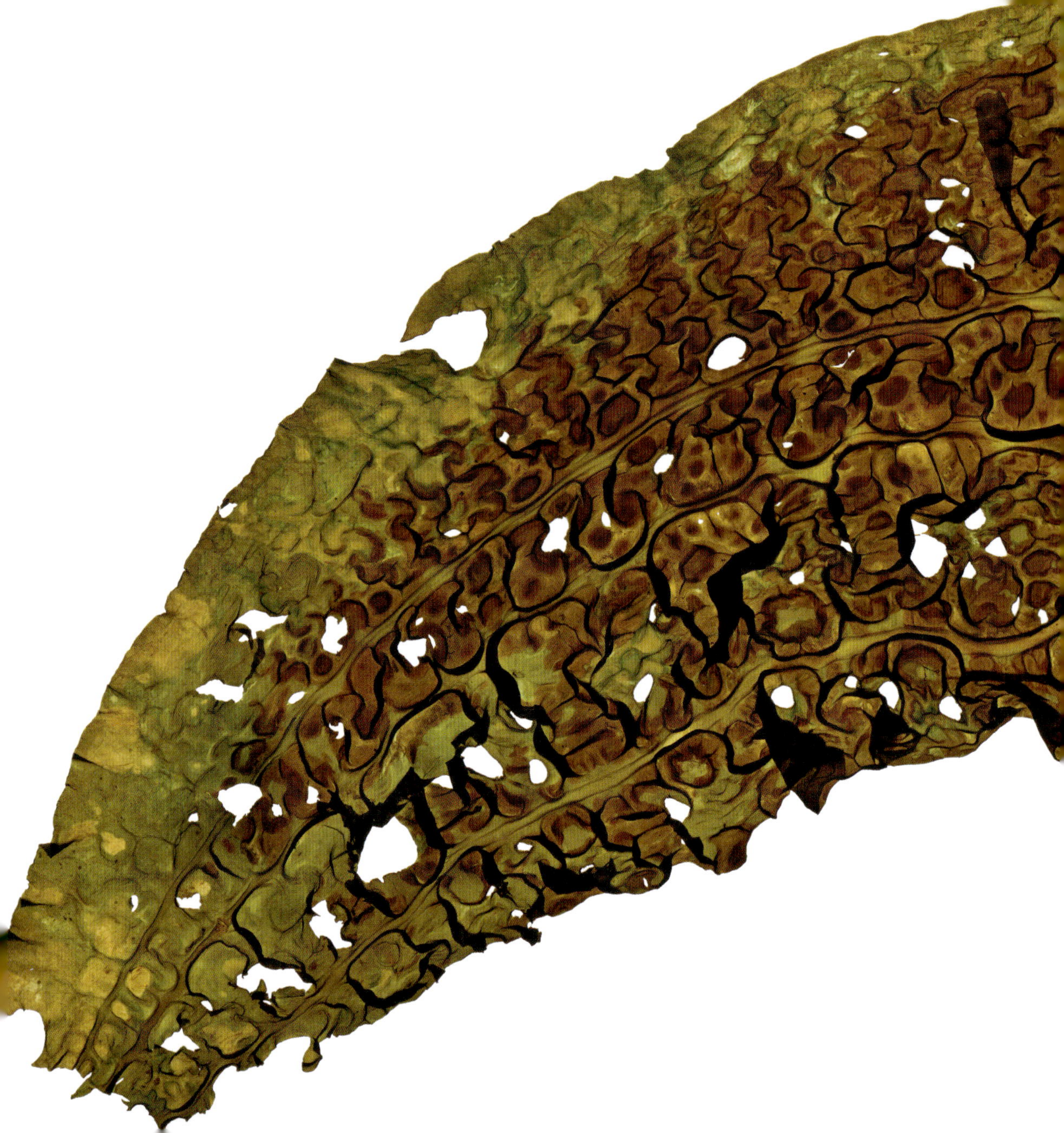

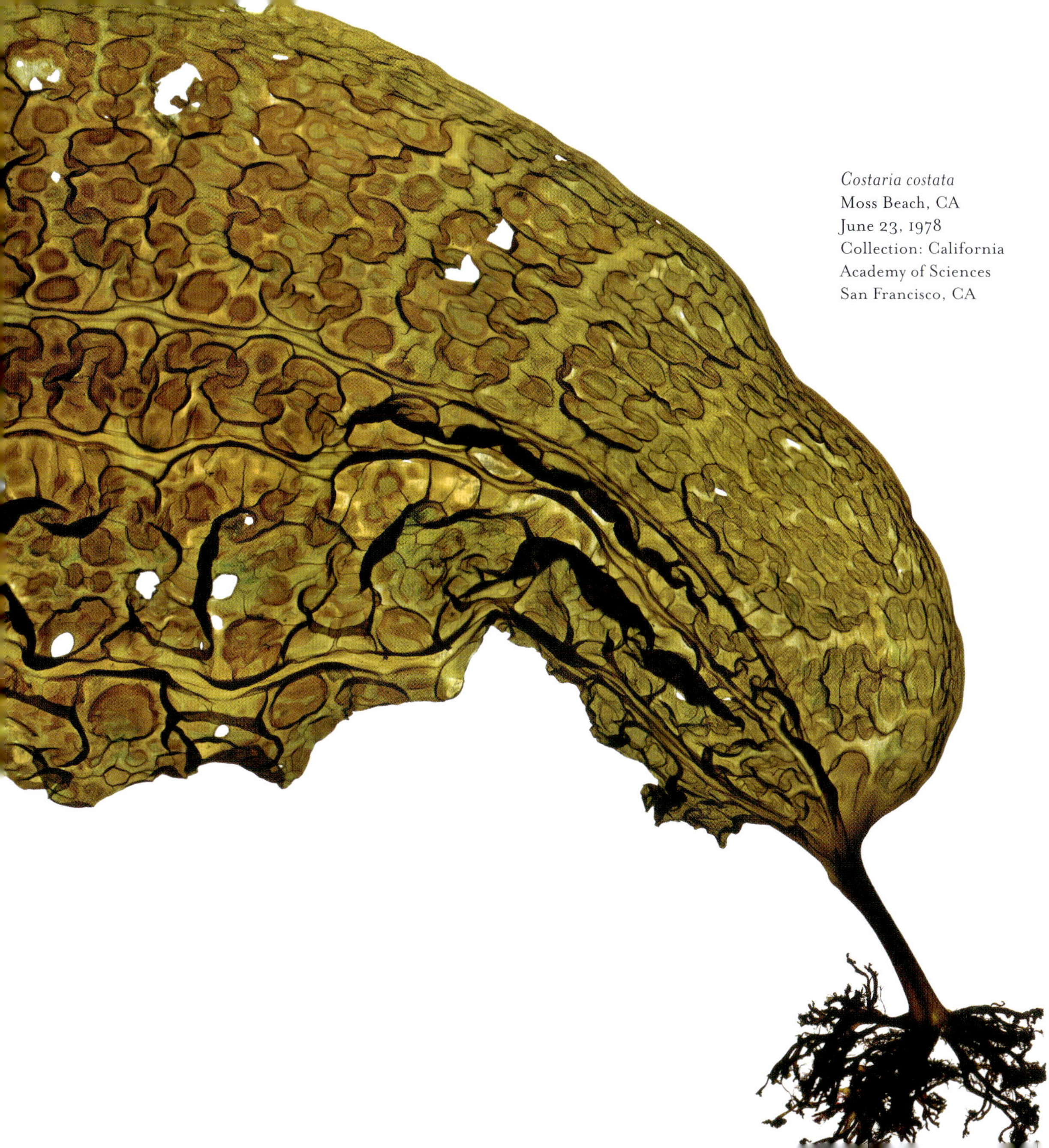

Costaria costata
Moss Beach, CA
June 23, 1978
Collection: California Academy of Sciences
San Francisco, CA

Osmundea spectabilis
PEPPER DULSE
Cambria, CA
May 12, 2012

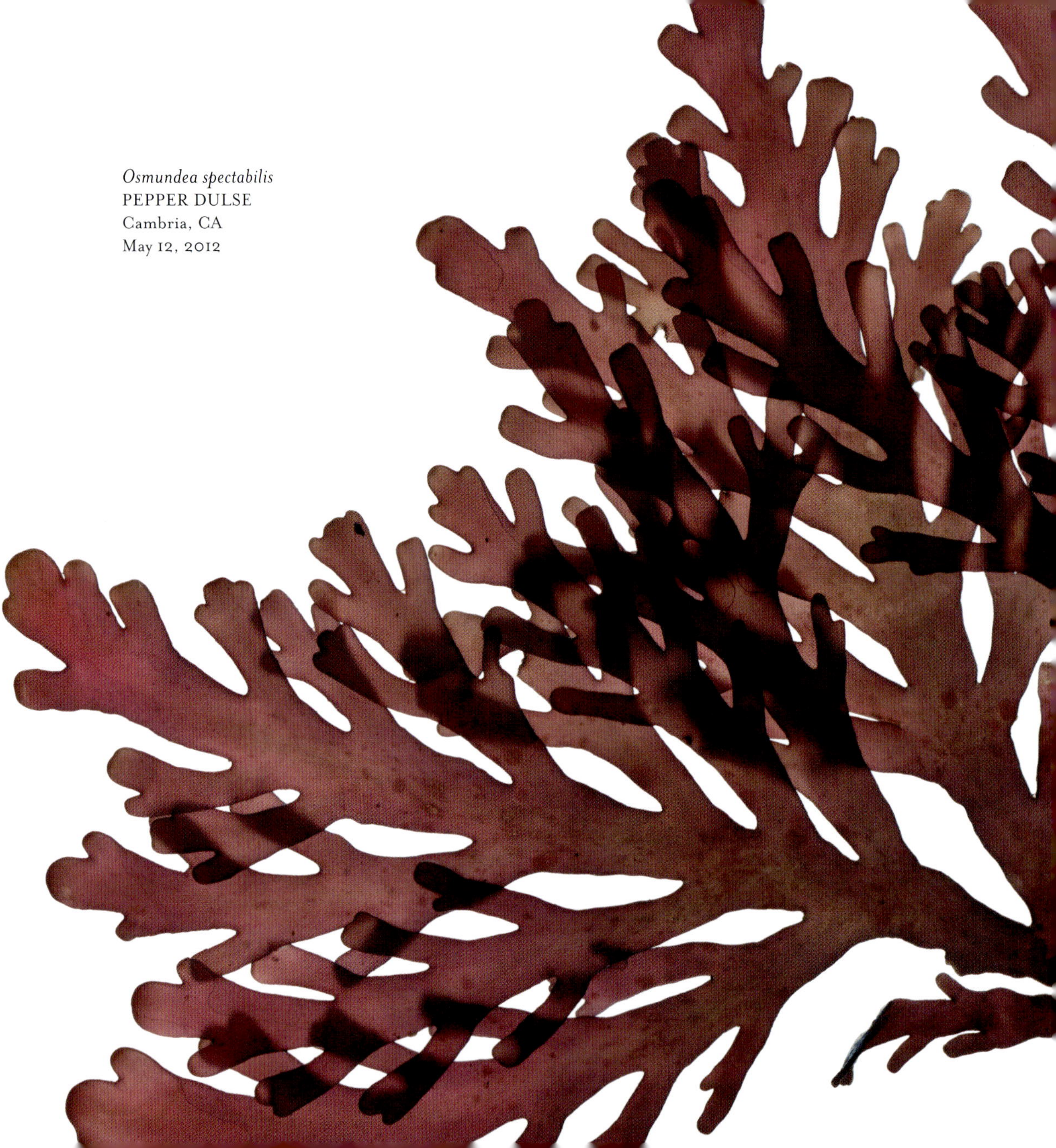

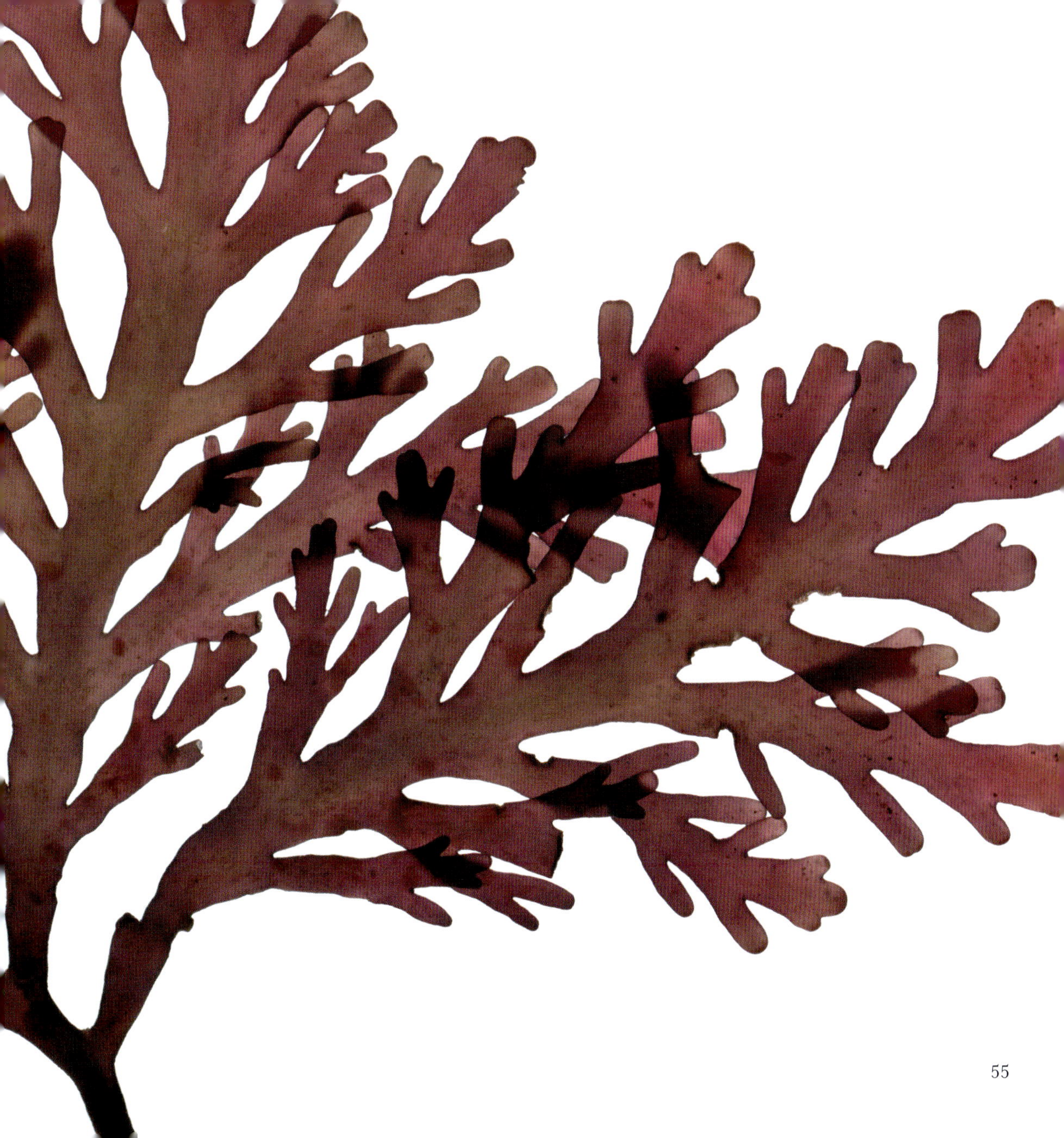

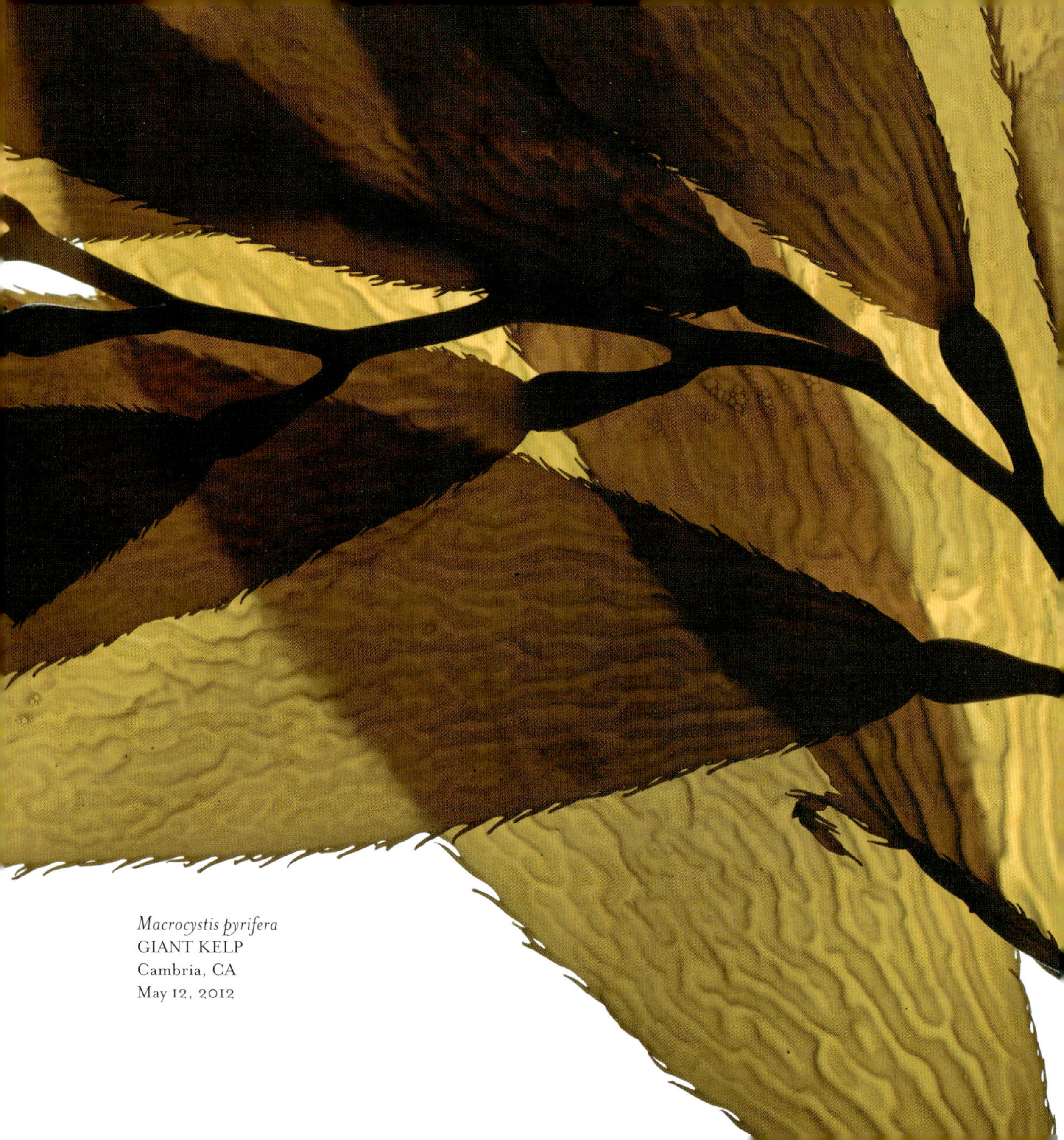

Macrocystis pyrifera
GIANT KELP
Cambria, CA
May 12, 2012

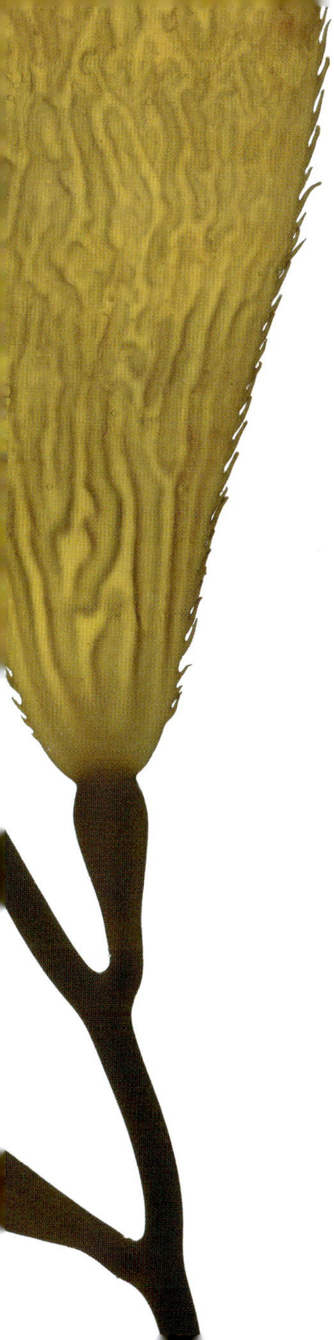

Macrocystis pyrifera

Giant Kelp

Macrocystis pyrifera, the amber giant of the kelp forests, is the most romantic of seaweeds. We should all want skin as resilient and flexible as the beautiful *Macrocystis*, frequently found among the wrack of a California beach. Its direct connection to the ocean makes it a powerful marketing image: Its blades adorn advertisements for high-end hand cream, and it's not a gimmick. Seaweed derivatives, such as the phycocolloid called "alginate," made from the cell walls of *Macrocystis*, have long been the emulsifying agent in skin-care products. But today, seaweed in toto is used as the active ingredient in many health-enhancing body lotions.

As anyone who swims in the ocean knows, seawater has magically rejuvenating powers. The waters of the ocean are a complex mix of water and minerals, salt (sodium chloride) being the most obvious, but the others—potassium, calcium, magnesium, chlorine, and iodine—make a rich medium in which to grow. The seaweeds and kelps that thrive along the edges of the earth's oceans soak up the sun's energy to make the complex sugar molecules that fuel growth. They also are self-sufficient in their environment, absorbing the nutrients they need directly from the seawater through their cell walls. Seaweeds have the sea and all its medicinal and psychic healing powers in every cell.

For humans, seaweed is perhaps the most powerful food on earth, containing, in concentrated form, most of the minerals and vitamins vital to strength and long life. While it is still a nose crinkler in most American kitchens, health spas and skin-lotion manufacturers have embraced it with enthusiasm as the active ingredient in antiaging treatments, and as a topical way to create balance and to revitalize body and soul.

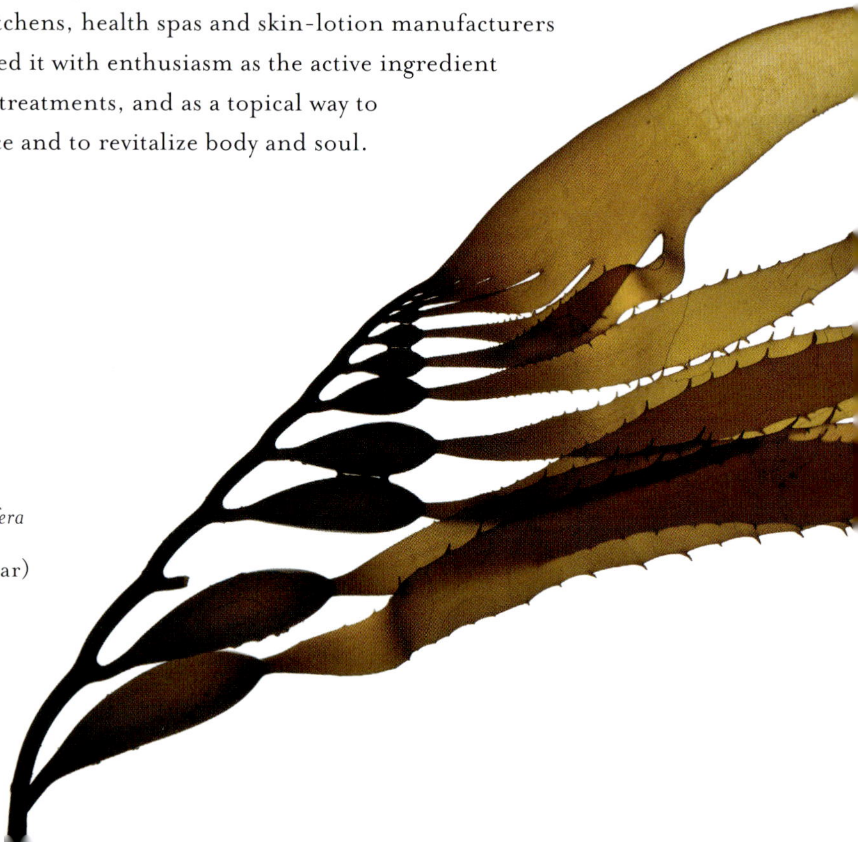

Macrocystis pyrifera
GIANT KELP
(apical scimitar)
Cambria, CA
May 12, 2012

Balance and harmony have everything to do with salt. It is a life-preserving element used in almost every aspect of our body's physiology, from hormone communication to muscle and nerve functioning. Sodium controls the balance of liquid in our own tissues and performs the same task for the seaweeds. The synchronicity between seawater and seaweed is best illuminated when the salt is removed, or a specimen is put into freshwater. I made this mistake once, dropping a large and beautiful *Macrocystis* into a bucket of freshwater.

Immediately, without the higher density of the mineralized seawater to keep osmosis in balance, the cell walls emitted their goo-like substances, the phycocolloids, turning the beautiful array of golden bladders and blades into a sticky, oozing mess.

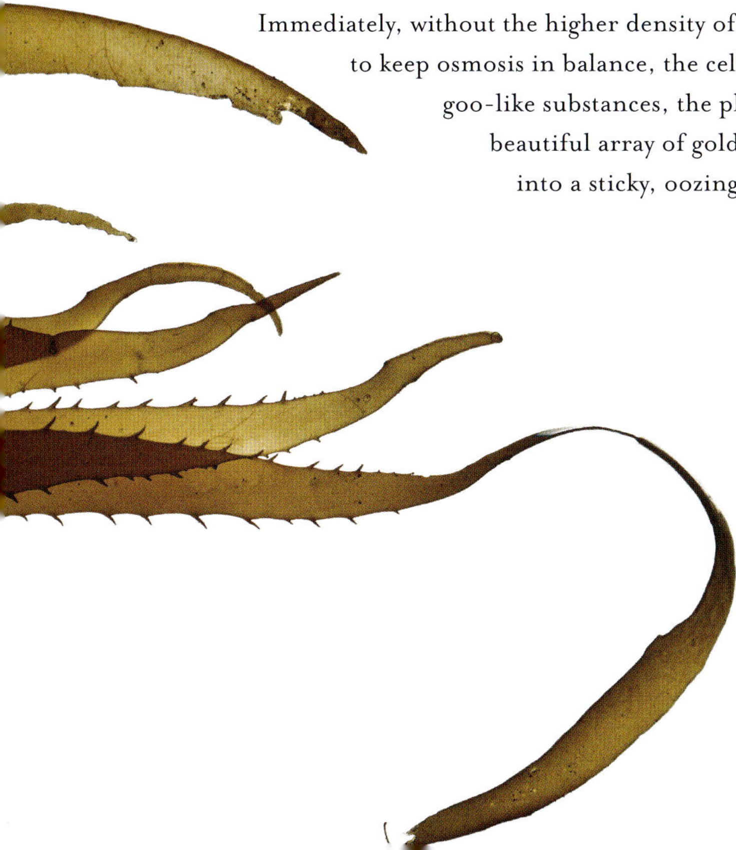

overleaf:
Macrocystis bladders

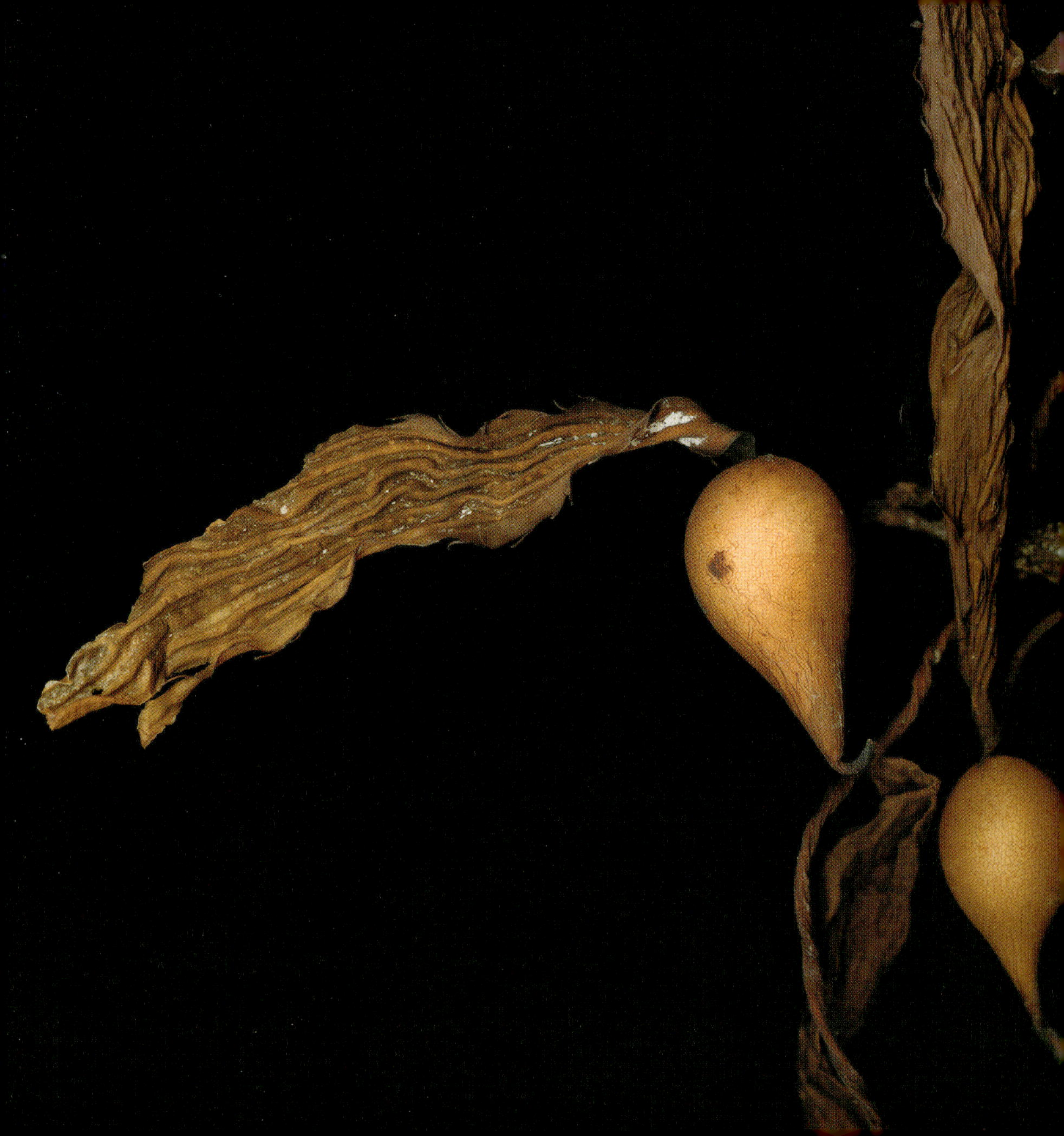

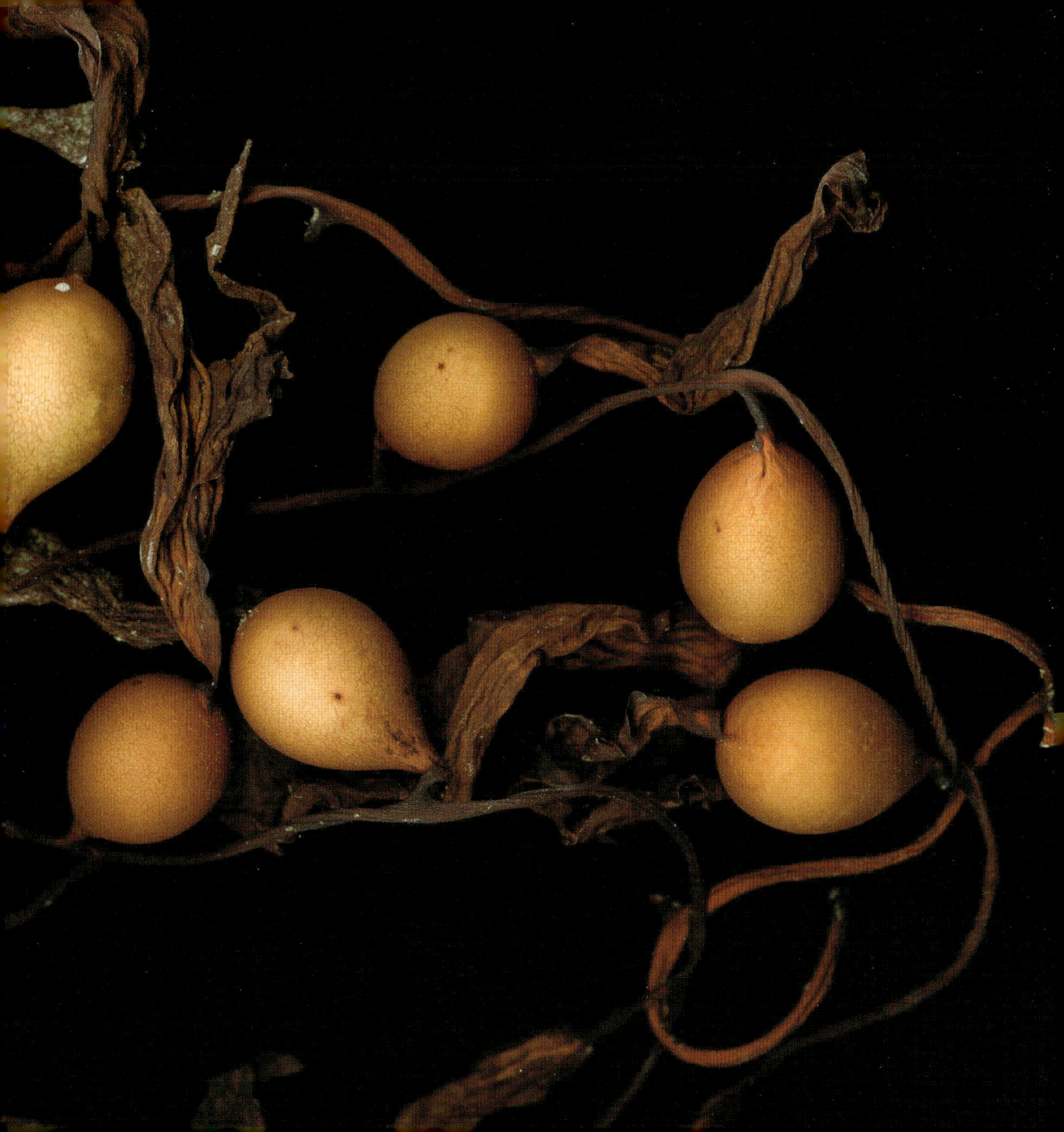

While the remarkable shapes of the giant kelp evoke the mystery and wonder of undersea life, there is functionality to this seaweed's form. The ovoid bladders, like tiny buoys, hold the blades upright toward the sun. The flat, wide blades maximize surface exposure for efficient photosynthesis, and the rugose (wavy) texture of ridges and rivulets along each blade creates a localized turbulence that brings fresh nourishment to each cell.

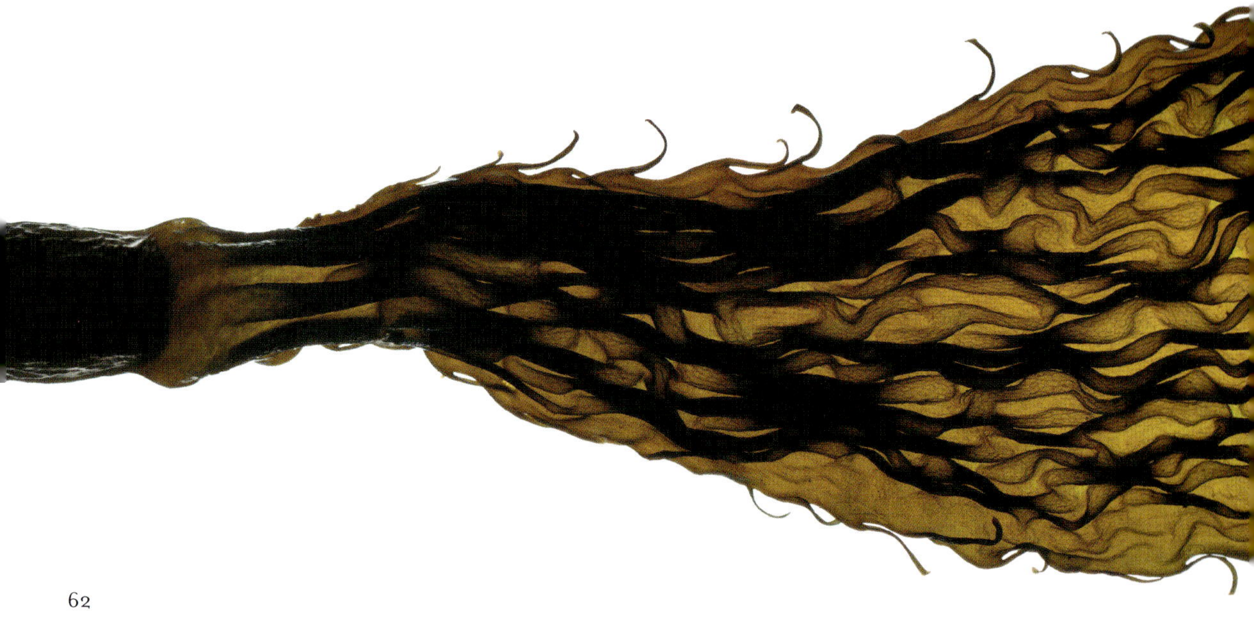

Macrocystis pyrifera
GIANT KELP
(single blade)
Cambria, CA
May 13, 2012

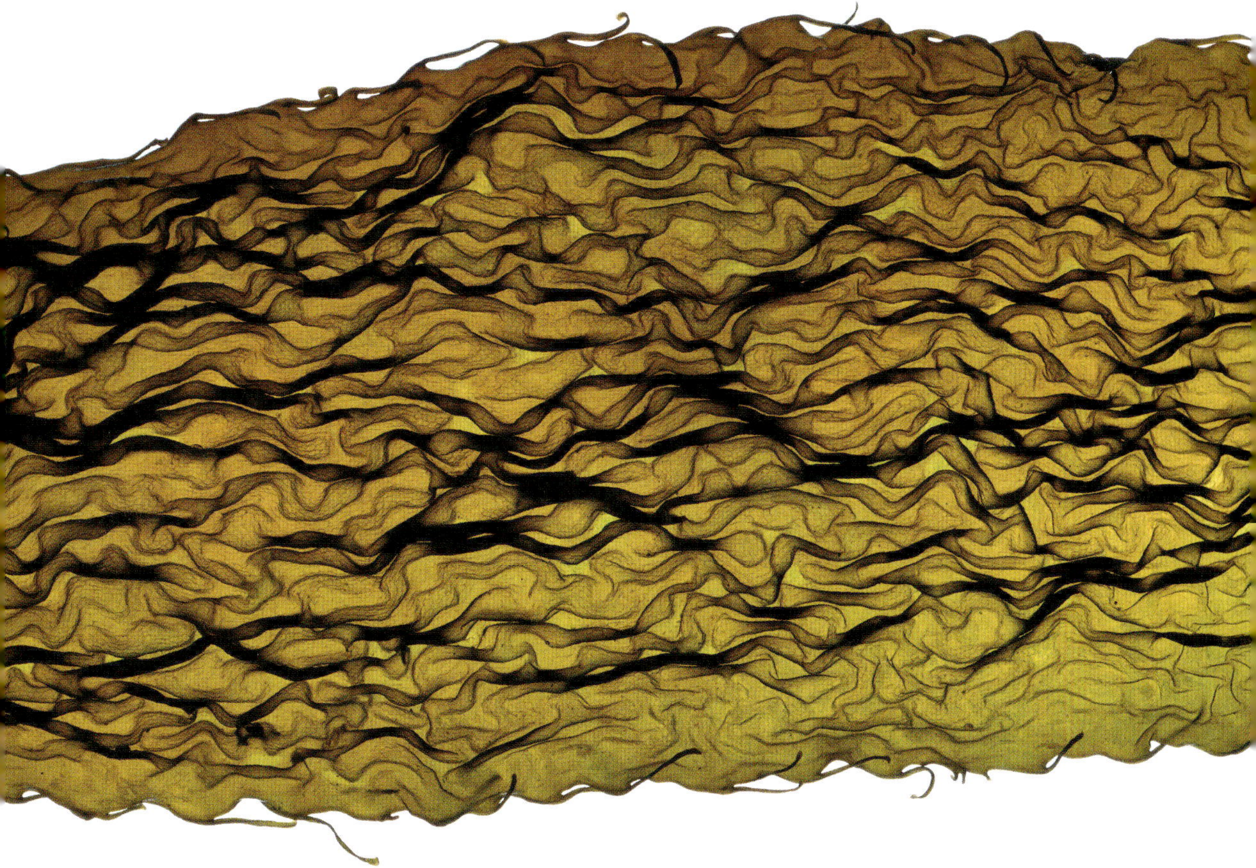

The giant kelp can live up to six years or more, but the reproductive cycle for this robust organism is complex—as it is for all seaweeds—and involves a discreet, sometimes invisible, generation. Spores are created by the specialized blades, which are called sporophylls, at the base of the kelp. The tiny spores disperse and settle on the ocean floor, and develop into male or female gametophytes, microscopic organisms that produce either an egg or sperm. Amazingly, a sperm follows a pheromone trail to find an egg, and once fertilized, the egg divides and begins growing in two directions at once, downward into the holdfast and upward into a tiny, single-bladed sporophyte, or baby kelp. This blade will

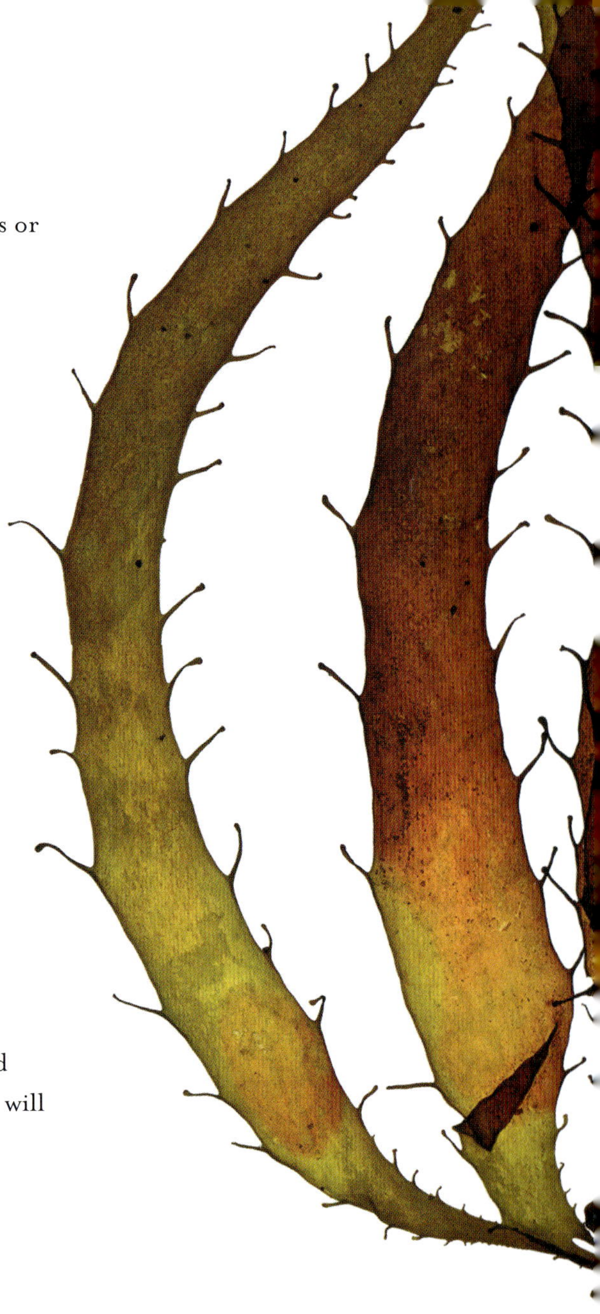

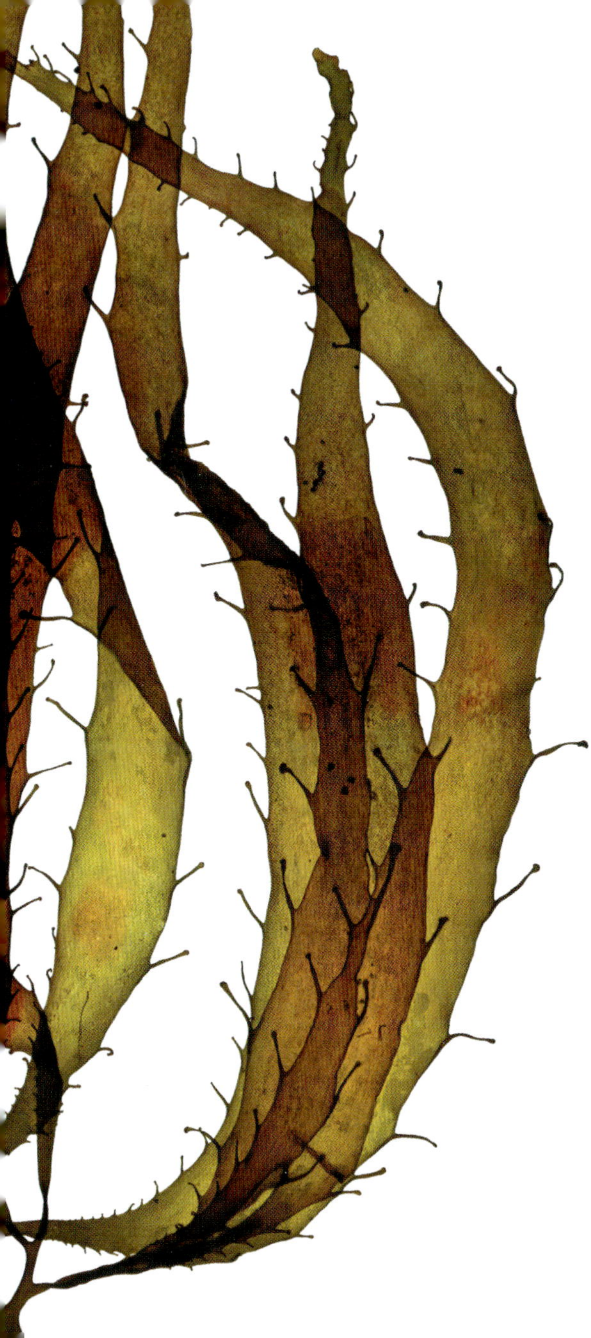

split in two and eventually develop into
the amber giant of the kelp forests.
These intricate steps have evolved
to occur in concert with the ebb
and flow of tide and current—
a miracle that is yet to be
completely understood.

Macrocystis pyrifera
GIANT KELP
(sporophyll blades)
Cambria, CA
May 12, 2012

overleaf:
Two *Macrocystis* holdfasts
(one fresh and one dried)

page 68:
Kelp holdfast

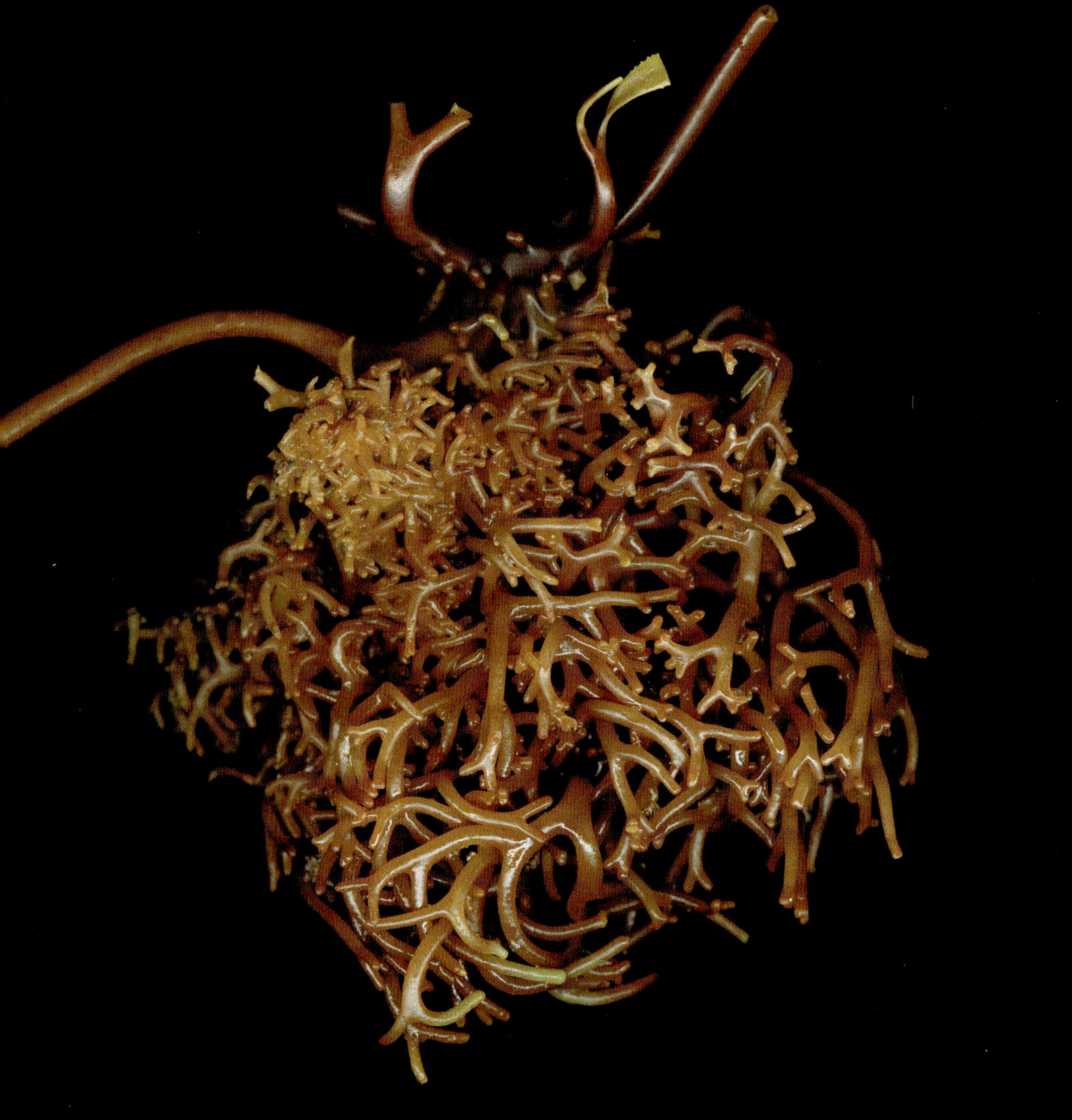

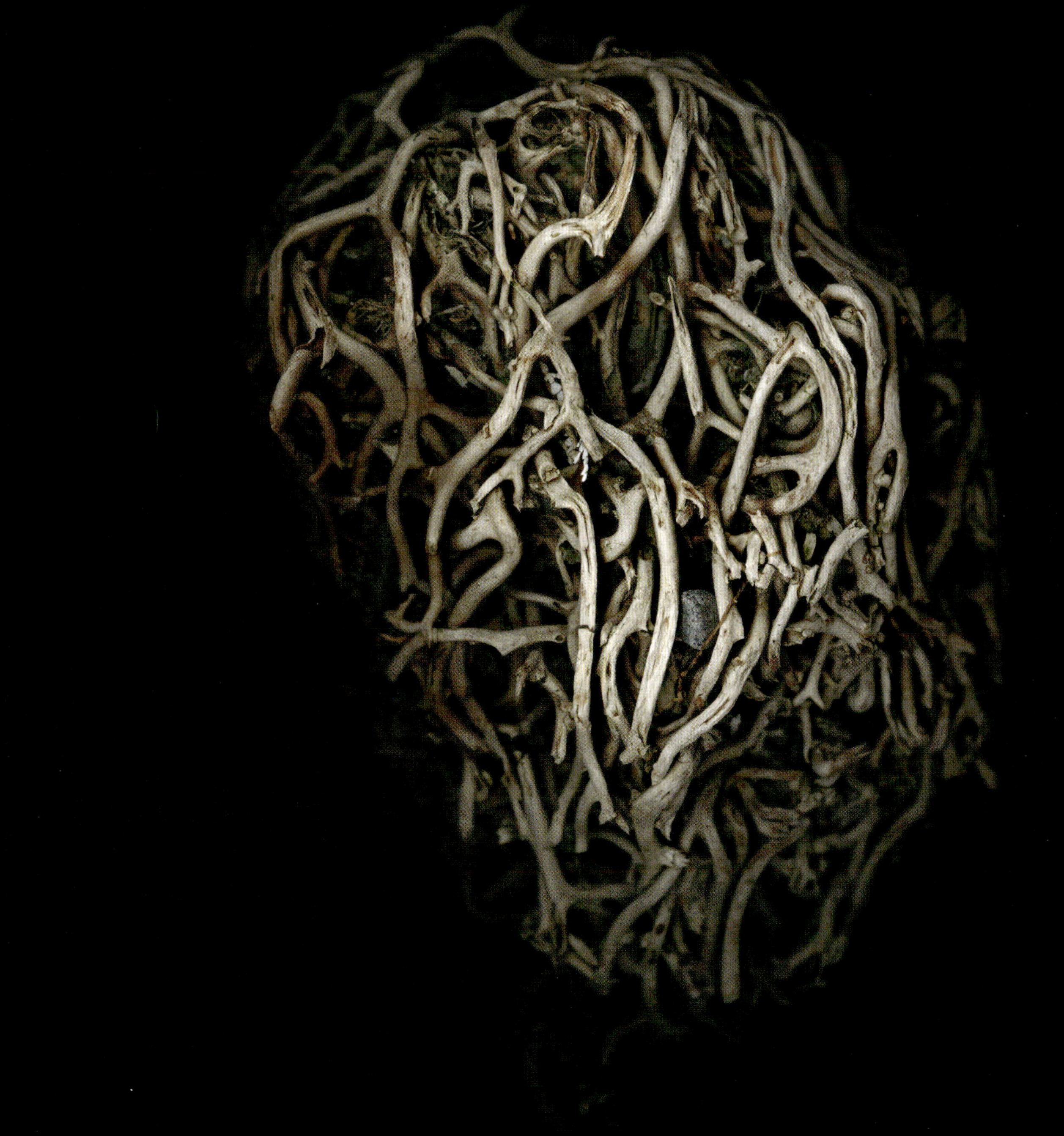

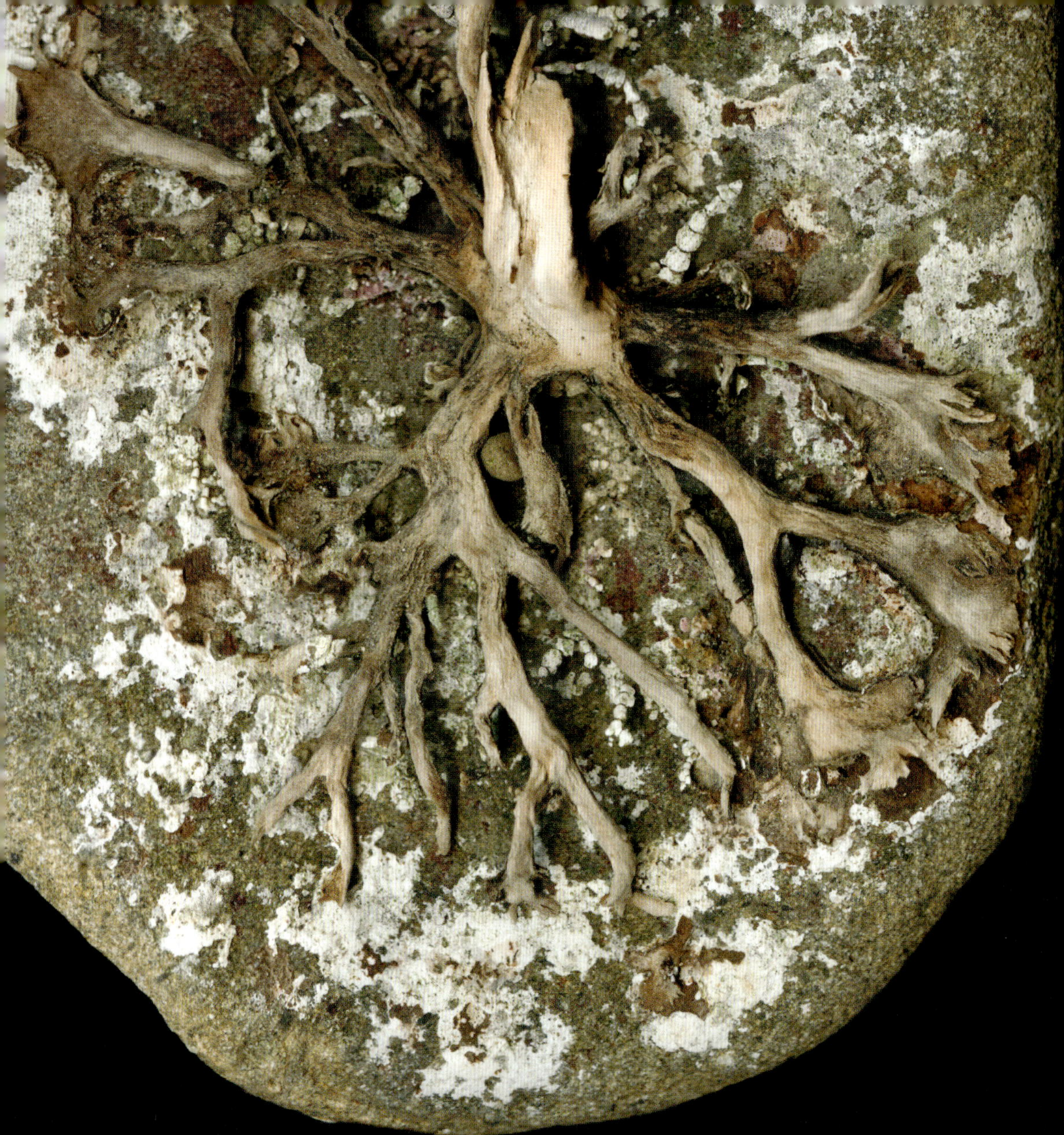

The Holdfast

The holdfast's connection to the sea floor is a magnificent thing—one of those feats of nature that far exceeds human engineering. Despite the immense torque and forces of ocean current and wave action, the holdfast's "glue" is strong.

The holdfasts of the giant kelp grow over many years into complex and persistent structures. The root-like strands (they are not actually roots), called "haptera," of the young plant spread out rapidly, grabbing either a rocky portion of the sea floor, or latching on to worm casings that penetrate into a sandy bottom. As the holdfast ages, the newer, colorful haptera—they can be red, pink, or even purple—grow over the inner core of older dead growth, making a massive, cone-shaped edifice. Over the years, this maze-like anchor expands upward, becoming an underwater cathedral to the hundreds of species that seek refuge in its catacombs. Research divers at the Scripps Institution of Oceanography exploring the massive kelp forests off San Diego, where entire cities of holdfasts dot the ocean floor, identified more than 175 species living on and in the holdfasts of the *Macrocystis* plants. These include kelp fish, anemones, brittle stars, snails, crabs, and something called a "kelp gibble," which lives exclusively in the dead, central portion, nibbling its way through the haptera. The purse-shaped egg casing of the swell shark secures itself with tendrils to the *Macrocystis* holdfast, allowing its single egg to develop inside while moored safely to home base.

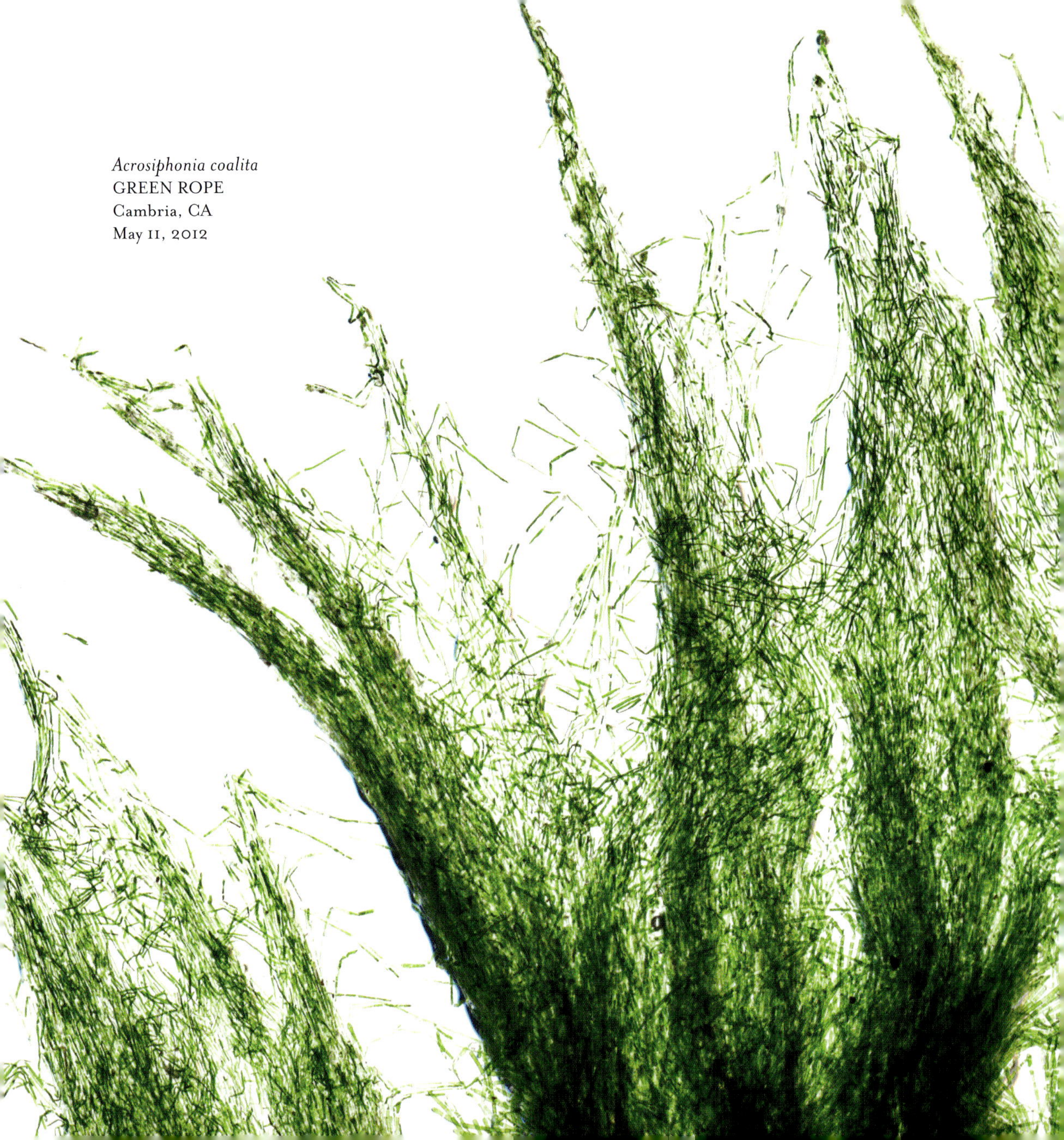

Acrosiphonia coalita
GREEN ROPE
Cambria, CA
May 11, 2012

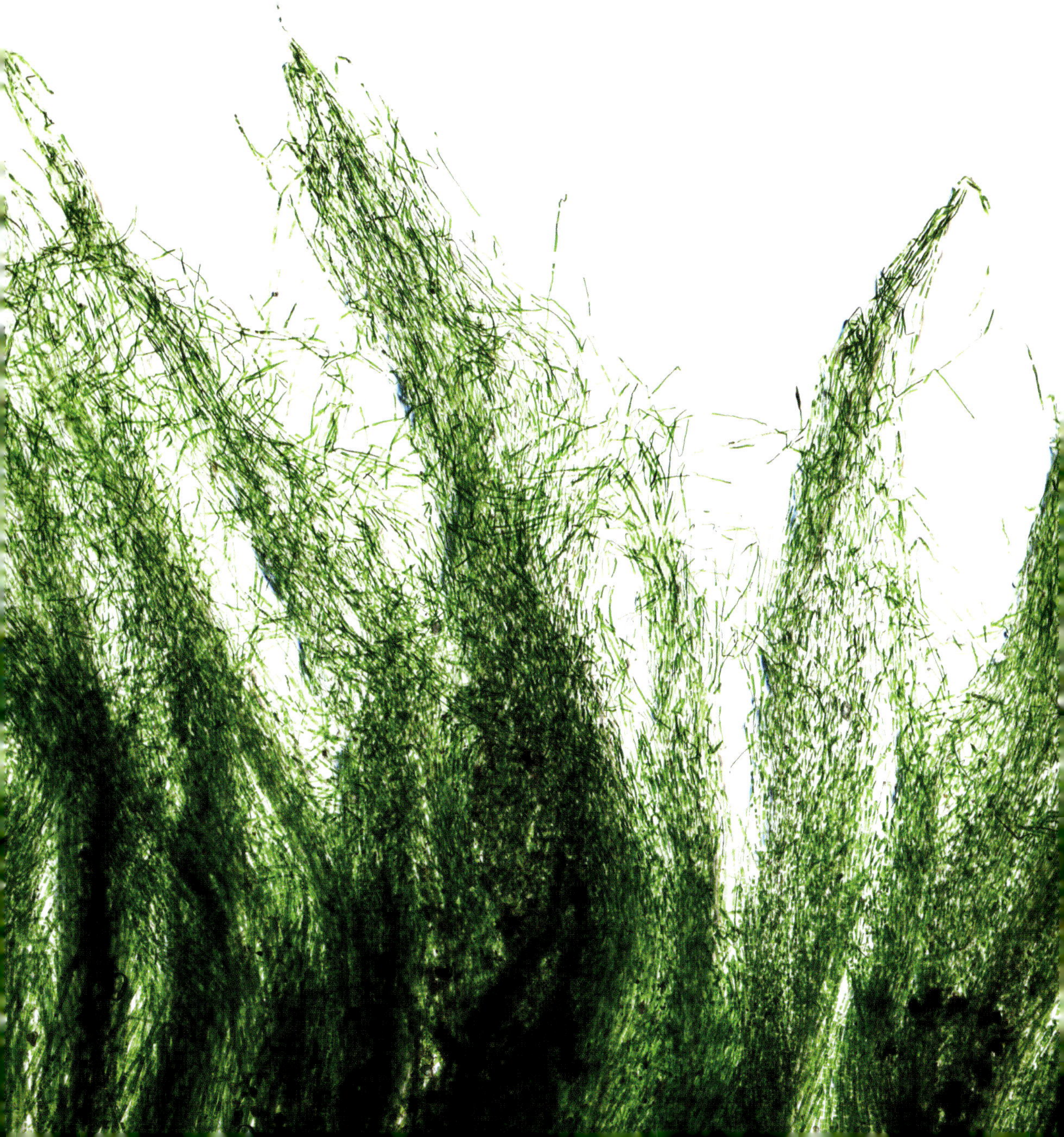

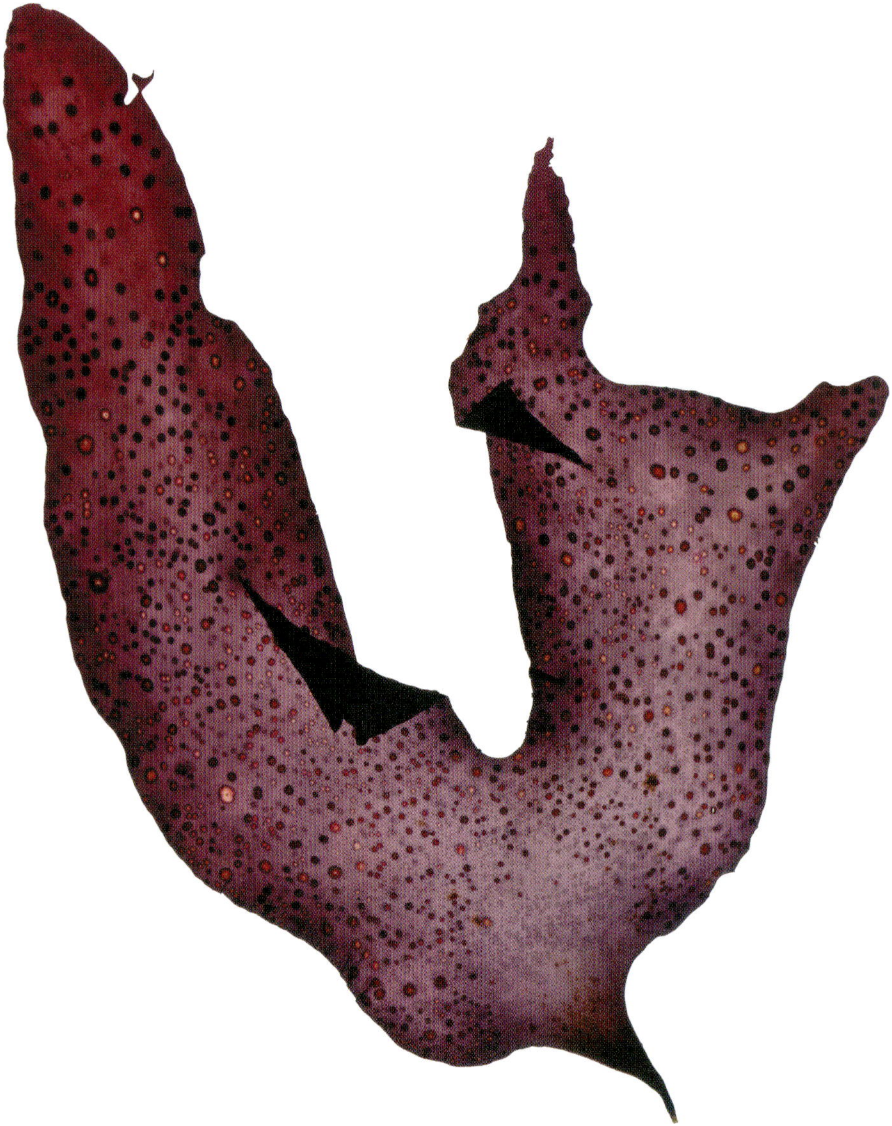

opposite and below:
Mazzaella oregona
Cambria, CA
May 11, 2012

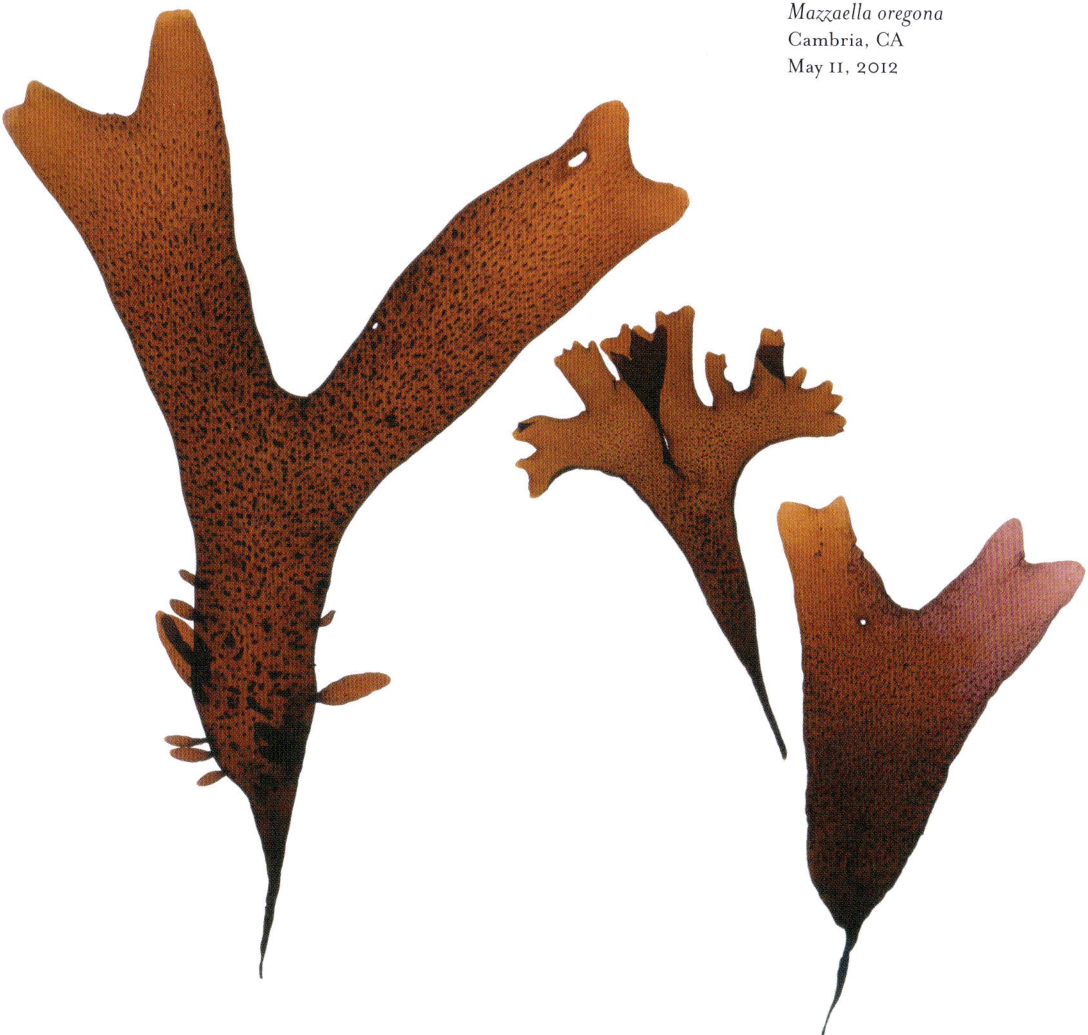

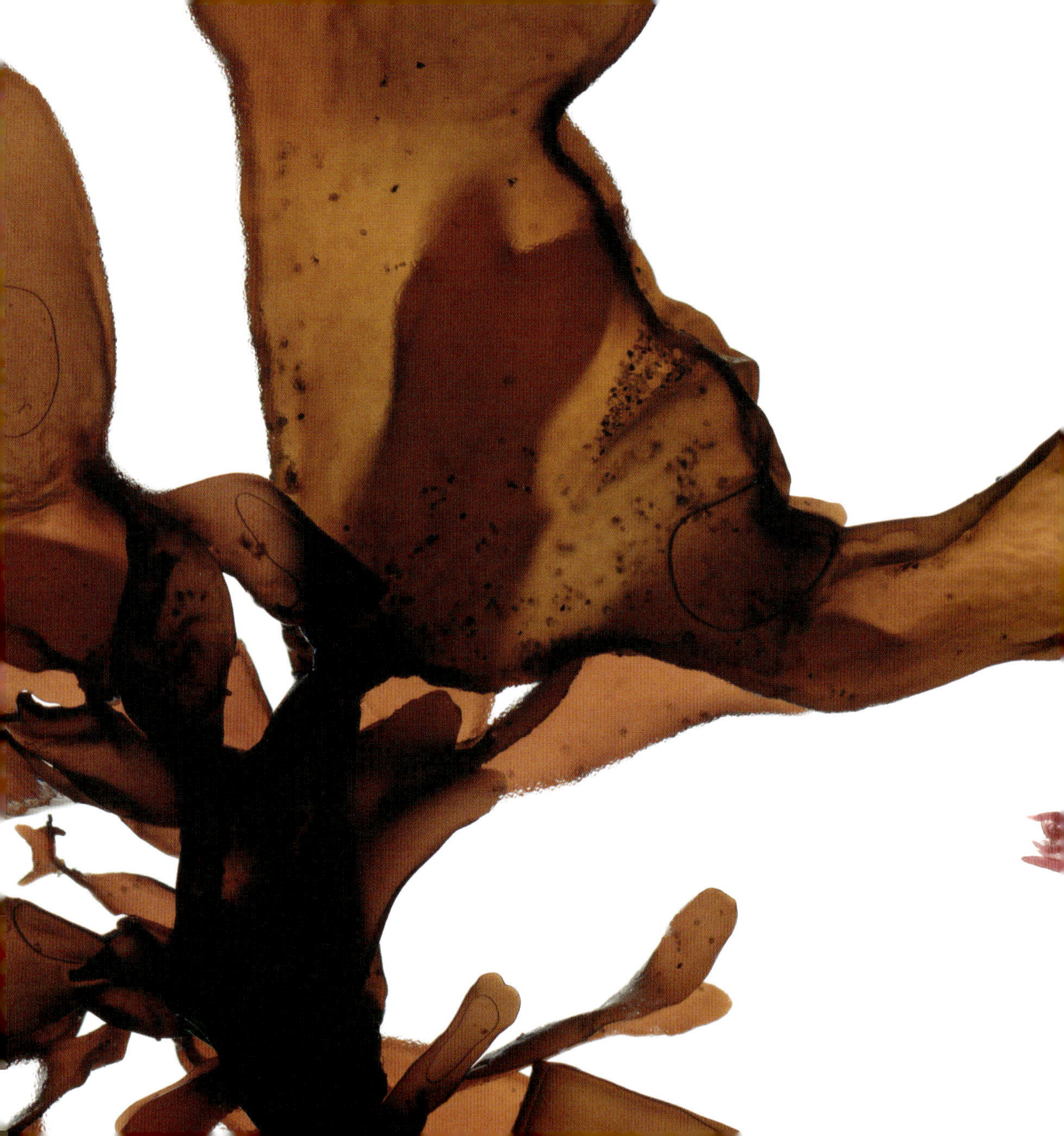

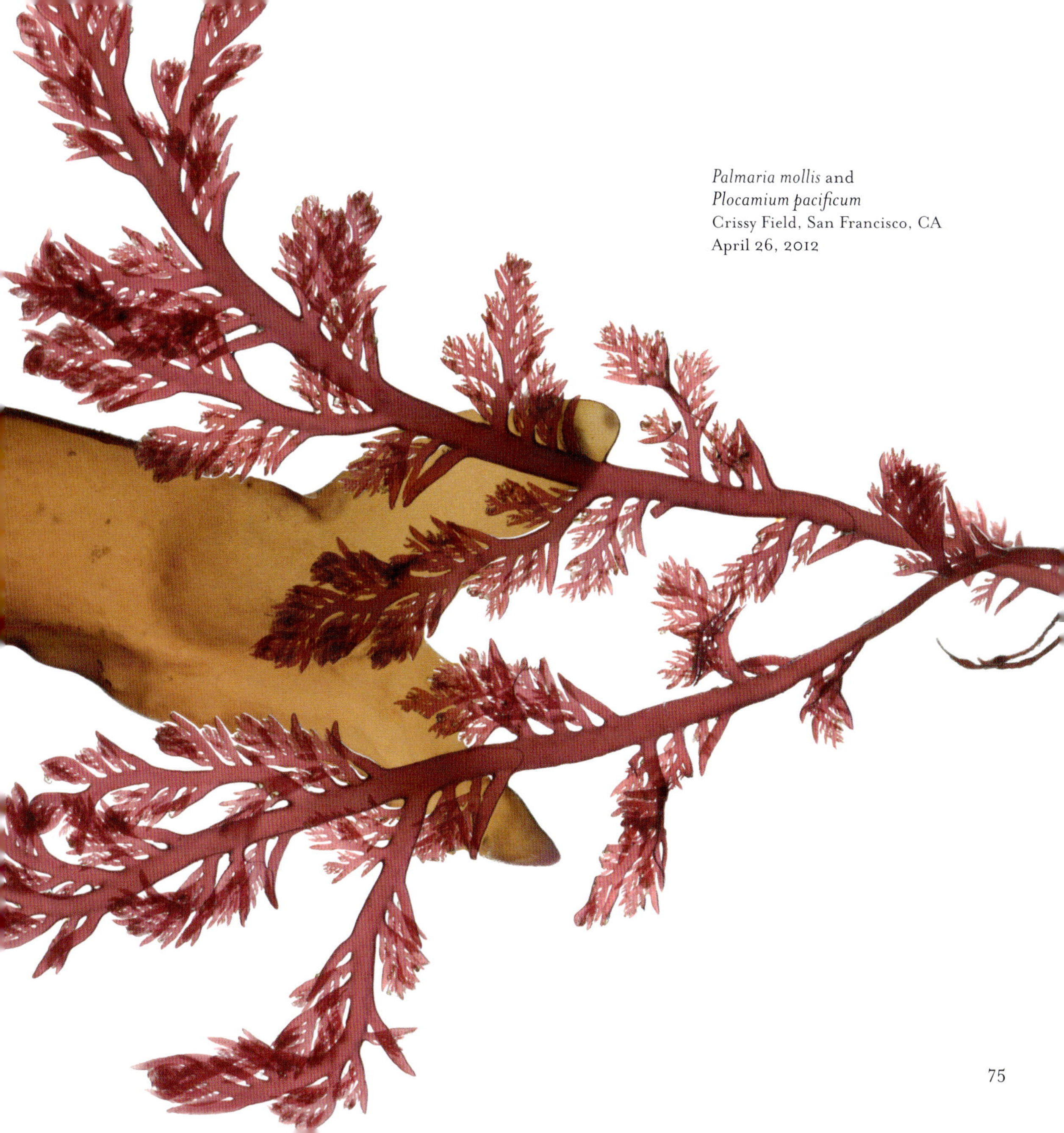

Palmaria mollis and
Plocamium pacificum
Crissy Field, San Francisco, CA
April 26, 2012

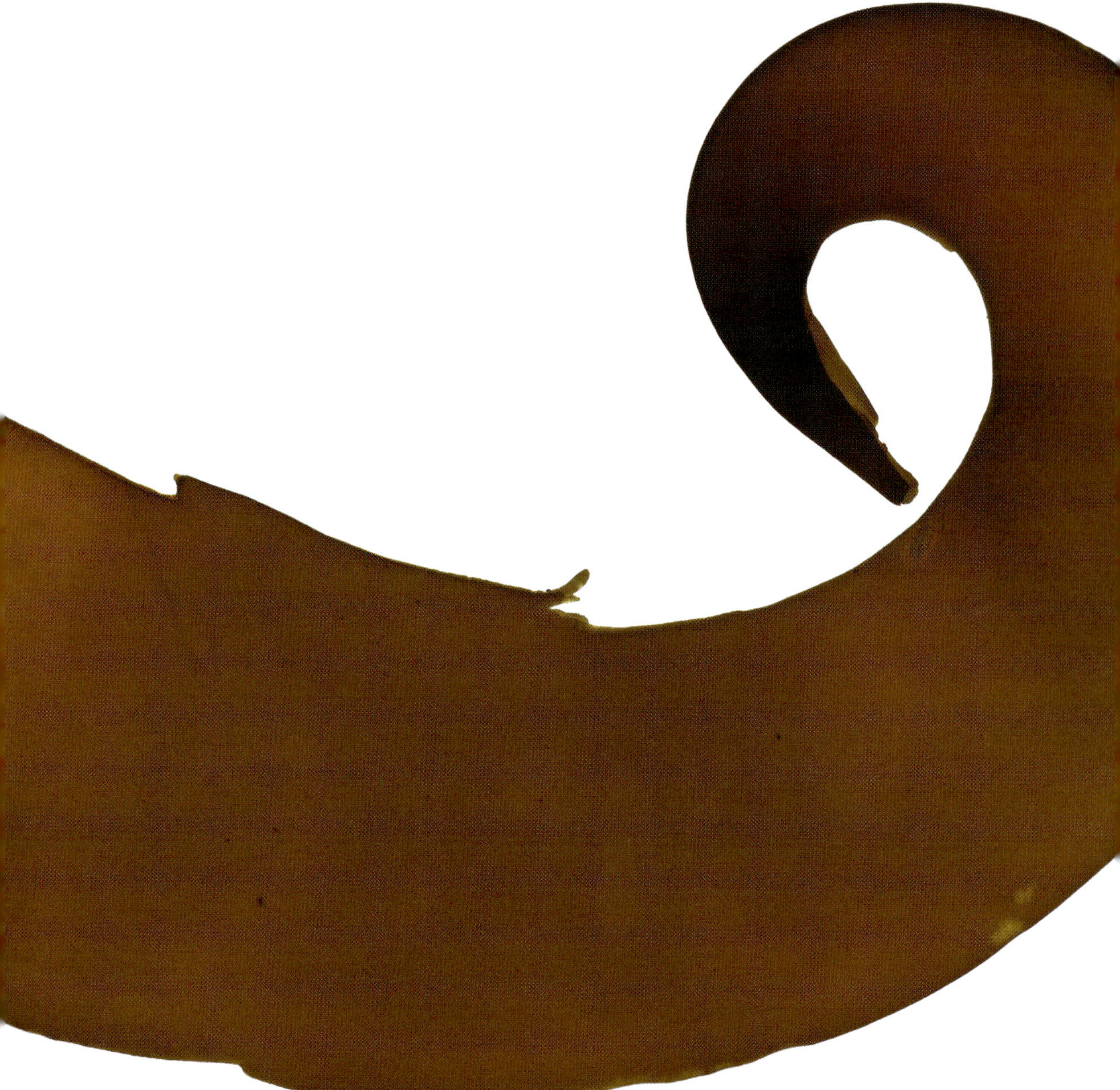

Community

AUGUST 2, FOX ISLAND THOROUGHFARE, ME. This curious specimen reminded me of the *Saccharina latissima* I found wound around the mooring line one morning last summer. Loosed from its bed, the majestic kelp streamed along the surface of the water, its curved, flouncing margin glinting golden in the morning sun. I hated to pull it out of the ocean because instantly, a degree of its fabulousness was lost, but there were bryozoan growths, known as sea lace, on it that warranted deeper investigation. These minute animals growing in star-shaped colonies are similar to yet different than the round-colonied bryozoans *Membranipora* on the delicate pink dulse, *Palmaria palmata*, which I had found nearby, clinging to the stone pier at the lowest tide (see pages 80–81).

The bryozoans clearly love their seaweed. Hitching a permanent ride on kelps and other seaweeds has many advantages for these tiny animals. Gaining motility as a sessile animal must make nearby barnacles envious. The constant motion provided by the host not only provides added access to food particles, but also a defense against predators. Living right on an oxygen source, with each cell of kelp exhaling oxygen ready for the animal's respiratory needs, is also a bonus.

In the chaotic environment of the intertidal landscape, these kinds of interrelationships are key to survival. As it turns out, a certain amount of disruption—by wave action or storm surges—makes for the most diverse marine ecology. Too little disruption leads to overcrowding while too much disruption leads to . . . well, being swept or blown away. Success in the littoral community is not found in the individual staking a claim, but rather through interrelationships and community-building.

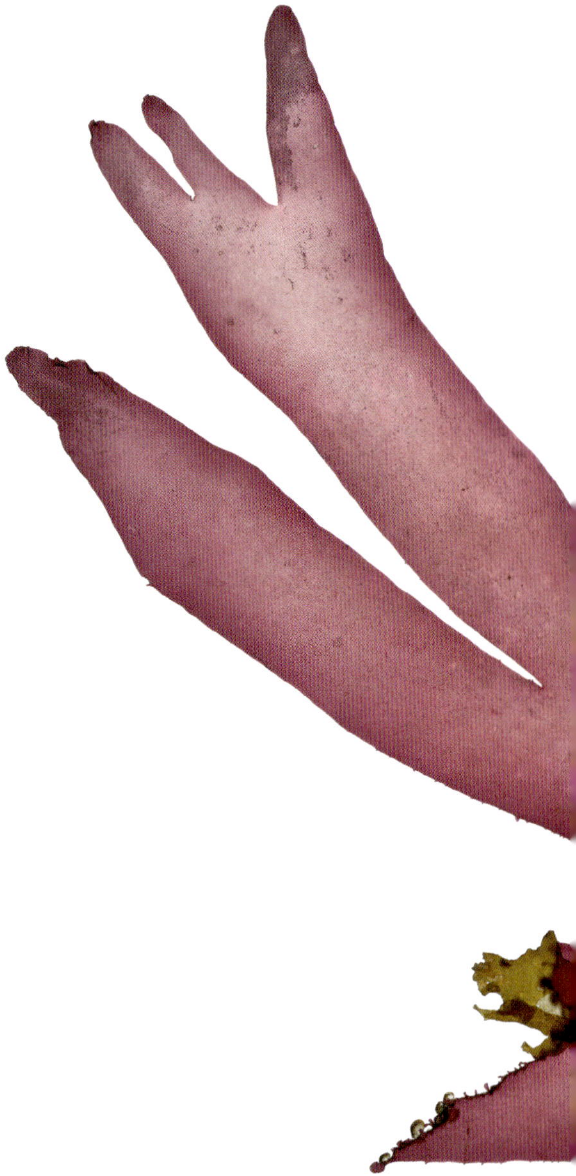

previous spread:
Kelp scrap

right:
Palmaria palmata
DULSE
and
Saccharina latissima scrap
SUGAR KELP
Fox Island Thoroughfare,
Penobscot Bay, ME
July 25, 2012

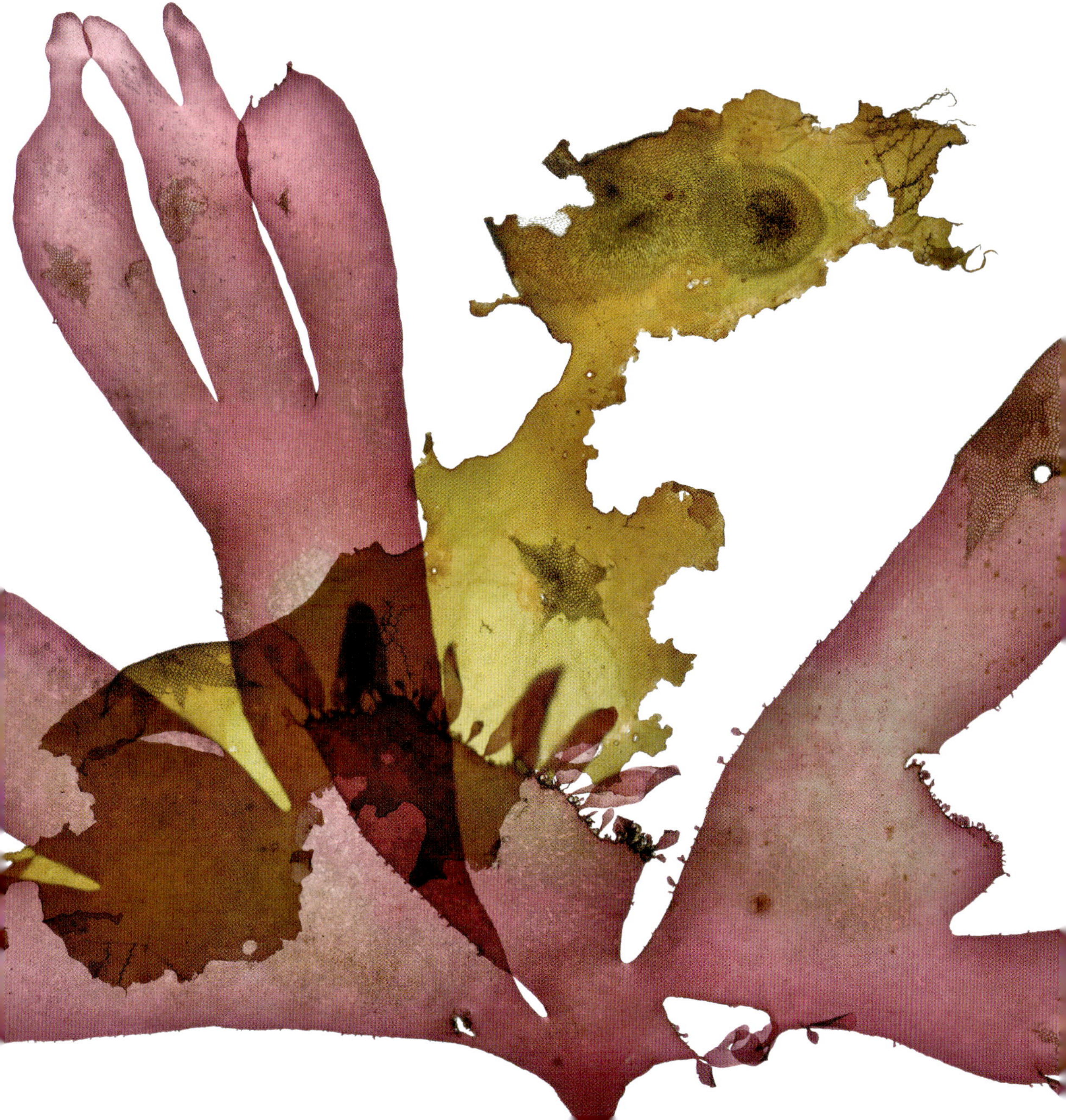

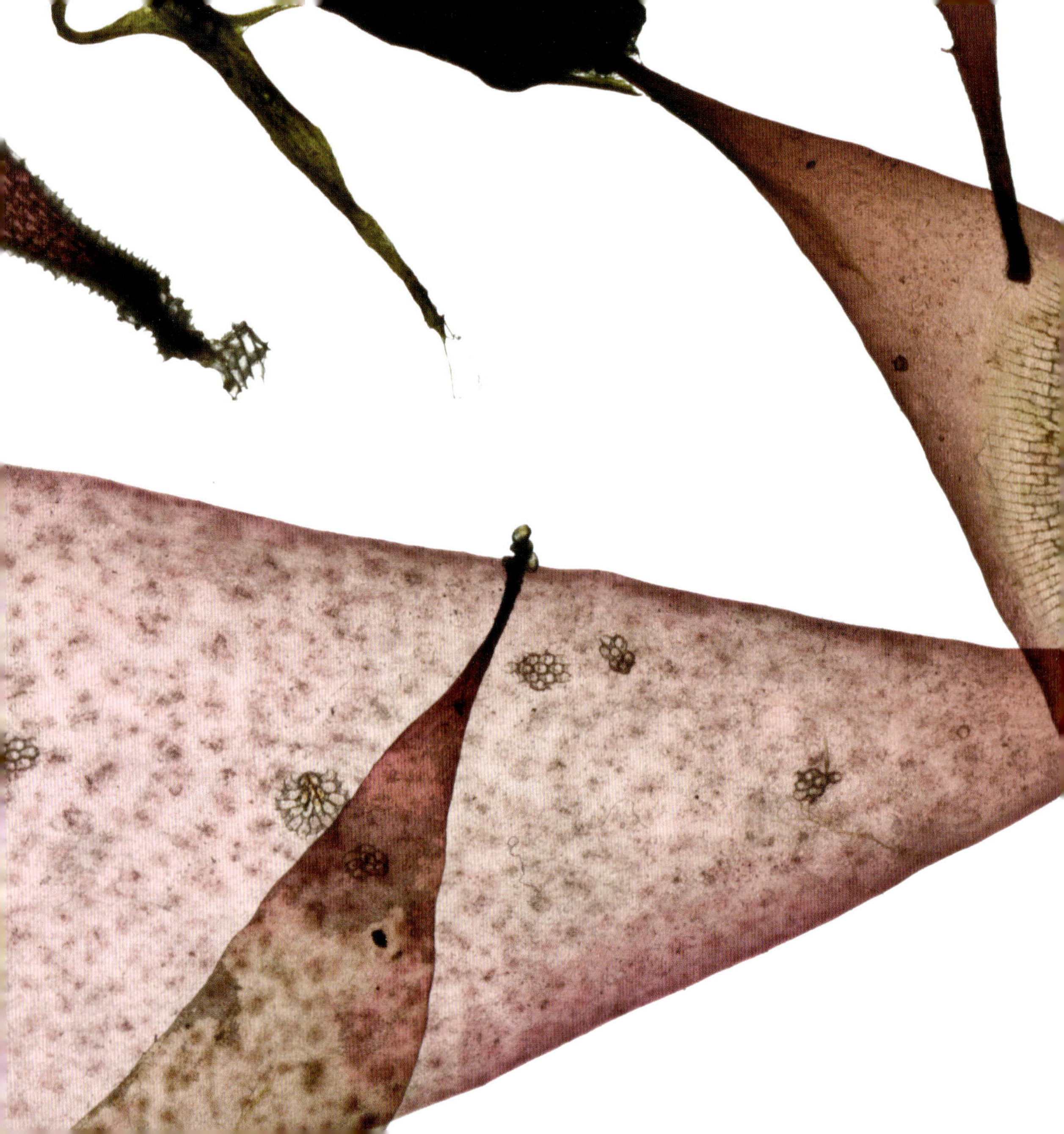

Palmaria palmata
DULSE
(with bryozoan colony)
Fox Island Thoroughfare, Penobscot Bay, ME
July 25, 2012

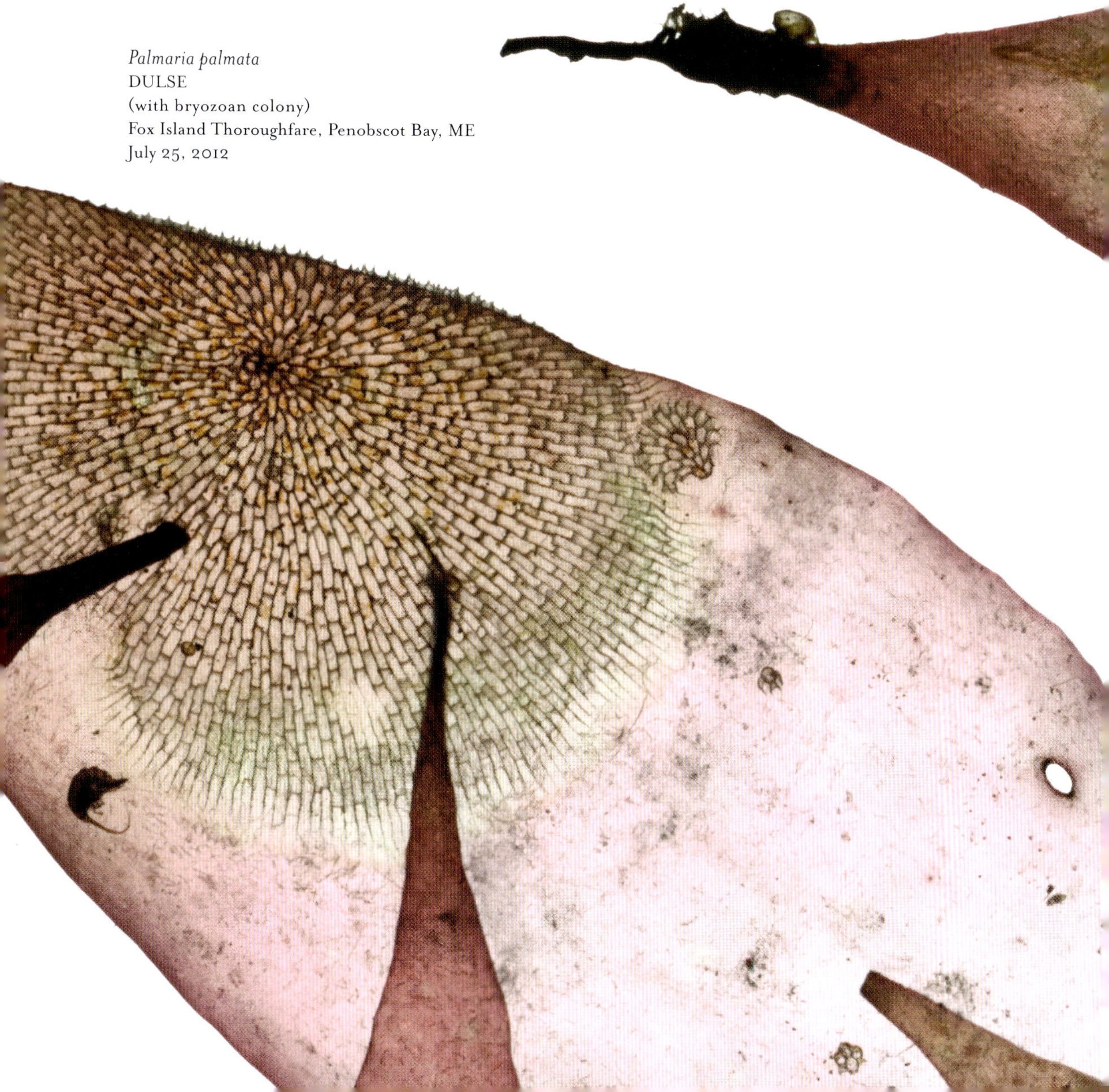

Phyllospadix scouleri and *Smithora naiadum*

Surfgrass and Its Epiphyte

Real estate in the intertidal zone can be a scarce commodity. Space on a given rock may be limited, and thus many seaweeds and sea creatures grow on top of each other. It is common to see certain seaweeds associated with others in this interdependent, nonparasitic relationship, but the classic epiphyte on the Pacific reefs is the beautiful and delicate *Smithora*, which grows exclusively on surfgrass (*Phyllospadix*) or the slightly wider eelgrass (*Zostera*). On Duxbury Reef at low tide, close inspection of the great mats of brilliant green surfgrass reveal dark patches on the long straight leaves (these are true leaves). When the grasses rise with the tide and sway with the current in their underwater meadow, the *Smithora*'s incredibly thin blades unfurl into lavender wings. Its spores will stick only to another blade of surfgrass—not to seaweeds, not to rock.

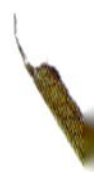

Phyllospadix scouleri
and *Smithora naiadum*
Cambria, CA
May 12, 2012

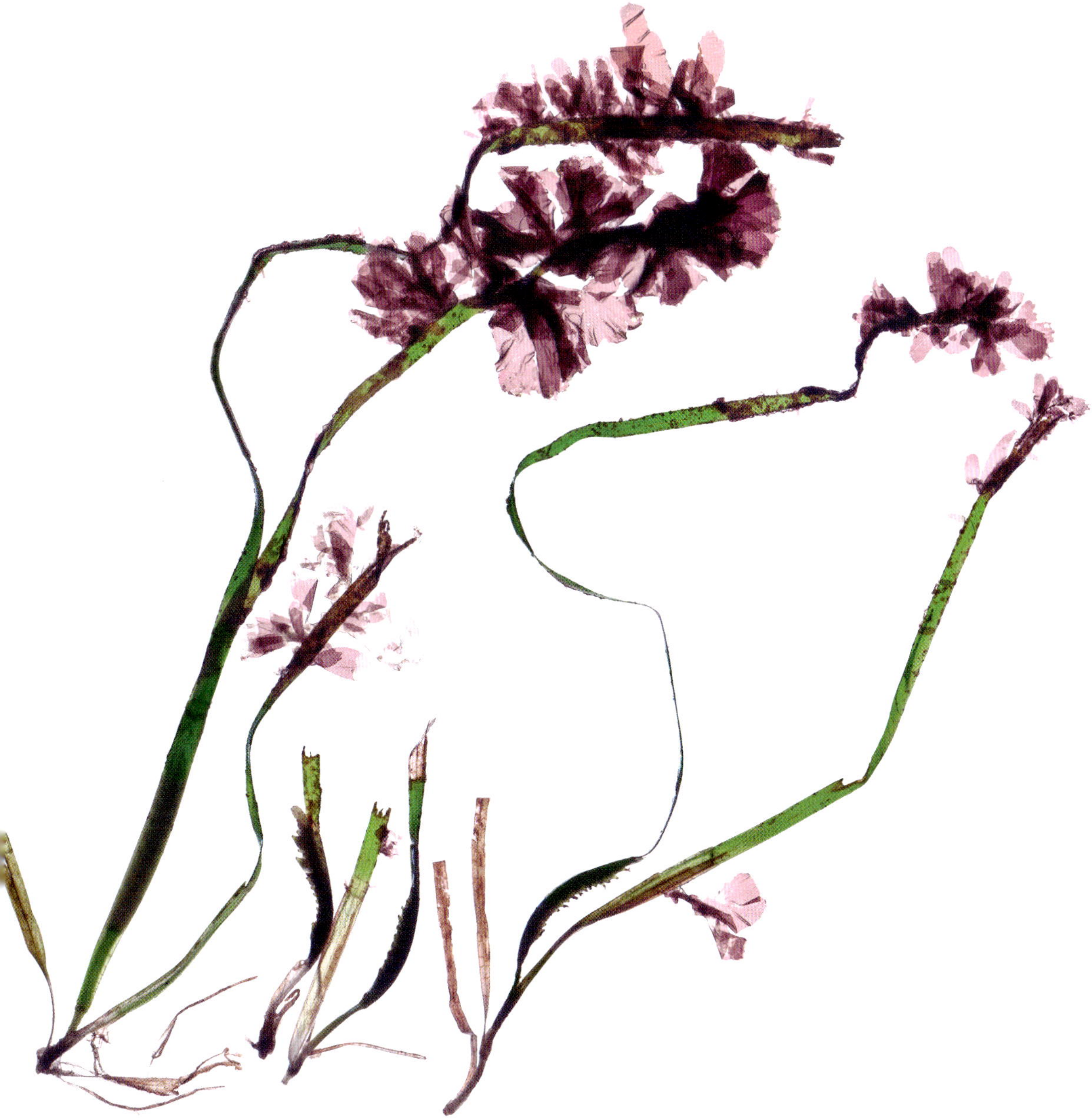

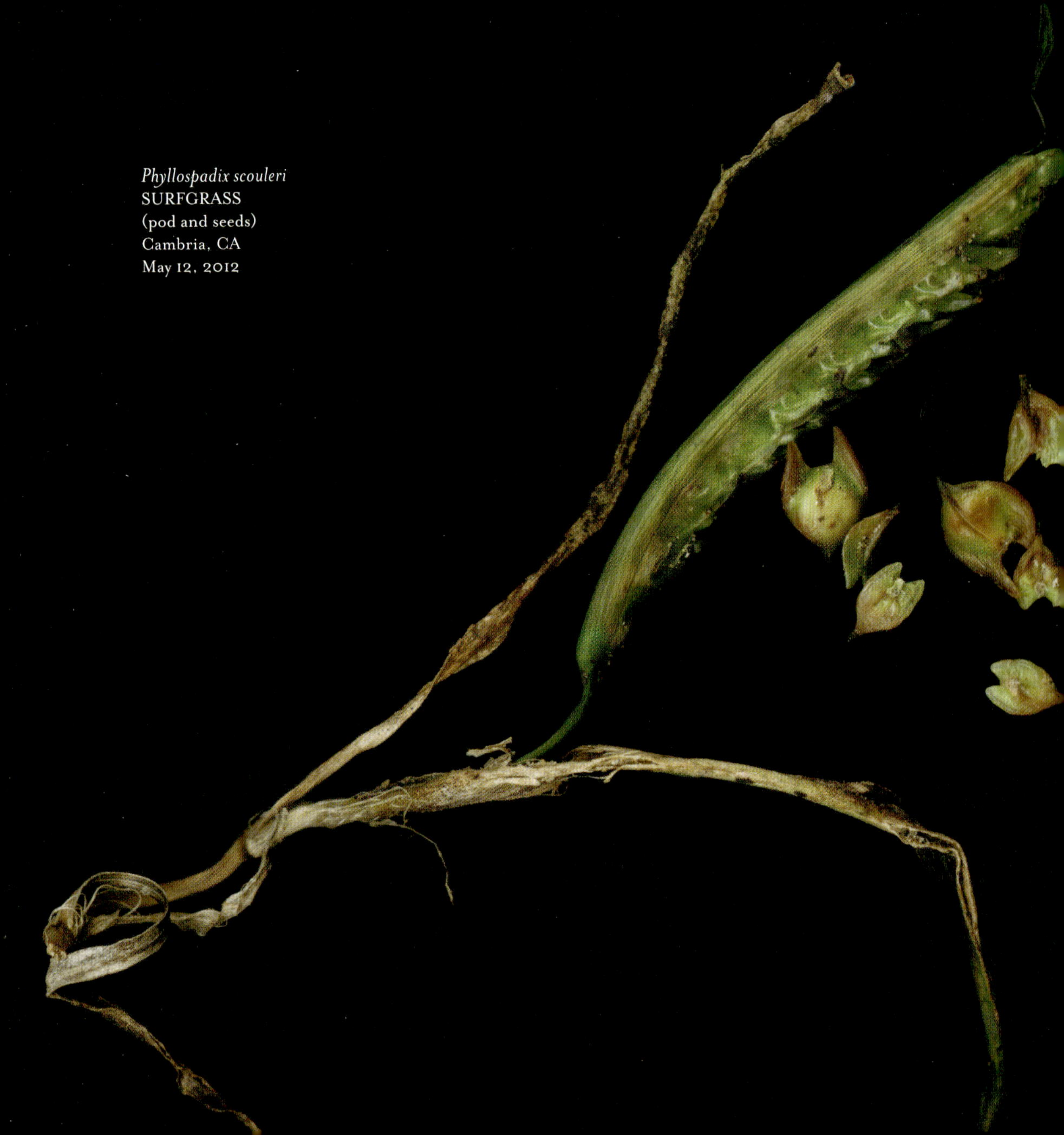

Phyllospadix scouleri
SURFGRASS
(pod and seeds)
Cambria, CA
May 12, 2012

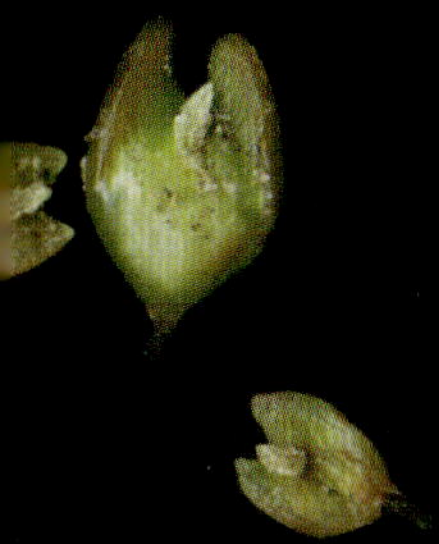

Surfgrass, or *Phyllospadix scouleri,* is commonly seen in the intertidal zone, from Alaska to Baja, California, and Mexico, especially on rocks exposed to surf. It likes to be in the middle of the action, where it is covered by the tide at least half of the time. Despite living in the salty ocean, *Phyllospadix* is a vascular plant with proper roots, a stem, leaves, and flowers. And while it acts like a seaweed in many ways, the *Phyllospadix* flower makes seeds like any flower in a backyard garden, except it all happens underwater and is timed to the period of spring tides.

A long strand of sticky pollen is released by the male flower and floats, either underwater or on the surface if the tide is low, until it snags the stigma of the female flower. The fertilized seed develops a seed coat with tiny wings or hooks that, once released, catch anything it can grab onto, giving the seed a chance to put down roots. Unlike a seaweed's holdfast, these really are roots.

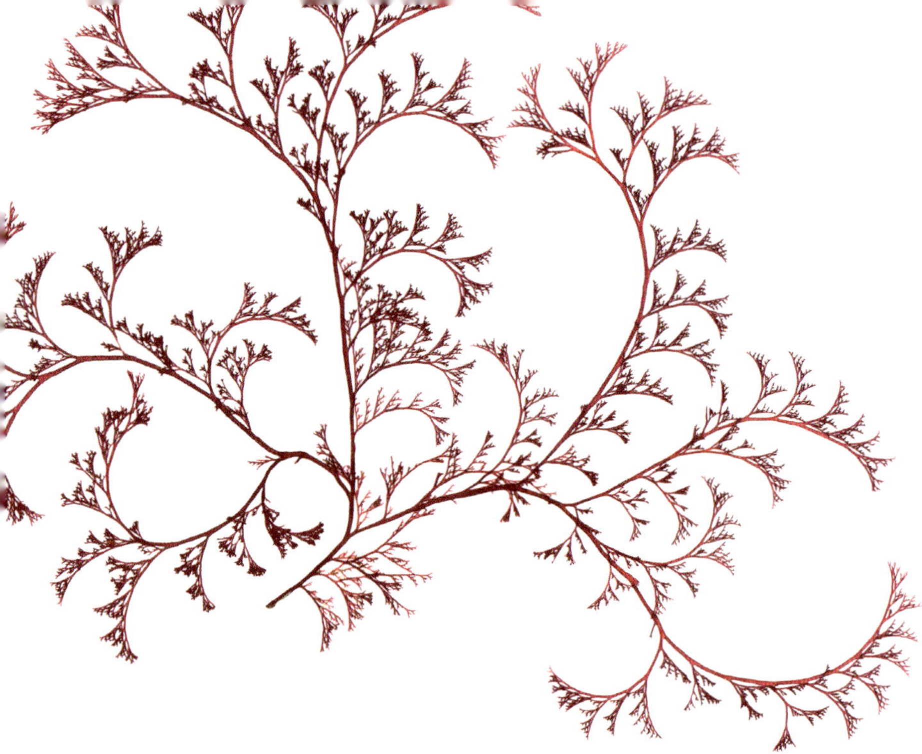

Microcladia borealis
Outlet Cove,
Bodega Head, CA
July 5, 2008

MAY 12, CAMBRIA, CA. How much seaweed is there in our oceans? A particular cove on the central coast of California gave me a sense. Here, tide, current, and coastline conspired to collect a fantastic quantity of cast-off marine algae. The pile of fresh seaweed and kelp was stupendous—a tangled mass of reds and browns and greens. Every shape and color and texture was represented. It must have been many tons of material, enough to cover a small house.

The cold waters of the northern and southern oceans are able to hold more nutrients than tropical seas and thus they promote a more exuberant growth; this is where the largest species of marine algae flourish. Each continent's coastline hosts a unique forest of kelp with different species predominating: *Ecklonia* off of New Zealand and southern Australia; *Saccharina* in the North Atlantic; *Lessonia* along the southern coasts of South America; and *Macrocystis* and *Nereocystis* along the coasts of California, Canada, and Alaska.

These prolific primary producers, by synthesizing organic matter from inorganic molecules (water and carbon dioxide), are responsible for the organic carbon (carbohydrates) that all living things need to convert into metabolic energy. But this cove of smelly seaweed represents the second, equally important part of the cycle, in which the carbon is put back into the system to be rebuilt anew into organic matter, making seaweeds a complex vehicle for discussing carbon sequestration. As seaweeds slough off and decompose, whether in the shallow ocean, out in the deeper seas, or here on the beach, they reduce to their constituent parts, remineralizing the oceans or, in this case, the whole shore ecology. Some of the carbon and nitrogen from this massive seaweed pile, with the help of all the bugs engorged in it, will migrate up into the meadow above the cove, adding nutrition to the wildflowers and shore vegetation. While some might shy away from this cove filled with goopy seaweed, I found it a fascinating and fecund sign of life.

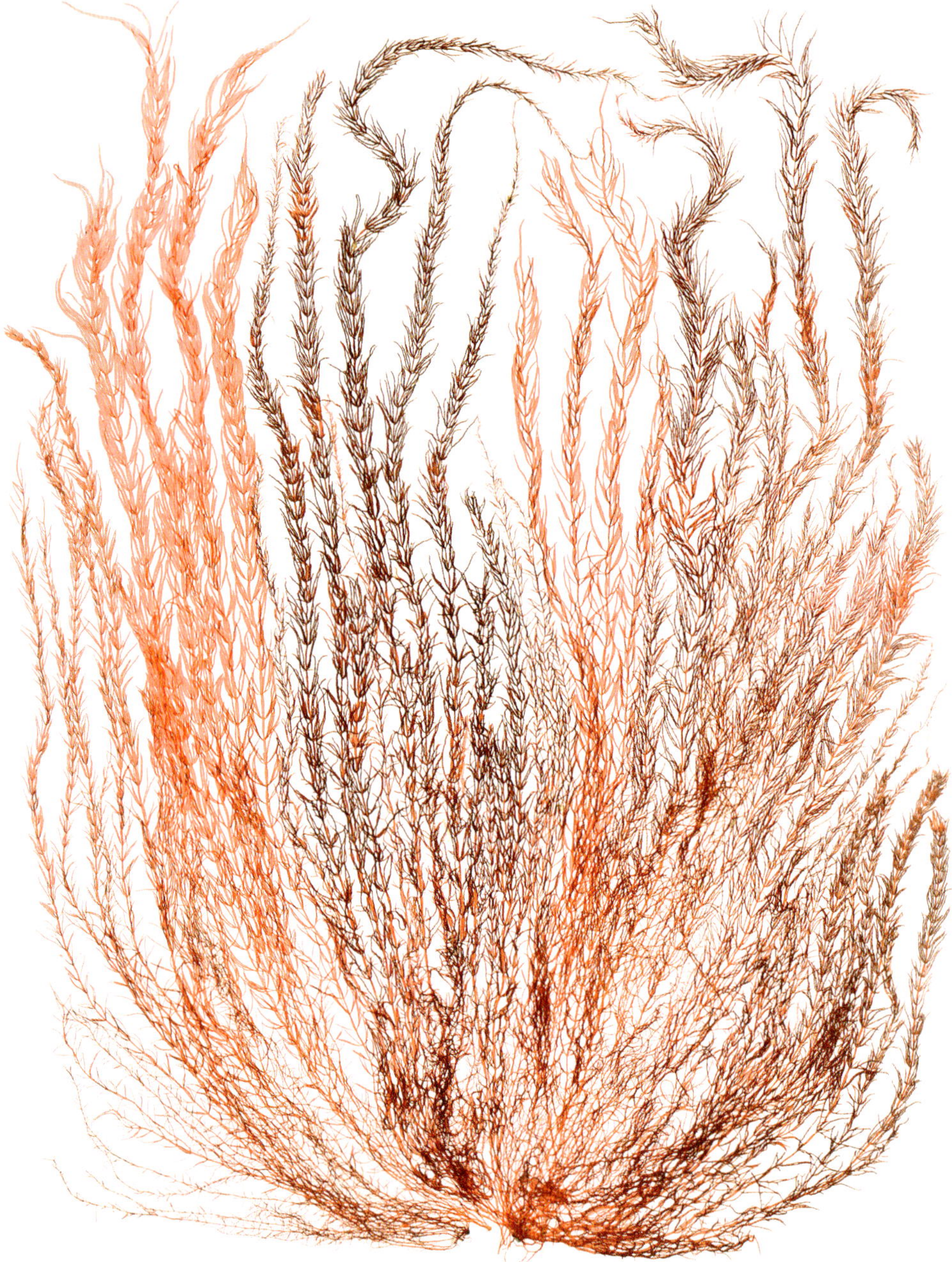

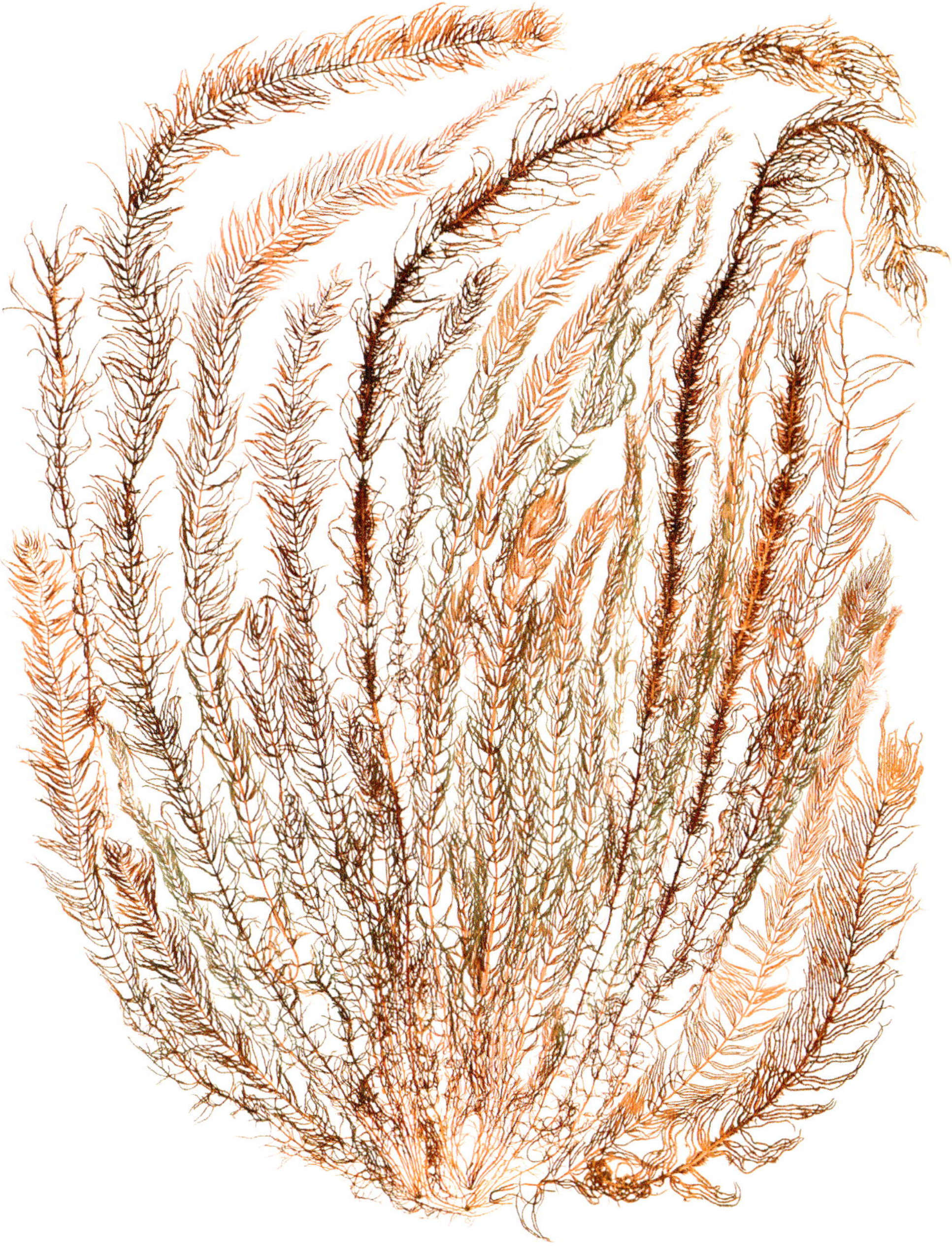

previous spread:
Gloiosiphonia verticillaris
Monterey Bay, CA
c. 1898
Collection: University Herbarium
UC Berkeley, CA

below:
Egregia menziesii
FEATHER BOA KELP
Duxbury Reef, Bolinas, CA
June 8, 2012

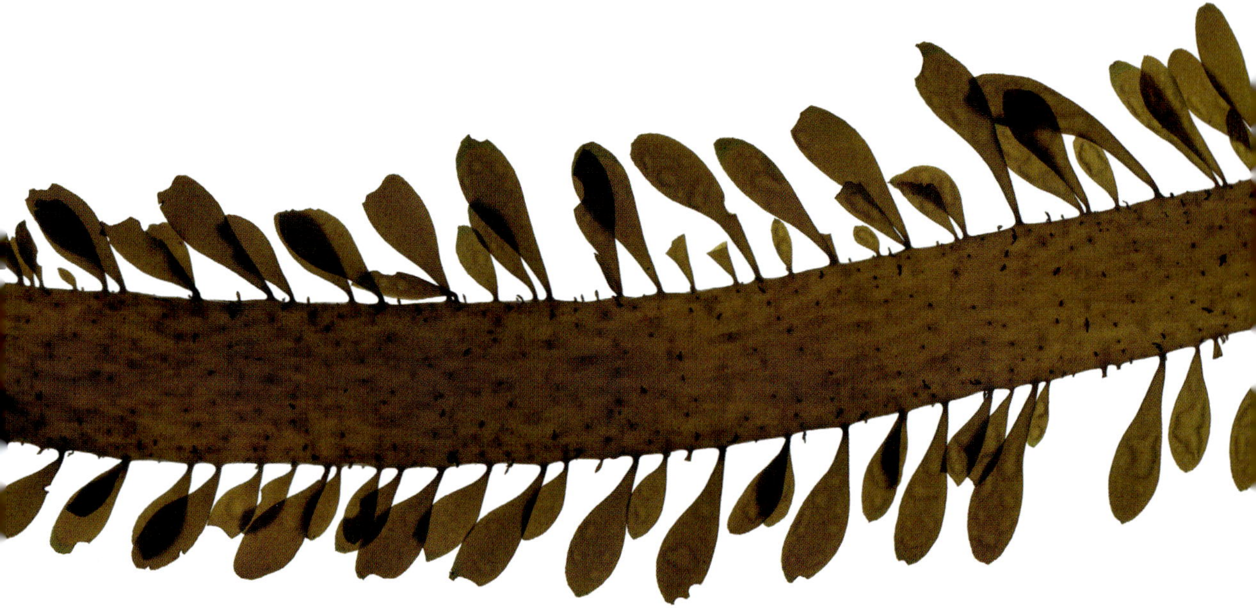

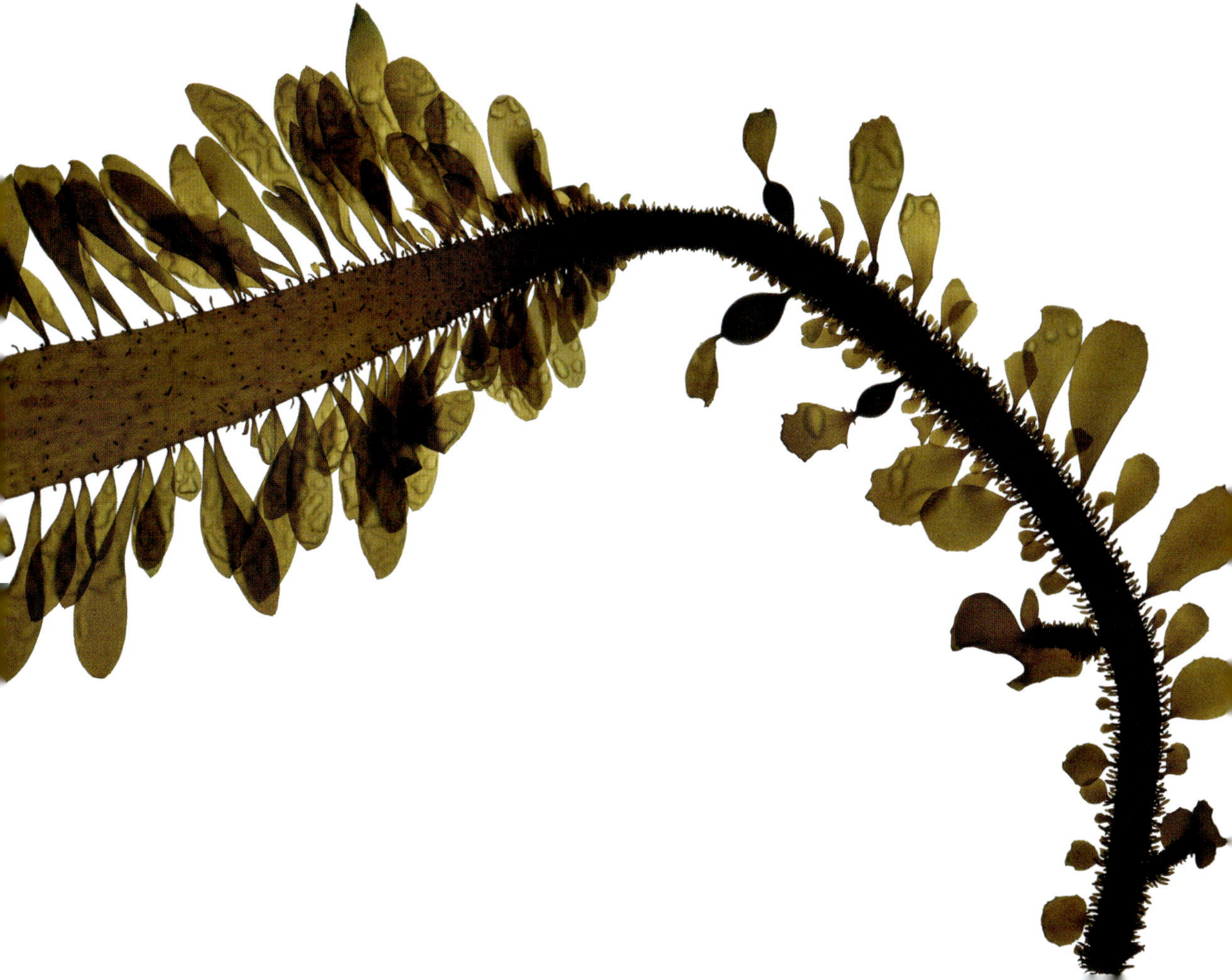

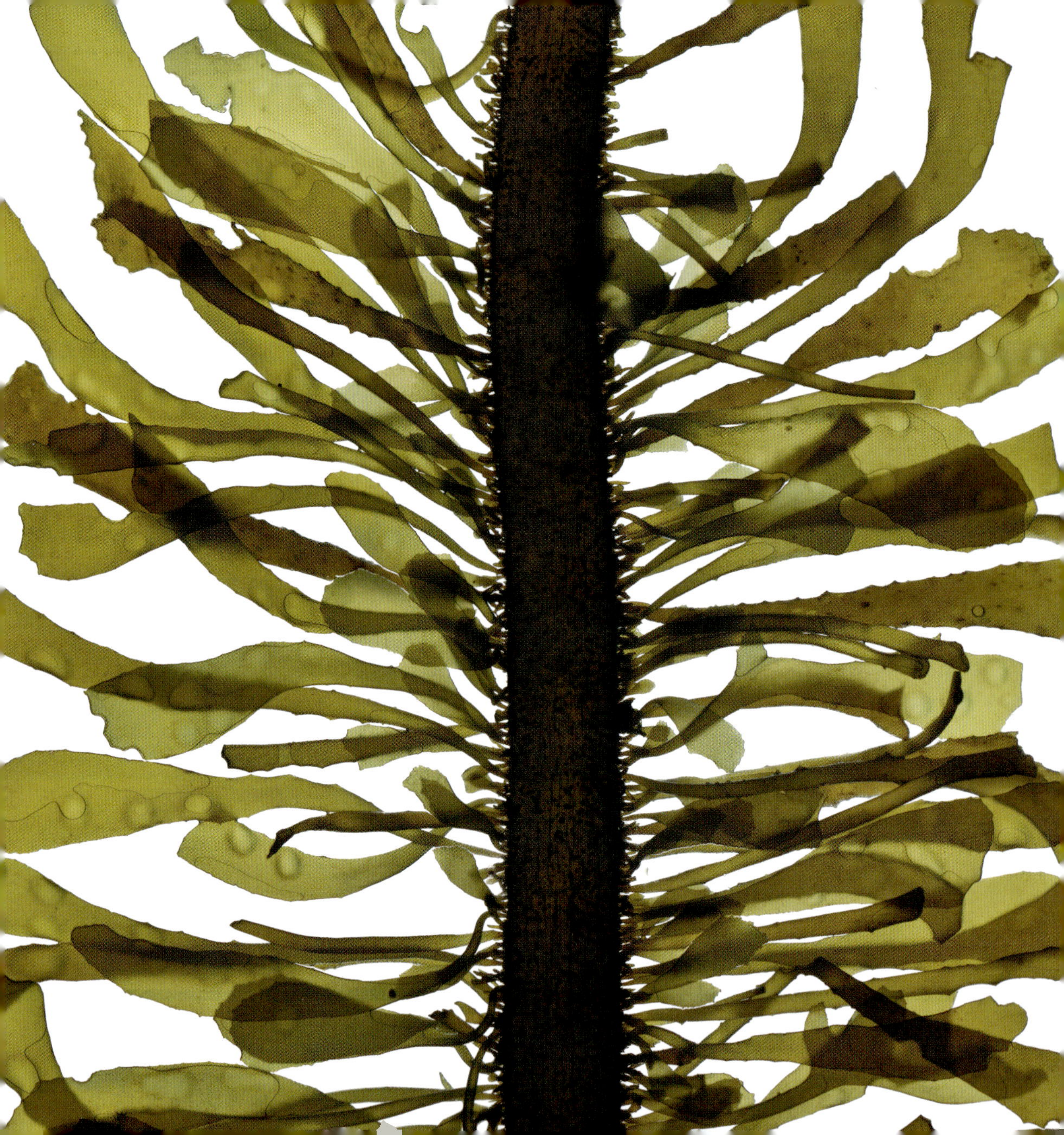

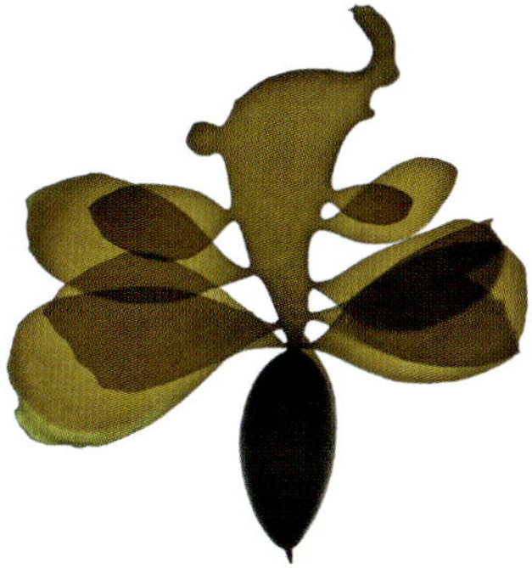

opposite and left:
Egregia menziesii
FEATHER BOA KELP
Princeton-by-the-Sea,
Half Moon Bay, CA
April 21, 2010

JUNE 8, DUXBURY REEF, BOLINAS, CA. I went out to the reef today. It was a minus tide, and the long stretch of exposed rock struck out into the Pacific, pointing south toward the Golden Gate Bridge. The zones of algae were immediately clear: *Fucus distichus* nearest the high-tide mark, masses of *Phyllospadix* or surfgrass a bit lower in the mid-tide zone, and *Mazzaella* and countless delicate reds such as *Cryptopleura* and *Chondracanthus* on the rocks, exposed only at low tide. Farther still, poking out from the surf at the lowest tides, were the rounded, dark stipes of *Laminaria setchellii* and *Laminaria sinclairii*, their golden blades bowing under each wave.

I looked for my favorite, the feather boa kelp, or *Egregia menziesii*. I went out to the far southern tip of the reef, where the lowest tide teases the rocks with a few hours of exposure and where there are a number of *Egregia* holdfasts. In February they were battered and worn. Now, from the same holdfasts, the *Egregia* emerged abundant and fresh, 20 to 40 feet long, olive green fronds splayed along the surf channels, devoted to these rocks for a few hours before

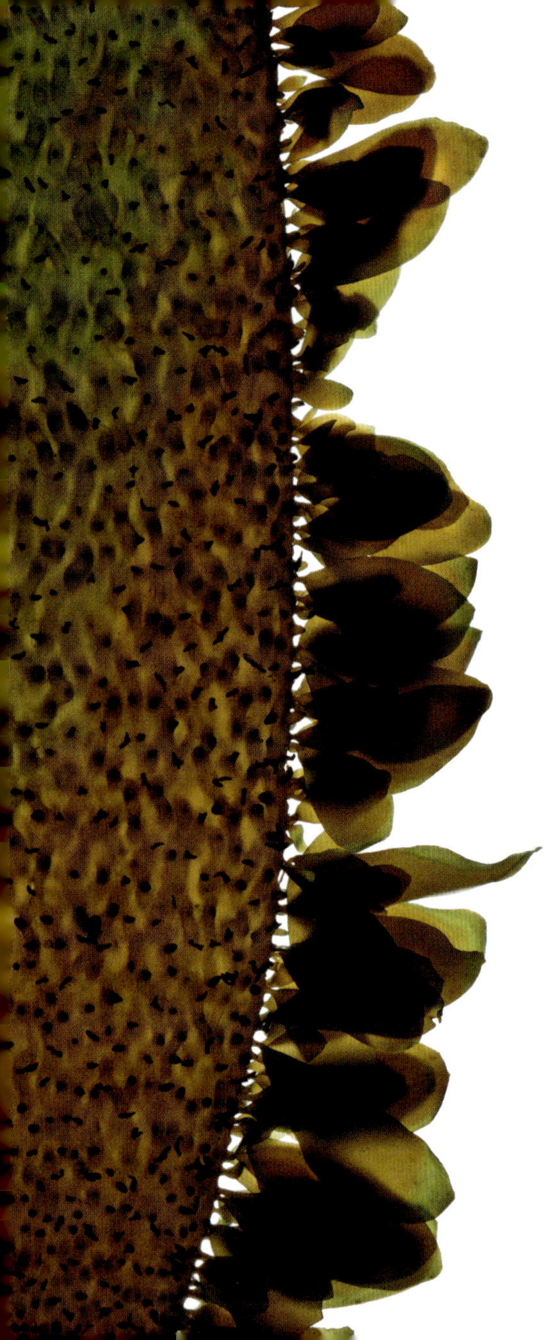

floating aloft with the rising tide. What a strange creation this kelp is. Like a bizarre feather boa, its paddle-shaped blades line the edges of a straplike midrib covered with tiny spikes. Intermittent rounded bladders, sporting whimsical, winglike blades, help to keep the massive rope afloat in its subtidal life, to catch the sun's rays and perform the work of photosynthesis.

How could something this funny looking be so successful? Without having to devote precious resources to combating gravity, it uses the buoyancy of water to its advantage. And always having the nutrients of the ocean available to it—like other kelps—*Egregia* is enormously efficient at producing more of itself. While the holdfast might be five years old, this 45-foot-long blade had grown in just a few months.

opposite:
Egregia menziesii (mature)
Duxbury Reef, Bolinas, CA
June 8, 2012

right:
Egregia menziesii (juvenile)
Cambria, CA
May 12, 2012

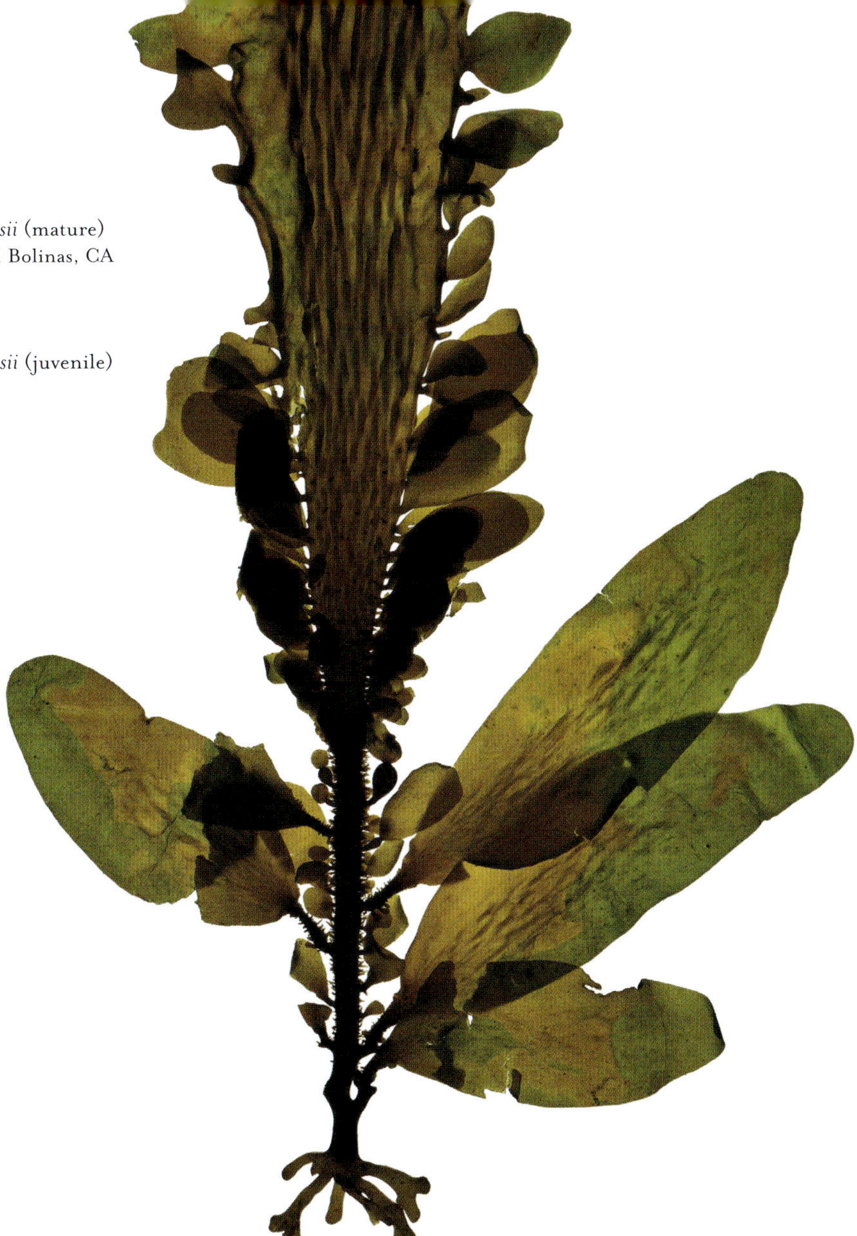

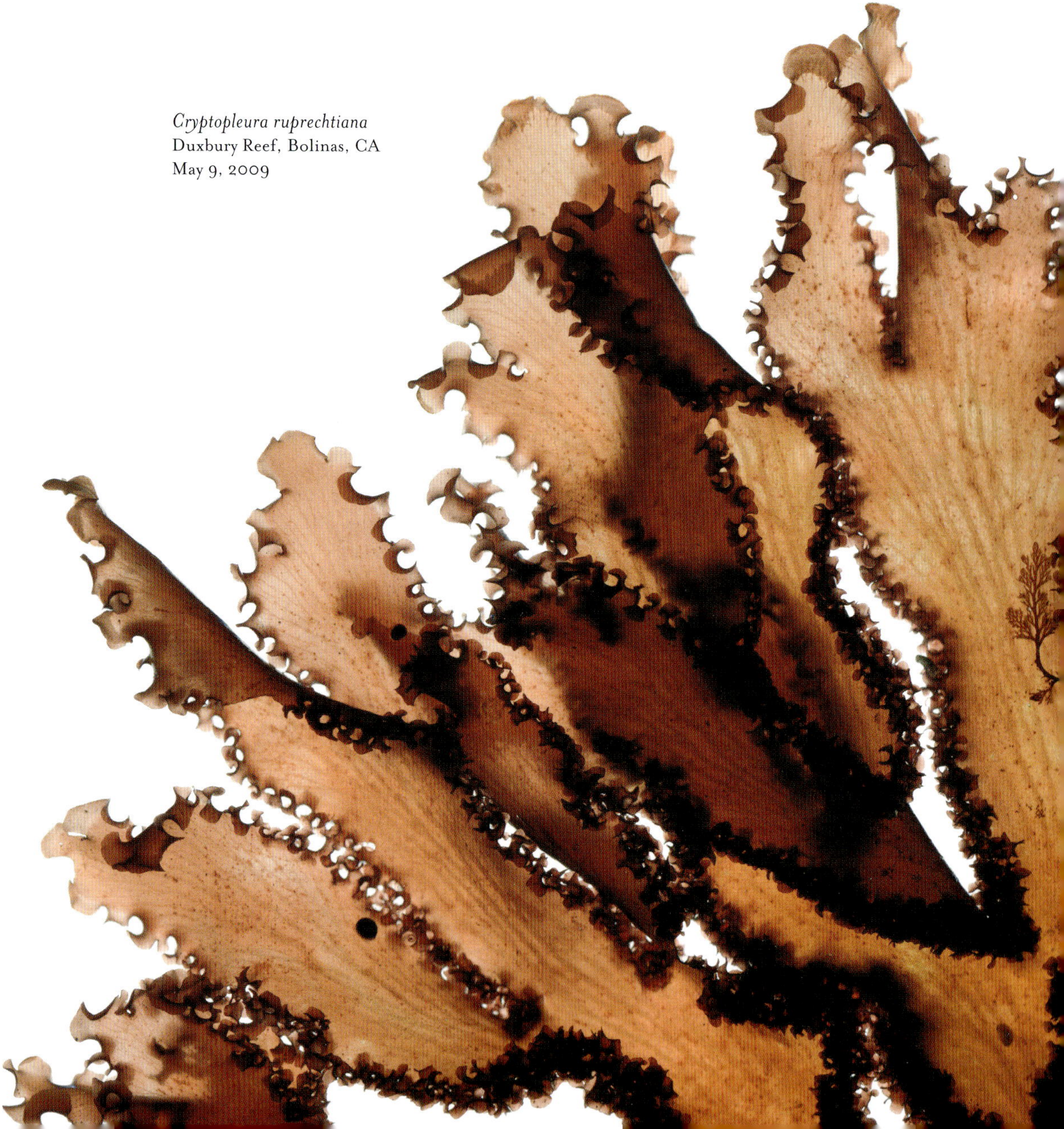

Cryptopleura ruprechtiana
Duxbury Reef, Bolinas, CA
May 9, 2009

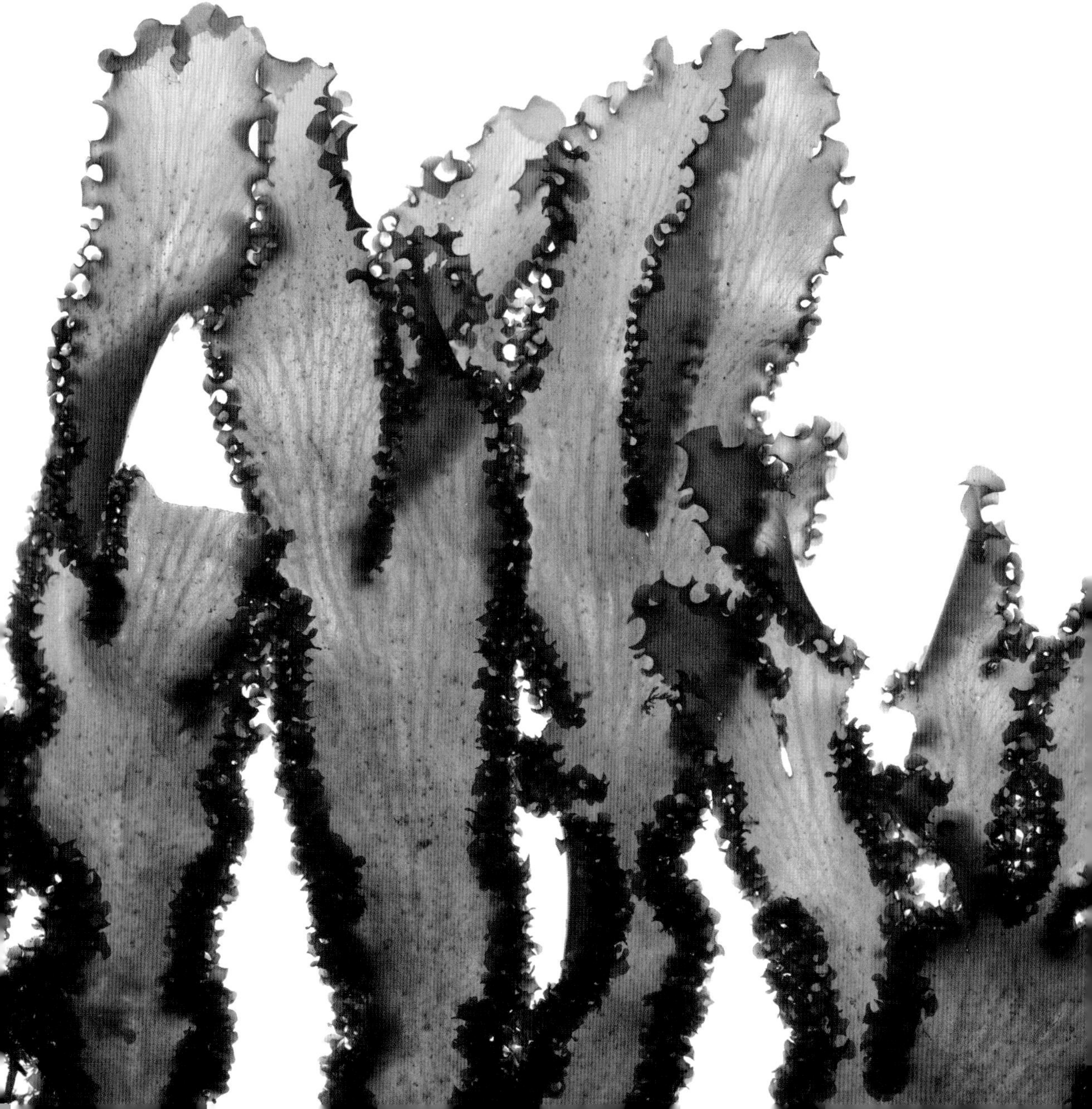

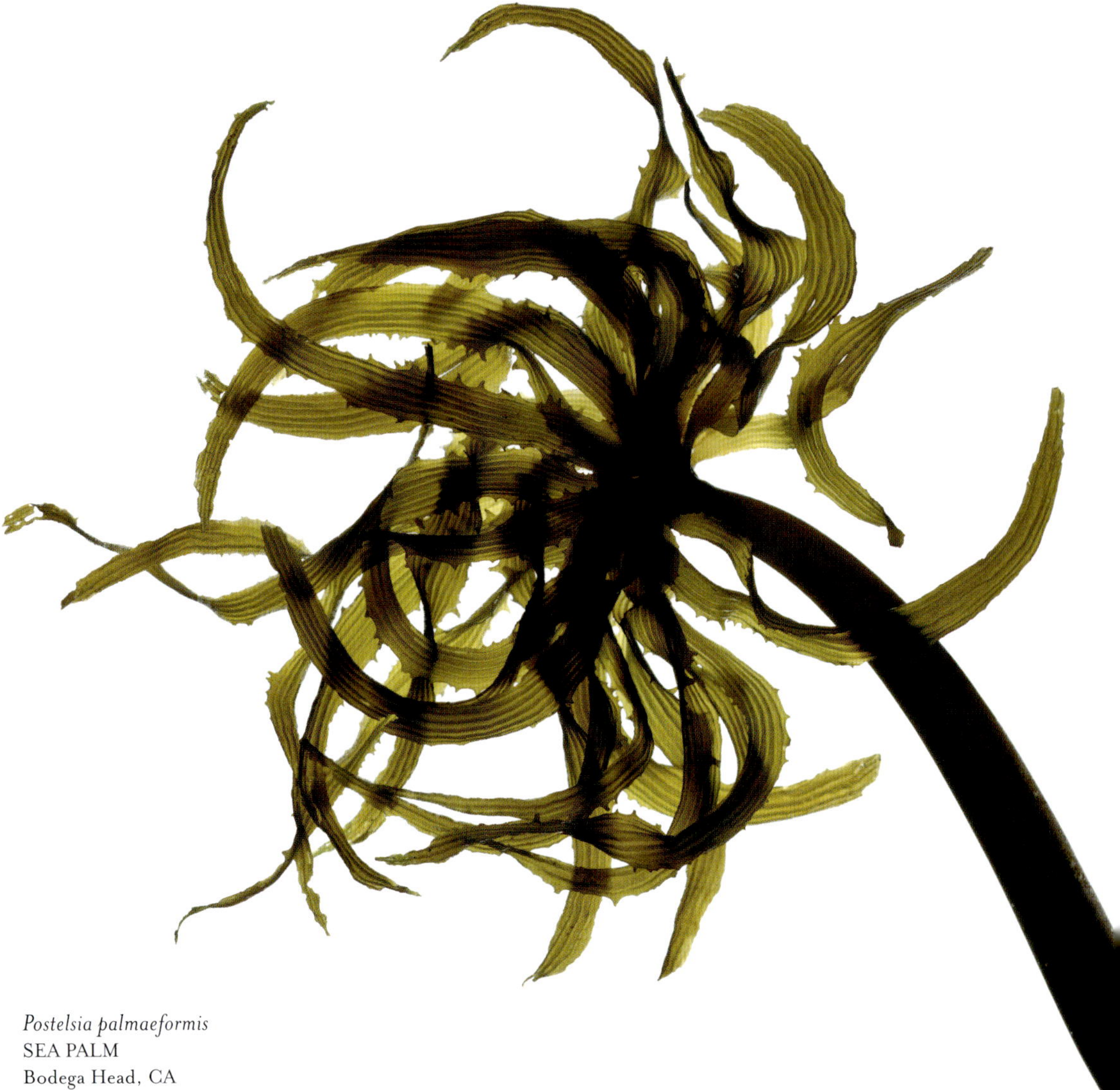

Postelsia palmaeformis
SEA PALM
Bodega Head, CA
May 30, 2010

Postelsia palmaeformis

Sea Palm

Postelsia palmaeformis grows only on the most exposed sections of the northern Pacific coast, from the northern tip of Vancouver Island down to San Luis Obispo in central California. Standing on the cliffs at Salt Point in Mendocino County, the small forests of palm tree–shaped algae can be seen on the wave-drenched rocks wrenched from the coast many eons ago. Bowing until prostrate under the crushing surf and popping upright as the white foam retreats, these seaweeds are examples of the strength, flexibility, and resilience that characterize seaweed in general and are so foreign to what we know on land.

But how does a species reproduce in such an extreme environment? Like many seaweeds, *Postelsia* is an annual; it goes through alternating generations in a complex life cycle that lasts just a single year. Its spores are held within the grooves of the blades. Knowing when the tide is low, these grooves direct the spores to drip down from the hanging blades onto the rock or mussels at the base of the parent. Spores are liberated in a mucilage made up primarily of polysaccharides. This sugary substance sticks to the substrate and quickly cures into a rubbery bonding agent, keeping the spores from being washed to sea.

With the spores deposited in such close proximity to the source, a clump of *Postelsia* is a tightly bred family. Space is created where the parent dies and is washed away, leaving an opening for the new *Postelsia* to take hold.

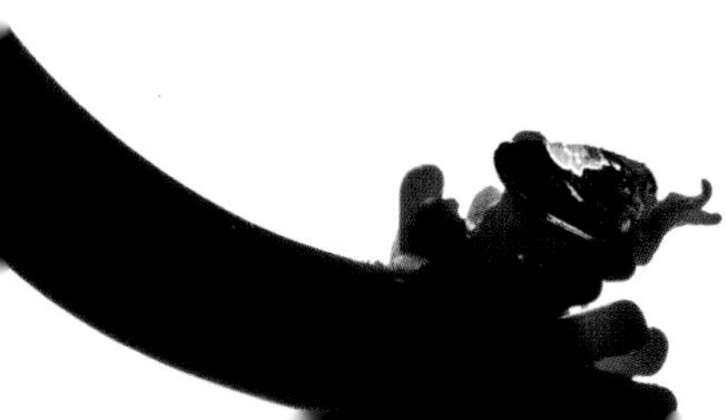

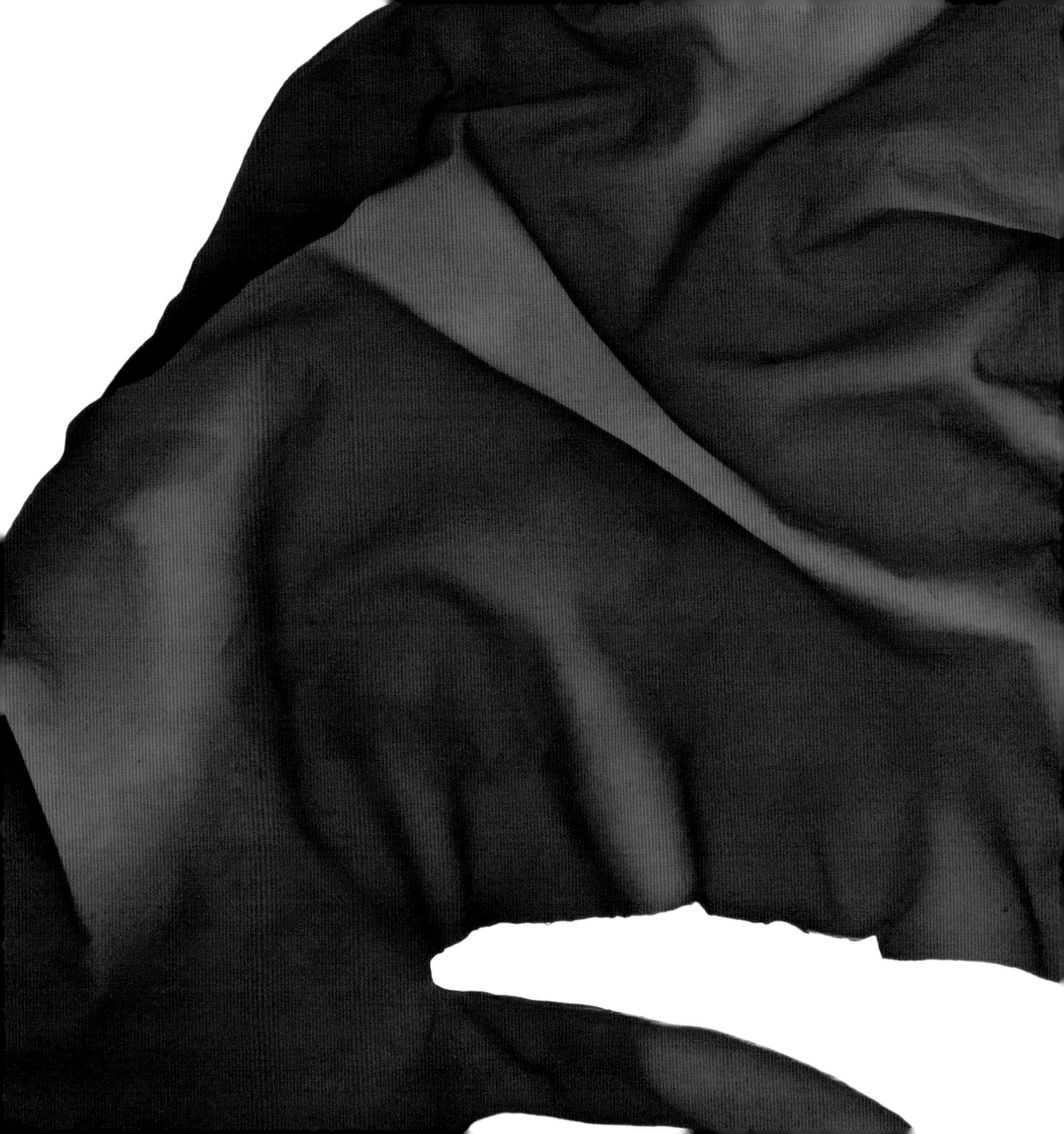

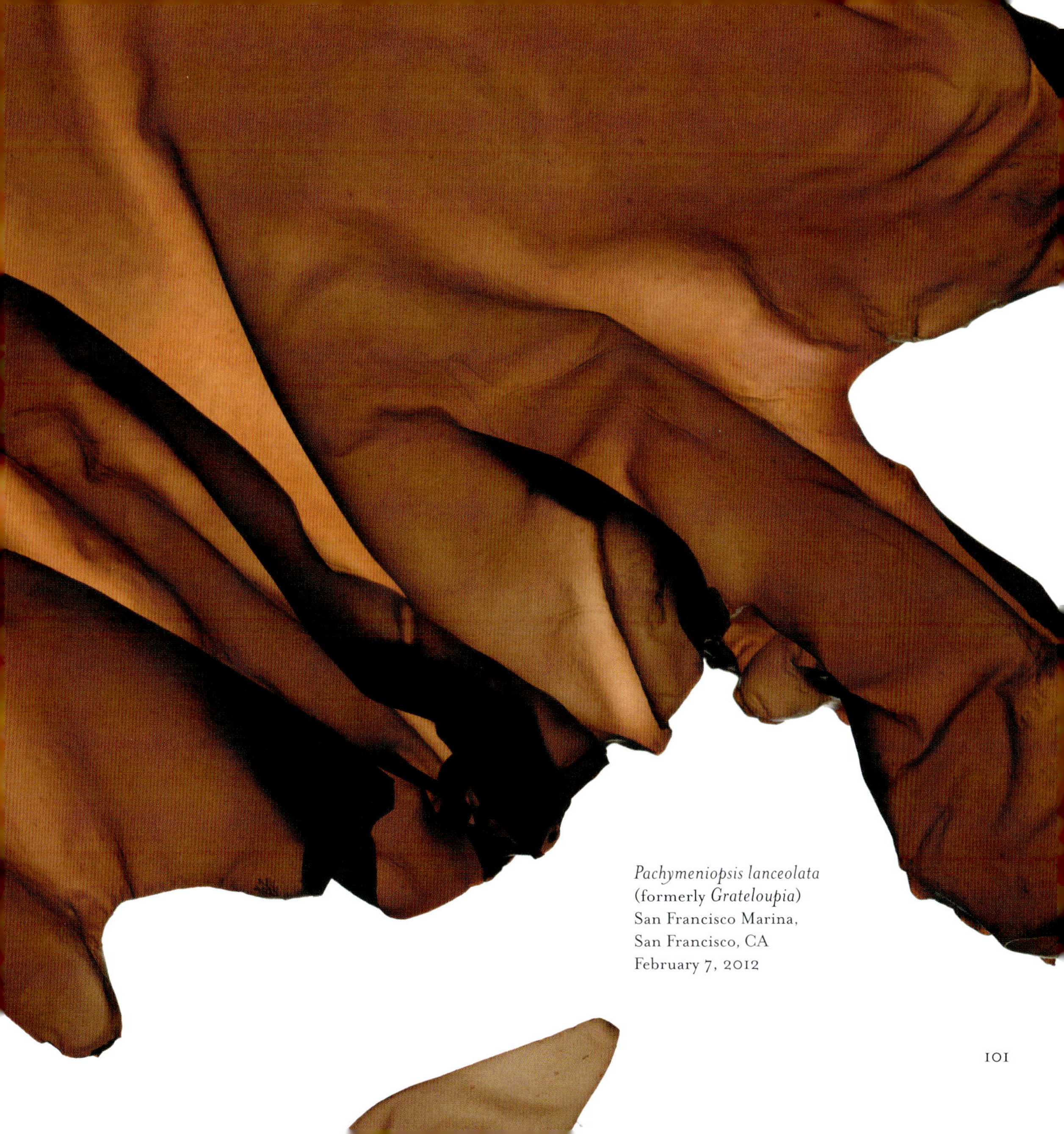

Pachymeniopsis lanceolata
(formerly *Grateloupia*)
San Francisco Marina,
San Francisco, CA
February 7, 2012

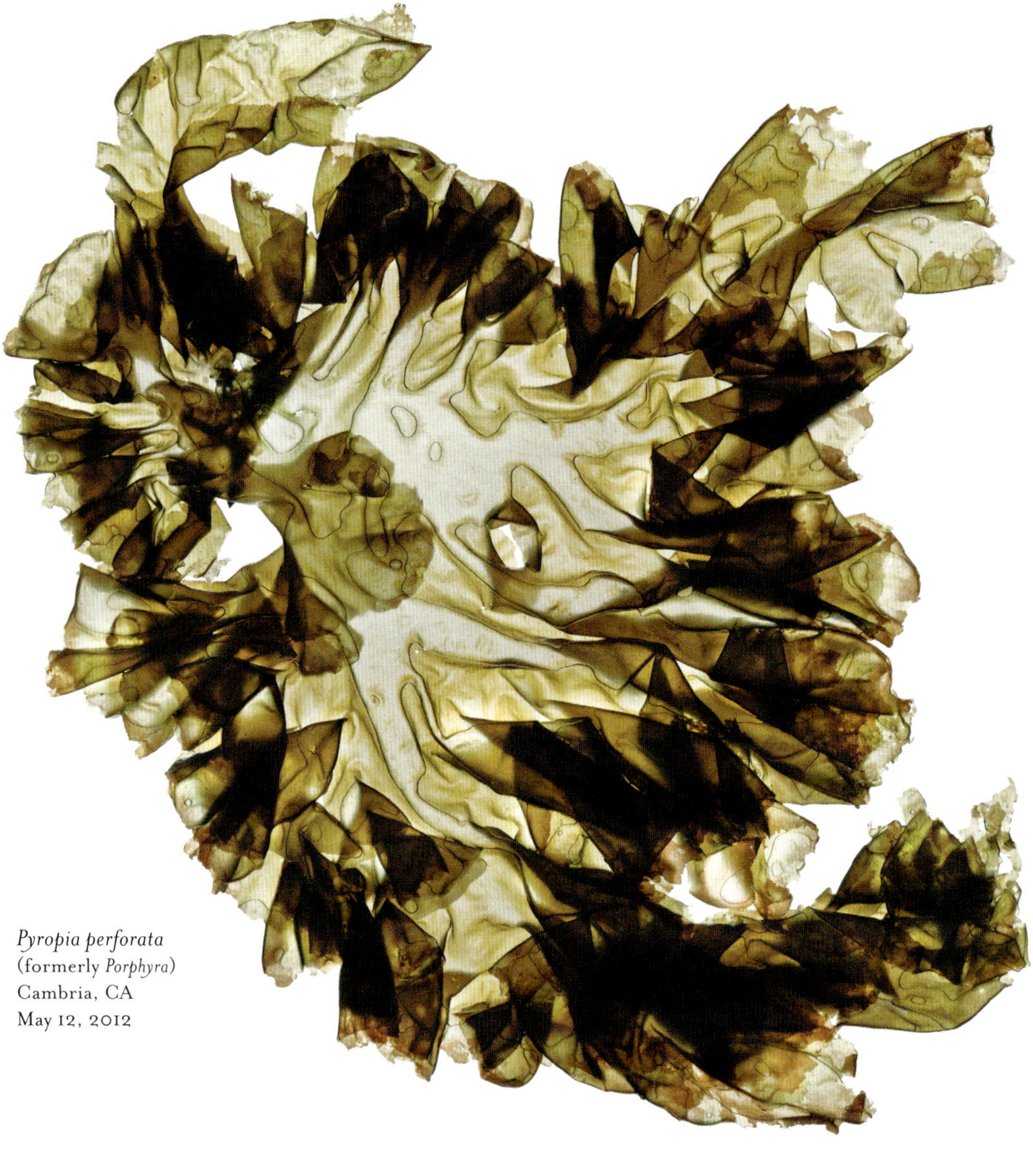

Pyropia perforata
(formerly *Porphyra*)
Cambria, CA
May 12, 2012

Dr. Kathleen Mary Drew-Baker

Overlooking the Ariake Sea, an inland waterway where much of Japan's nori farming takes place, there is a monument dedicated to Dr. Kathleen Mary Drew-Baker, a woman known locally as the "Mother of the Sea." Every year, on April 14, a festival in her honor takes place at the Sumiyoshi shrine because the nori farmers of Japan owe her their livelihoods. The honoree, an Englishwoman born in 1901, never set foot in Japan, but in 1949, after years of studying the species native to the coast of Wales, she solved the riddle of seaweed reproduction, thereby giving Japanese scientists the clue to cultivating nori.

The southwestern coast of Japan and the coast of Northern Wales both sustain the common red algal genera *Porphyra* and *Pyropia* (which until recently fell under the single heading of *Porphyra*). There are close to seventy related species in these genera, varying in color from dusky green to deep red and purple, but they are all characteristically sheer—as thin as film—and, despite the impression of fragility, tough and stretchy. It was assumed by the Japanese that the spores of nori would float in the seawater, land on a place to grab hold, and grow into new seaweed. But no one had actually seen it happen.

Throughout the centuries, nori harvests in Japan would fluctuate wildly; it was a luxury item some years and flooded the markets in others. In 1948 disaster struck the industry when a series of typhoons, combined with fertilizer and pollution runoff, devastated the nori beds, which would not regrow. No one in Japan could figure out what to do.

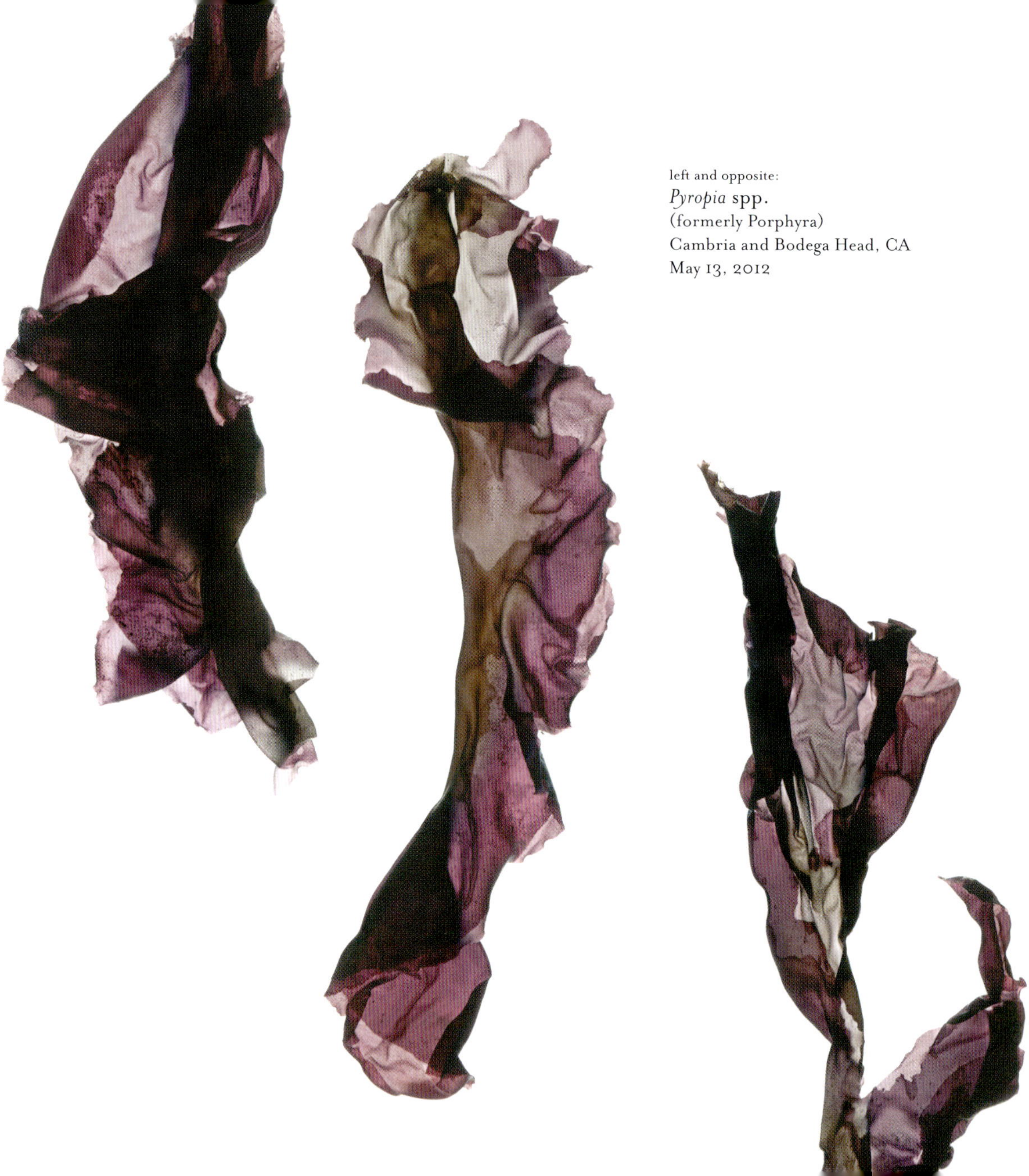

left and opposite:
Pyropia spp.
(formerly Porphyra)
Cambria and Bodega Head, CA
May 13, 2012

In 1922, before marriage constrained her career options, Kathleen Drew became the first woman to graduate with honors from Manchester University. She had become fascinated with the biology of marine algae and, once married, managed to secure an unpaid laboratory research position. Her husband built her a quirky but functional tidal tank, certainly one of the first of its kind and an essential tool for closely observing the thousands of species of seaweed she collected from the rocky shores of the Irish Sea. She had noticed with intrigue the fall bloom of *Porphyra umbilicalis*, which she studied along with a filamentous alga named *Conchocelis*. Her great discovery was that these two are not different species but different life stages of the same one. The familiar "laver" in the local laverbread (and what the Japanese press into sheets of nori) was but one stage of an alternating generational cycle. Unknown before then to scientists and harvesters alike was the multiphased reproductive techniques of most algae involving spores in one generation and egg and sperm in another. These interim generations can have completely different forms, some of which look nothing like "seaweed."

Scientists in Japan, upon reading a simple, 150-word article by Drew-Baker that appeared in *Nature* magazine in 1949, were able to experiment themselves and set up a system, using beds of seashells, to seed and grow nori systematically, and thus the modern-day, multibillion-dollar nori industry was born. While Drew-Baker's microscopes are enshrined in the museum at the University of Manchester, her memory is honored on the other side of the globe near the acres of crosshatched ropes that are the tidal nori farms.

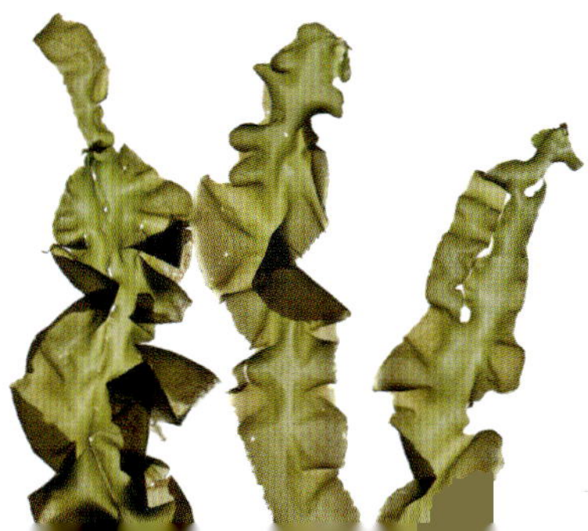

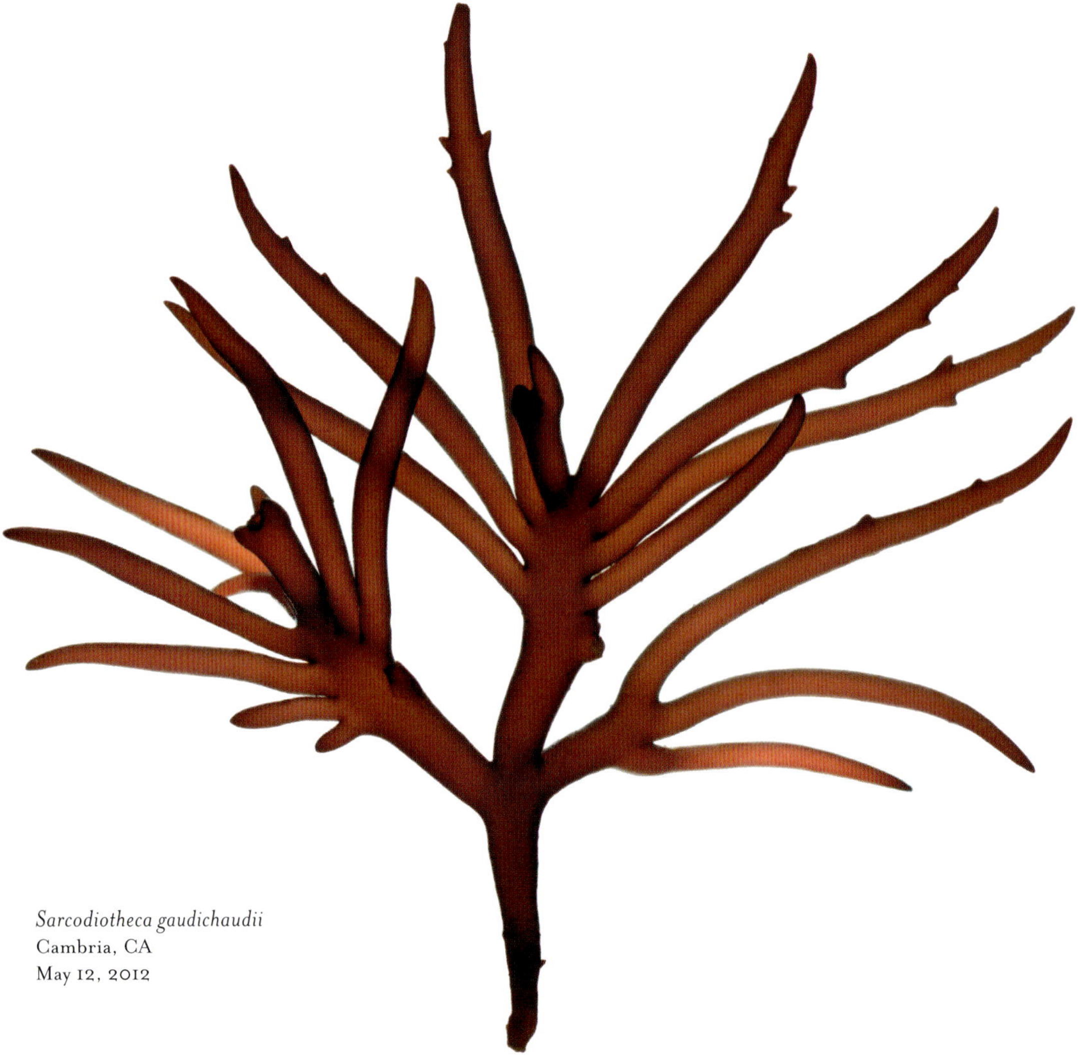

Sarcodiotheca gaudichaudii
Cambria, CA
May 12, 2012

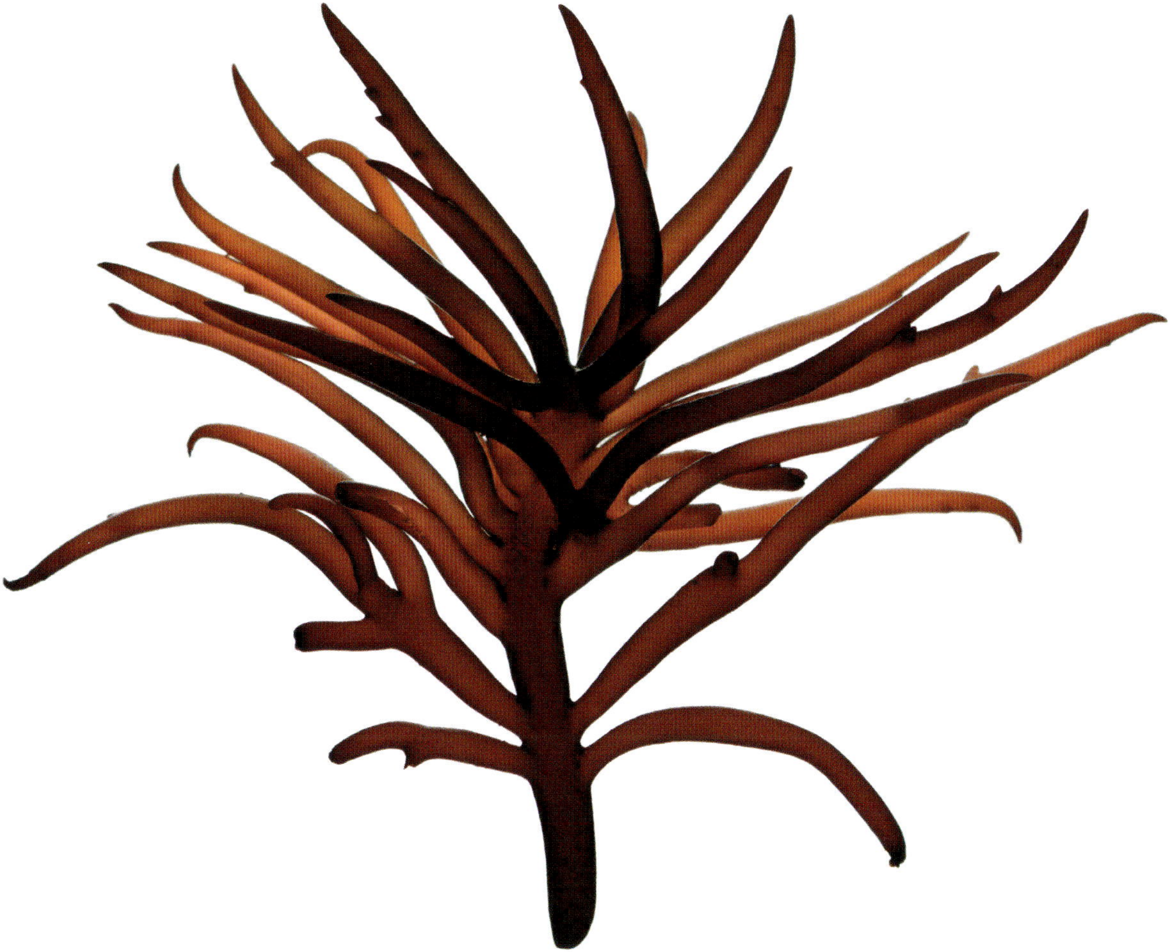

Nereocystis luetkeana

Bull Kelp

SEPTEMBER 12, FORT FUNSTON, SAN FRANCISCO, CA. The great Pacific Ocean never fails to offer up treasure. Today, thousands of *Nereocystis* were washed up along the sandy expanse of Fort Funston. The giant, mature bull kelps, with hard bulb, sturdy stipe, and streaming blades, collected in huge entanglements tumbling in the surf, their staggering size and quantity only hinting at the profusion of growth beyond the waves. As I veered between the bundles of wrack, I noticed single kelps washed up on the sand at my feet, but most of them were tiny, miniature versions of the giants, their perfectly spherical bulbs only as wide as a fingernail, their blades like golden wings, delicate and luminous in the morning sunshine. While the scale differential is as a seedling to an ancient redwood, the transformation from the tiny kelp to the giant does not take centuries but merely weeks and months. The remarkable transformation of the inorganic into the organic—of sunlight and seawater into the long stipe, substantial bladder, and winged blades that grow up to 100 feet from the ocean floor toward the surface—happens in a single season. But this tremendous growth happens out of sight, in the deep subtidal domain of the cold northern Pacific.

Nereocystis luetkeana was brought into the Linnean system of nomenclature when an 1826–27 Russian expedition of naturalists explored the shores of present-day Alaska, collecting seaweeds and plants, and bringing them back to be recorded and described in the herbaria of Europe. The bull kelp was named after the expedition captain, Fedor Petrovich Lütke. Alexander Postels was the gifted illustrator aboard, and in 1840 he and Franz Joseph Ruprecht, a Russian botanist, formed a famous partnership by creating a stunning elephant folio of the "algarum vegetatio" (seaweed community) found on this expedition.

I had the privilege of seeing the giant, hand-colored lithographs of this folio, which resides in Special Collections at the University of Southern California. The light from the high library windows filtered across the detailed renderings of *Fucus* and *Alaria*, *Agarum*, *Nereocystis*, and *Macrocystis*, perhaps as it might filter through the shallow ocean waters. Of course, the folio had to be big. How could one tame these wild and massive creations onto a smaller page? Postels was clearly enraptured by their magnificence, and the text by Ruprecht, undecipherable in Latin and Cyrillic, added to my sense of mystery and awe.

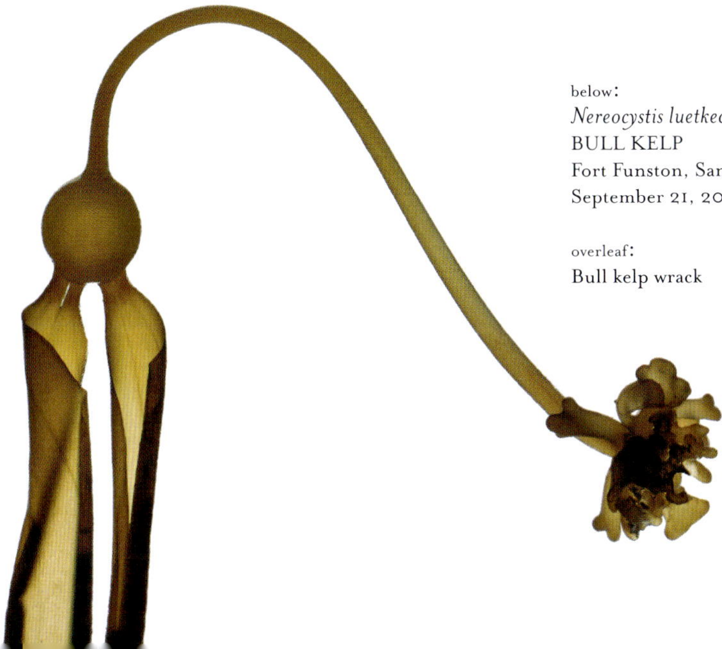

below:
Nereocystis luetkeana
BULL KELP
Fort Funston, San Francisco, CA
September 21, 2012

overleaf:
Bull kelp wrack

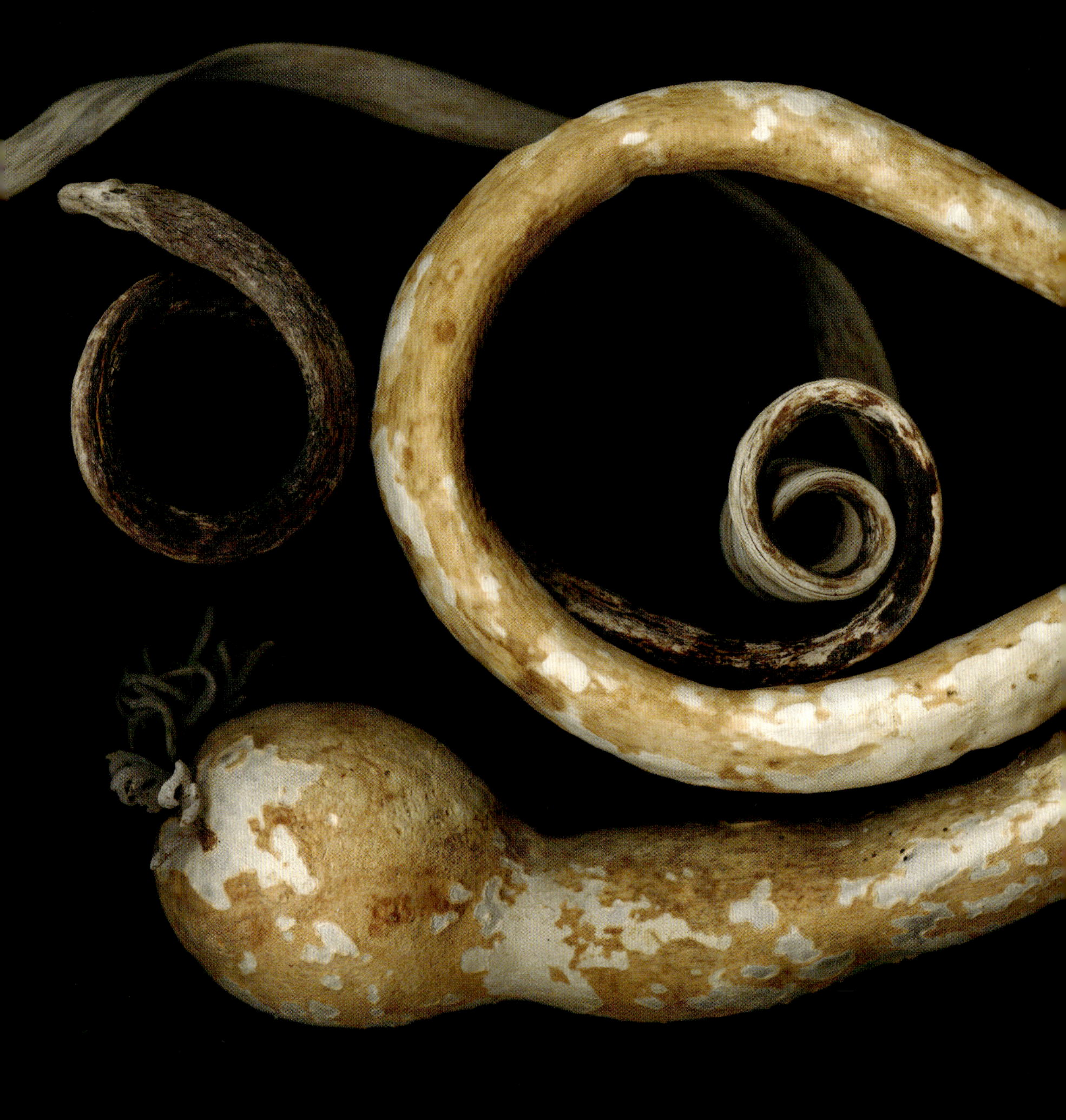

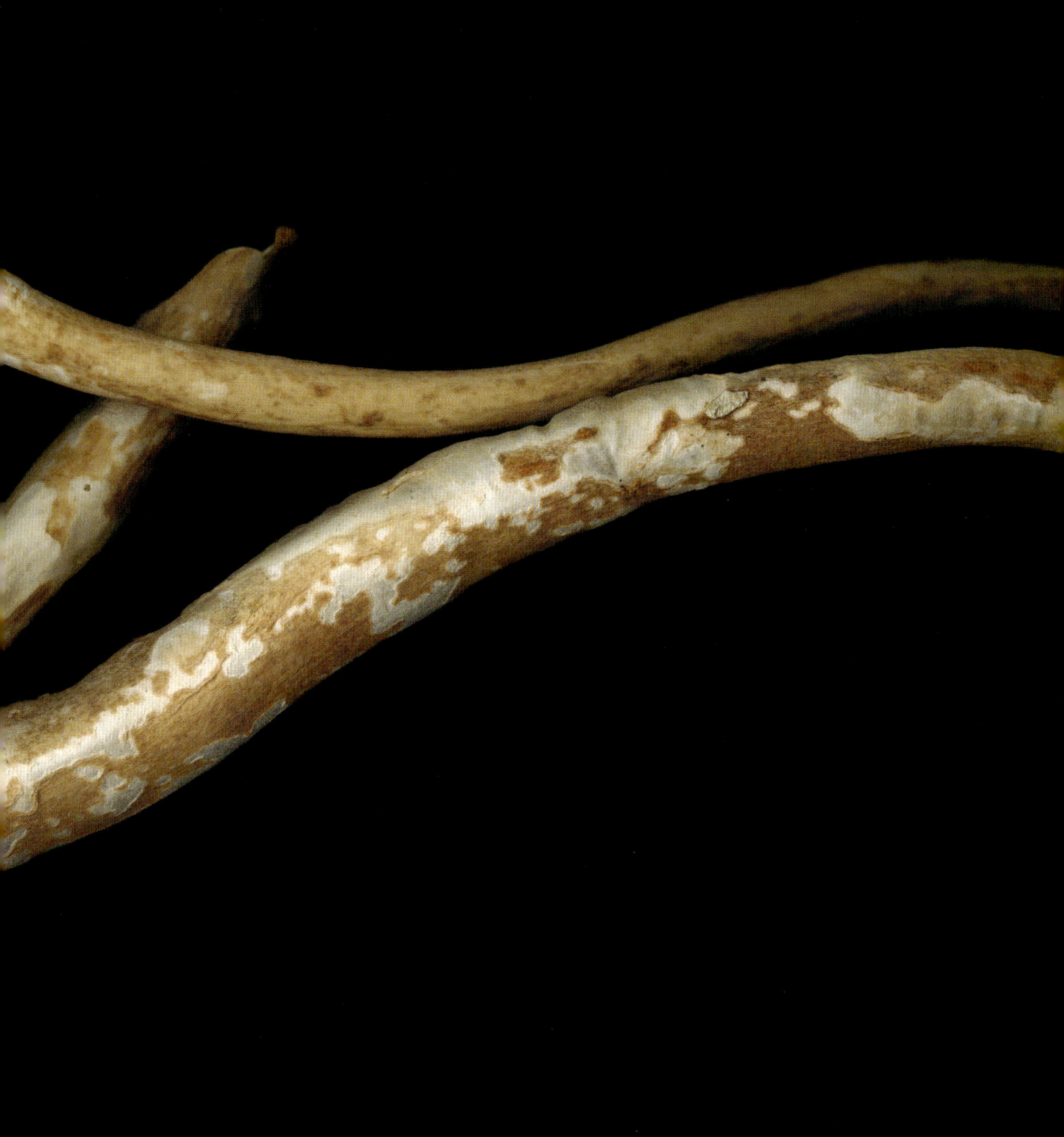

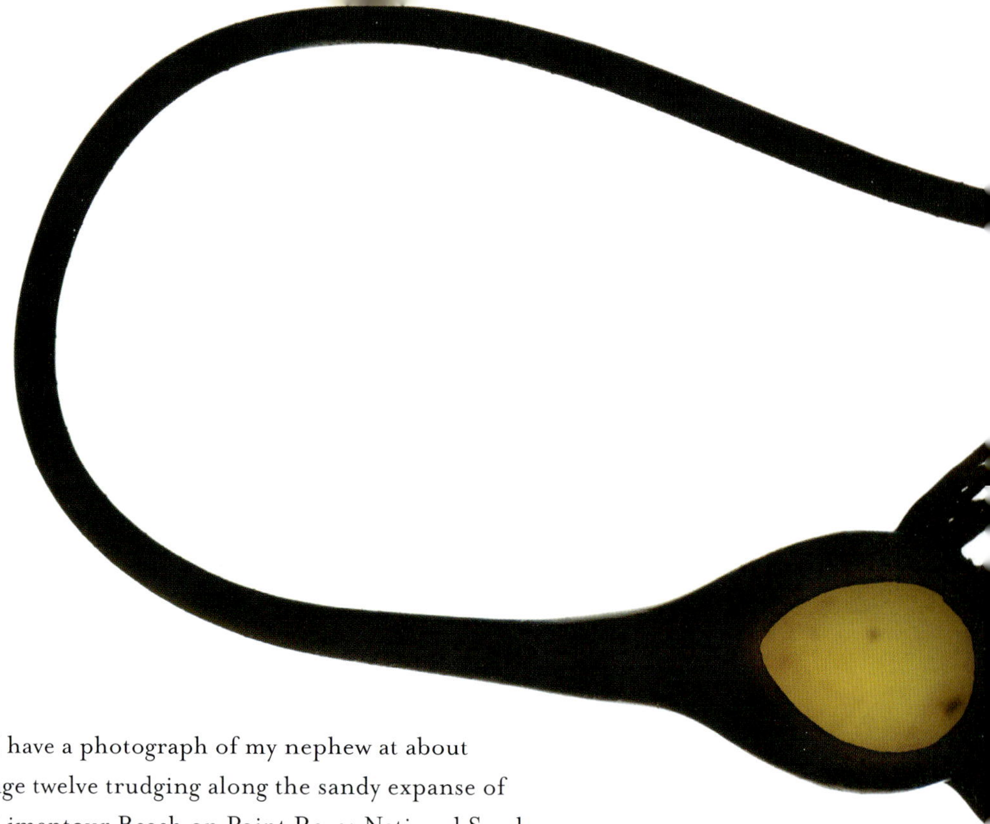

I have a photograph of my nephew at about age twelve trudging along the sandy expanse of Limantour Beach on Point Reyes National Seashore. He has the stipe of a great bull kelp draped over his shoulder, and he is leaning into the weight of it, the bulb and blades trailing behind him 30 feet or more. I think he must have fancied himself a slave in ancient Egypt, hauling stones to the pyramids. The scale of the enormous kelp brings that kind of thing to mind.

Nereocystis luetkeana
BULL KELP
Fort Funston,
San Francisco, CA
June 5, 2012

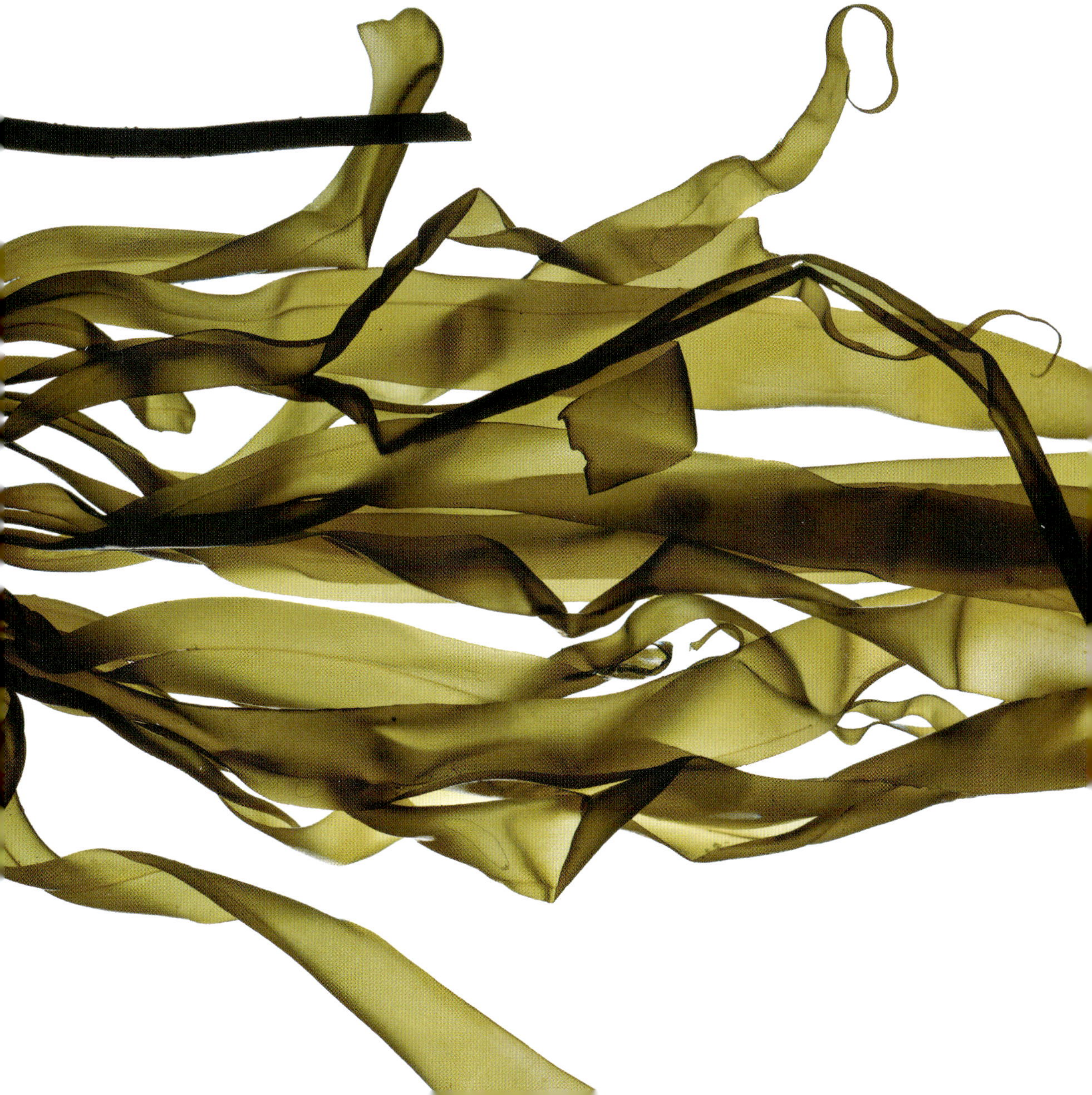

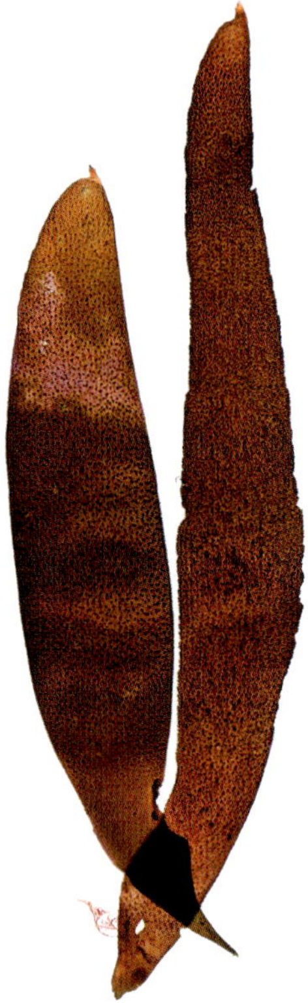

above:
Chondracanthus harveyanus
Cambria, CA
May 11, 2012

opposite:
Chondracanthus exasperatus
TURKISH TOWEL
Duxbury Reef, Bolinas, CA
November 23, 2012

Chondracanthus spp.

Turkish Towel

Cryptopleura ruprechtiana, Chondracanthus harveyanus, Postelsia palmaeformis, Nereocystis luetkeana . . . If one stood on the beach and loudly recited the Latin names of the algae in this book, it would be a powerful poem, with the syllables of genus and species rolling off the tongue in a lyrical cadence. But these names do more than label species. They also record the lineage of passionate explorers, collectors, observers, and academics who have built the knowledge base explaining this secret garden of the sea. The big names in nineteenth-century marine botany, or phycology, are well represented in the second half of the algae binomials: *menziesii* (Archibald Menzies), *harveyanus* (William H. Harvey), *ruprechtiana* (F. J. Ruprecht), *setchellii* (William A. Setchell) and *farlowii* (William G. Farlow) are just a few. But so, too, within the names of the seaweeds are found the fastidious seaside collectors, often women, clamoring in long skirts and slippery shoes, curious and deliberate, who would send their carefully pressed specimens by horse or boat or train to the academies for identification: *Weeksia, Binghamiae*, *snyderae*, *bushiae*, and *johnstoniae* were all named for nineteenth-century California women who were collectors of seaweed.

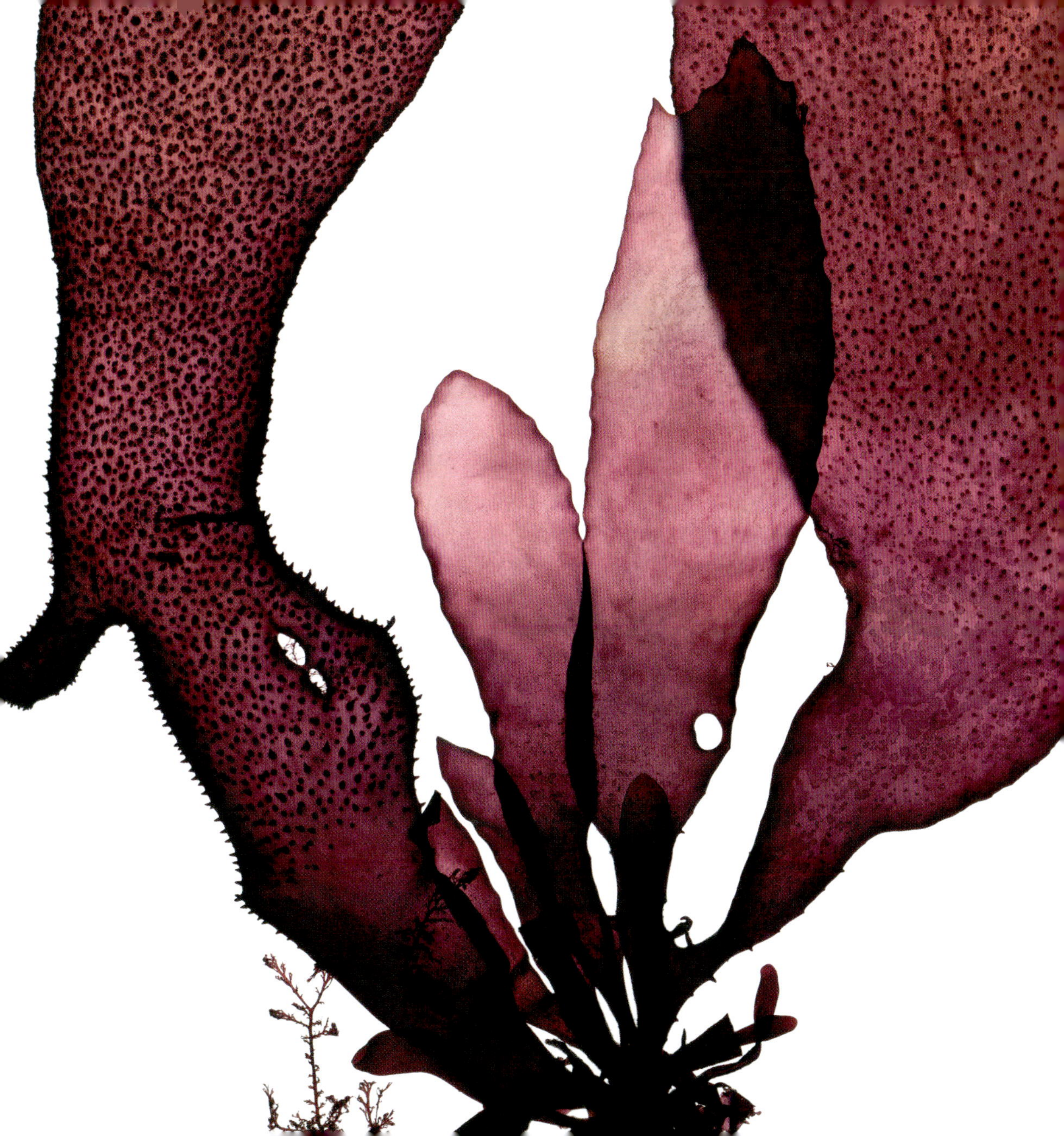

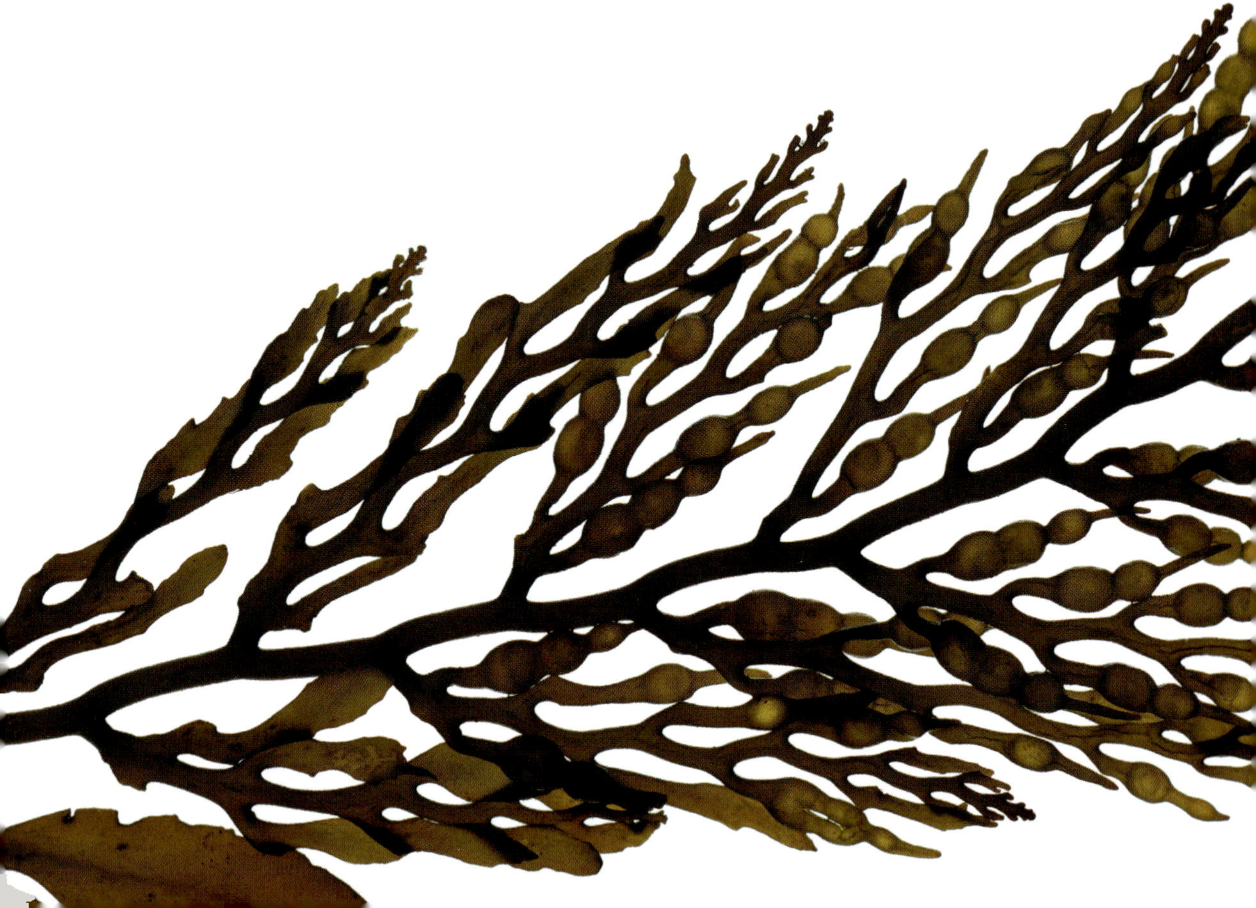

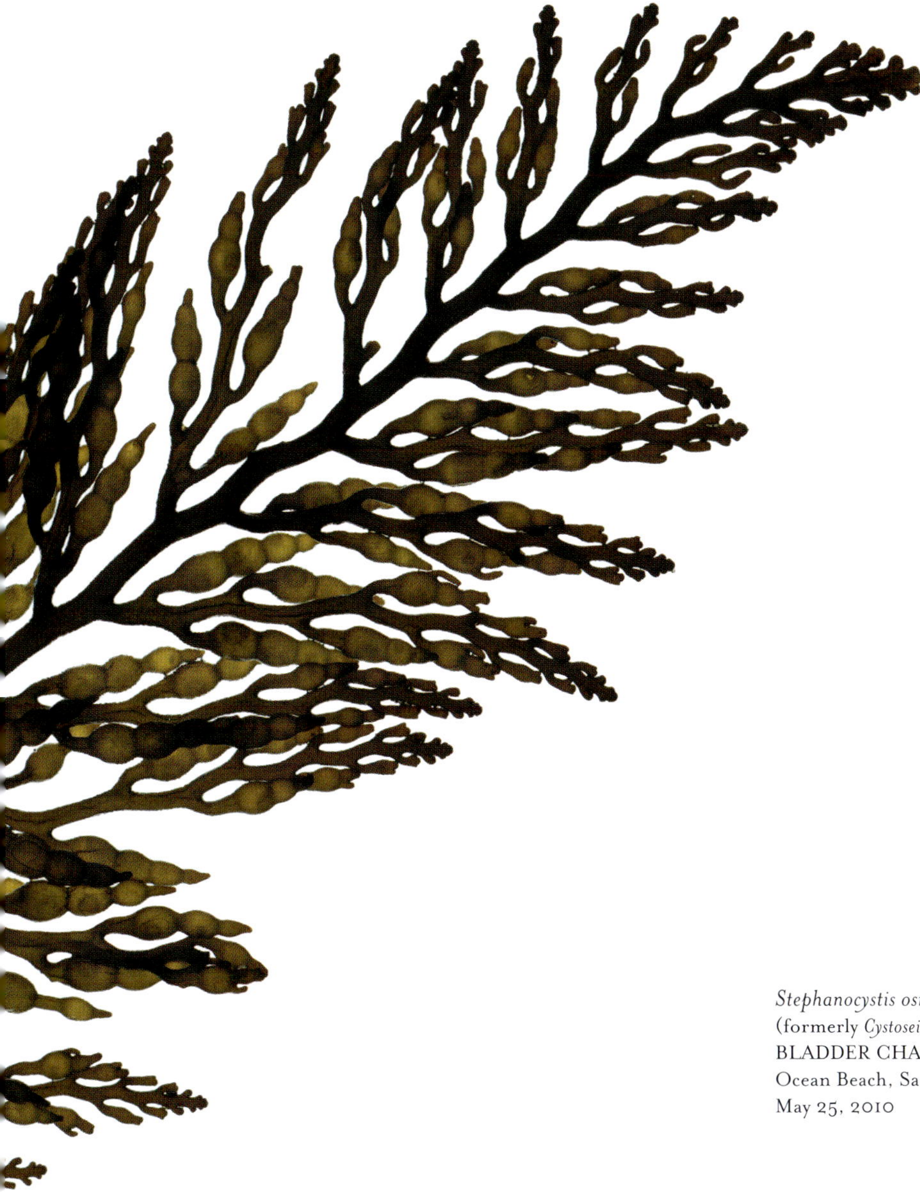

Stephanocystis osmundacea
(formerly *Cystoseira*)
BLADDER CHAIN WRACK
Ocean Beach, San Francisco, CA
May 25, 2010

Undaria pinnatifida

Wakame

Wakame is the Japanese common name for *Undaria pinnatifida*. It is "delicate and sweet with a clean flavor and aroma," reports Valerie Cooksley in her book *Seaweed*, good for soups and stews, and full of healthful fucoxanthin (a brown pigment), calcium, and iodine. *Undaria* is native to the seas of Japan and Korea, and it has been harvested there for centuries. In Korea, *Undaria* soup is served to new mothers for the two weeks after they give birth, the vital minerals passing to the new baby via breast milk for an auspicious beginning. Thereafter, it is served on birthdays as a reminder and celebration of this healthy and lucky first food.

Wakame, nori, kombu, and arame have not penetrated the American kitchen in any real way, despite the efforts of kelp farming advocates, the health consciousness of many Americans, and a love for sushi and Asian cuisine.

Among the places *Undaria* has landed with full force, however, are the bays and coasts where it is not native. This specimen was found on the docks of San Francisco Bay where, as in Santa Barbara, Monterey, and Half Moon Bays, it is considered a noxious invasive. Despite floating tastefully in your miso soup, *Undaria* is on the list of the world's one hundred worst invasive species. By outcompeting native species, algal invasives can prove disastrous to coastal ecosystems.

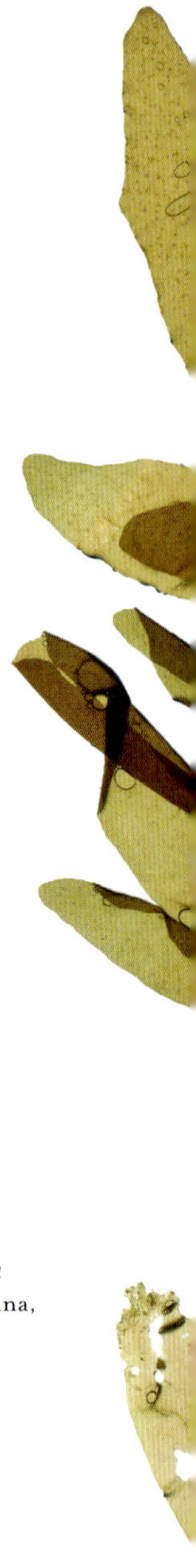

Undaria pinnatifida
San Francisco Marina,
San Francisco, CA
February 7, 2012

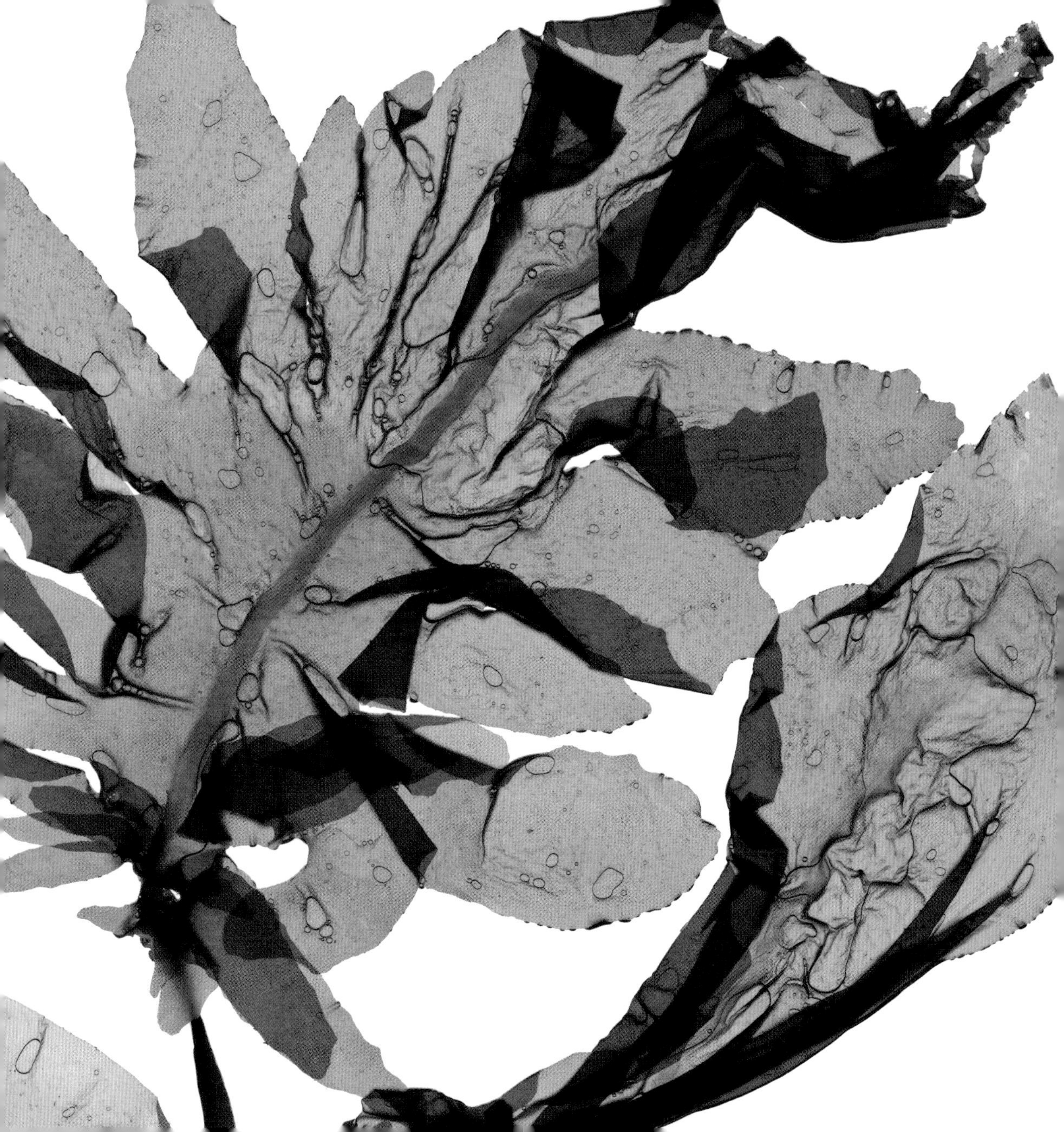

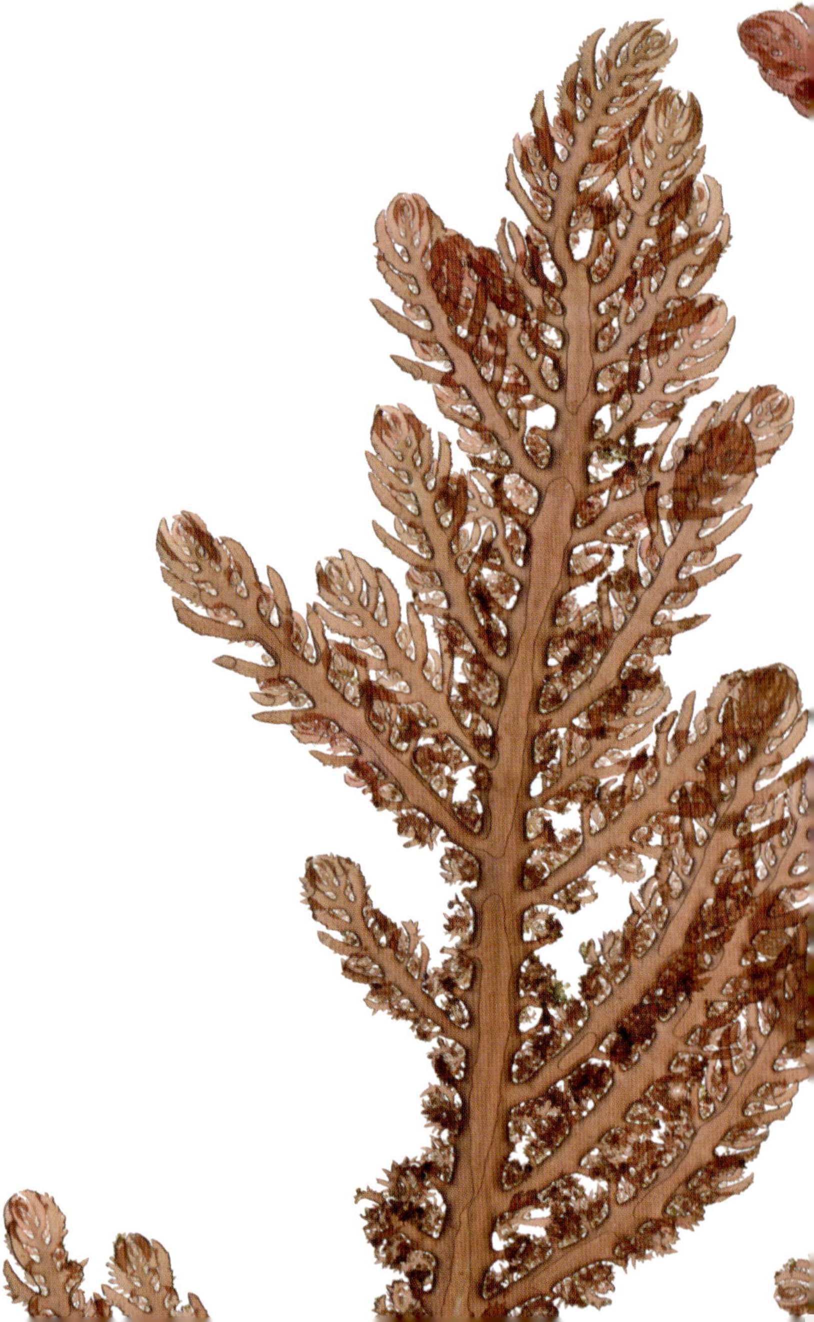

Ptilota densa
Cambria, CA
May 13, 2012

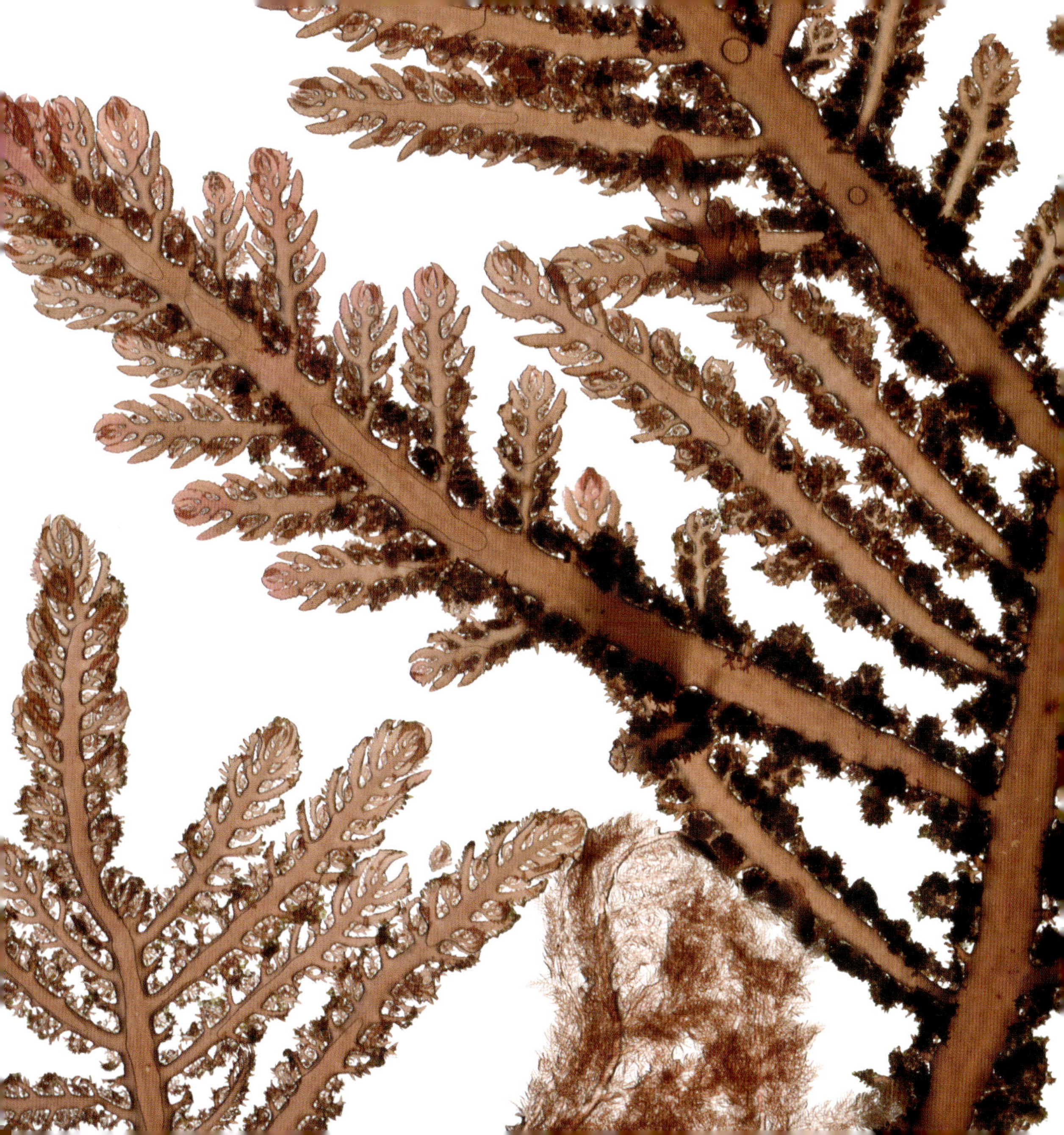

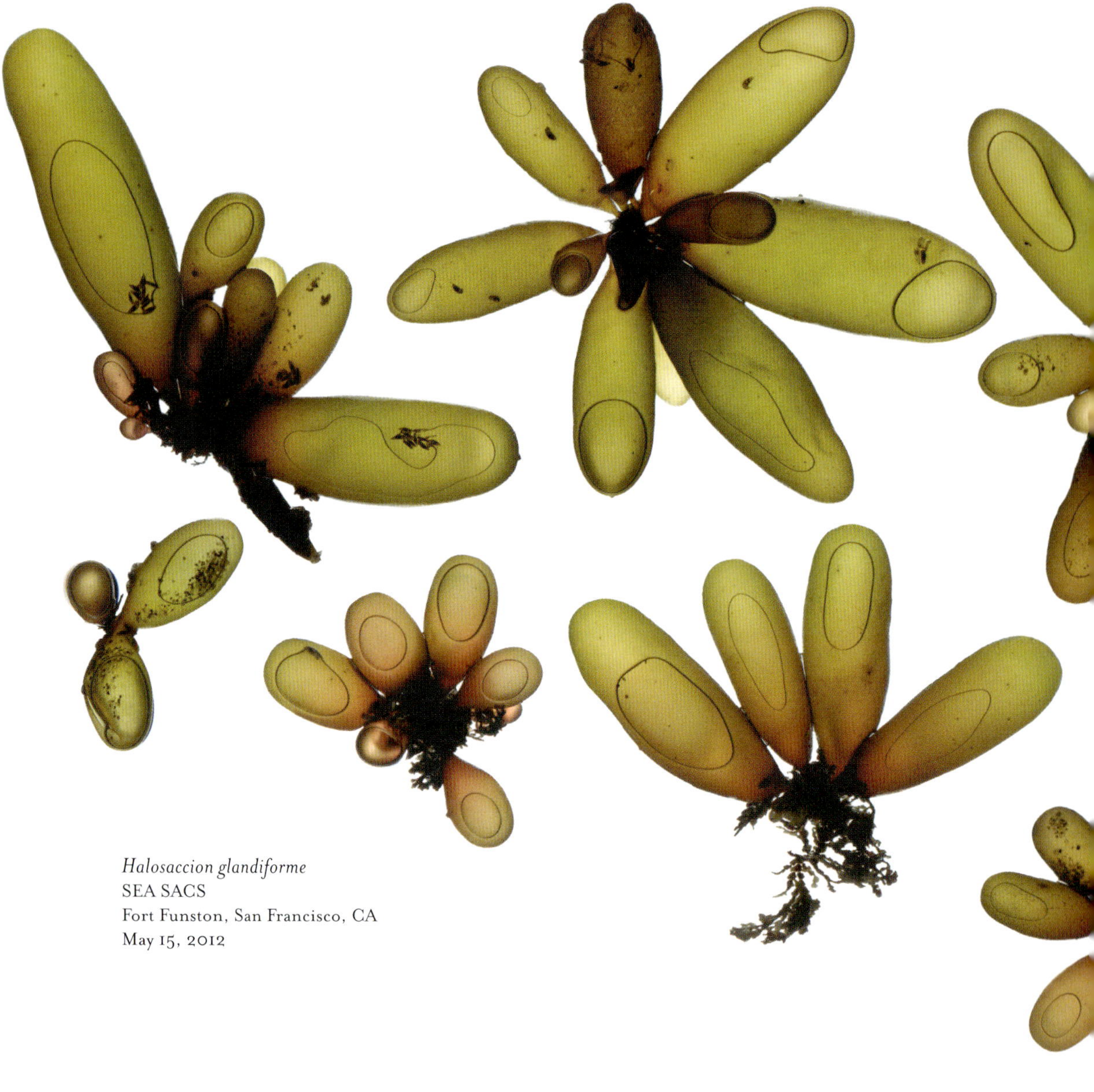

Halosaccion glandiforme
SEA SACS
Fort Funston, San Francisco, CA
May 15, 2012

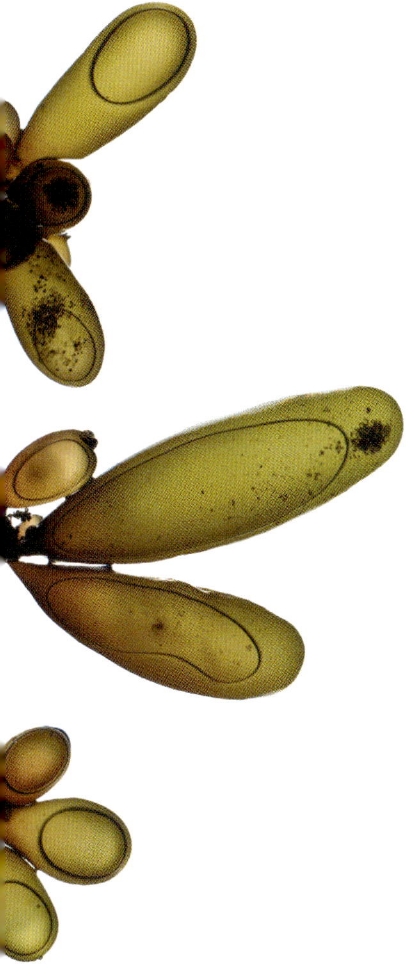

Halosaccion glandiforme

Sea Sacs

MAY 15, FORT FUNSTON, SAN FRANCISCO, CA. I have been descending the cliffs to walk the shore at Fort Funston twice a week for many years now, and every day the beach is different.

This morning, the halfway marker of my walk had reappeared. The fossil-studded rocks, buried and nearly forgotten over the past months, had returned, excavated to a rising massif by recent storms. Standing with the rocks looming sculpturally beside me, it was hard to imagine they had been underfoot just the week before. This massive transfer of sand is why there is no seaweed growing between the tides on this beach—there is nothing to hold on to. But there are plenty of seaweeds in the vicinity. The piles of jumbled wrack today include the funny sea sacs that fill up like water balloons to keep hydrated. Mysteriously, they litter the beach on this day and no other, reminding me of how little we know about the vibrant forests just out of sight beyond the breaking waves.

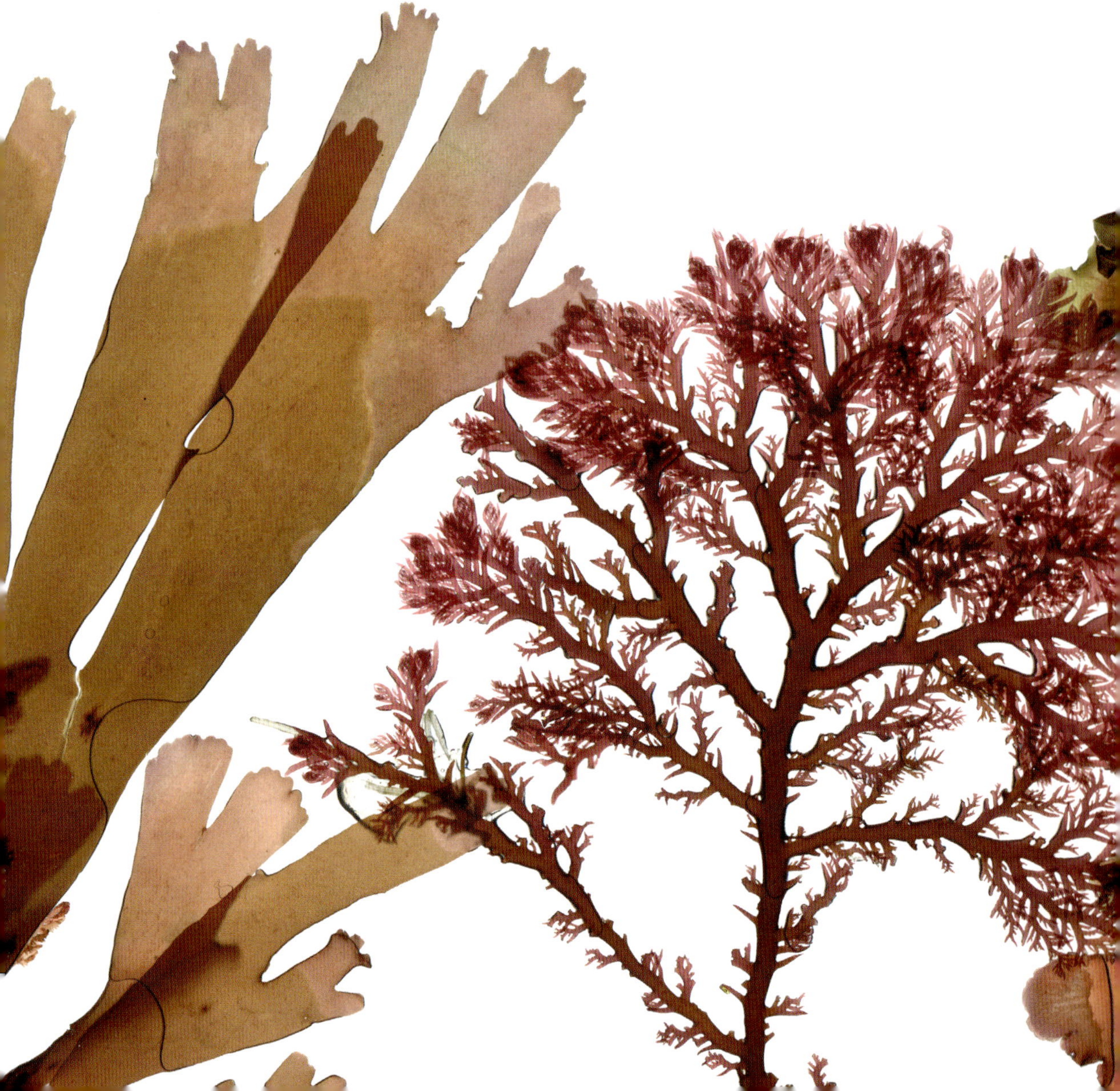

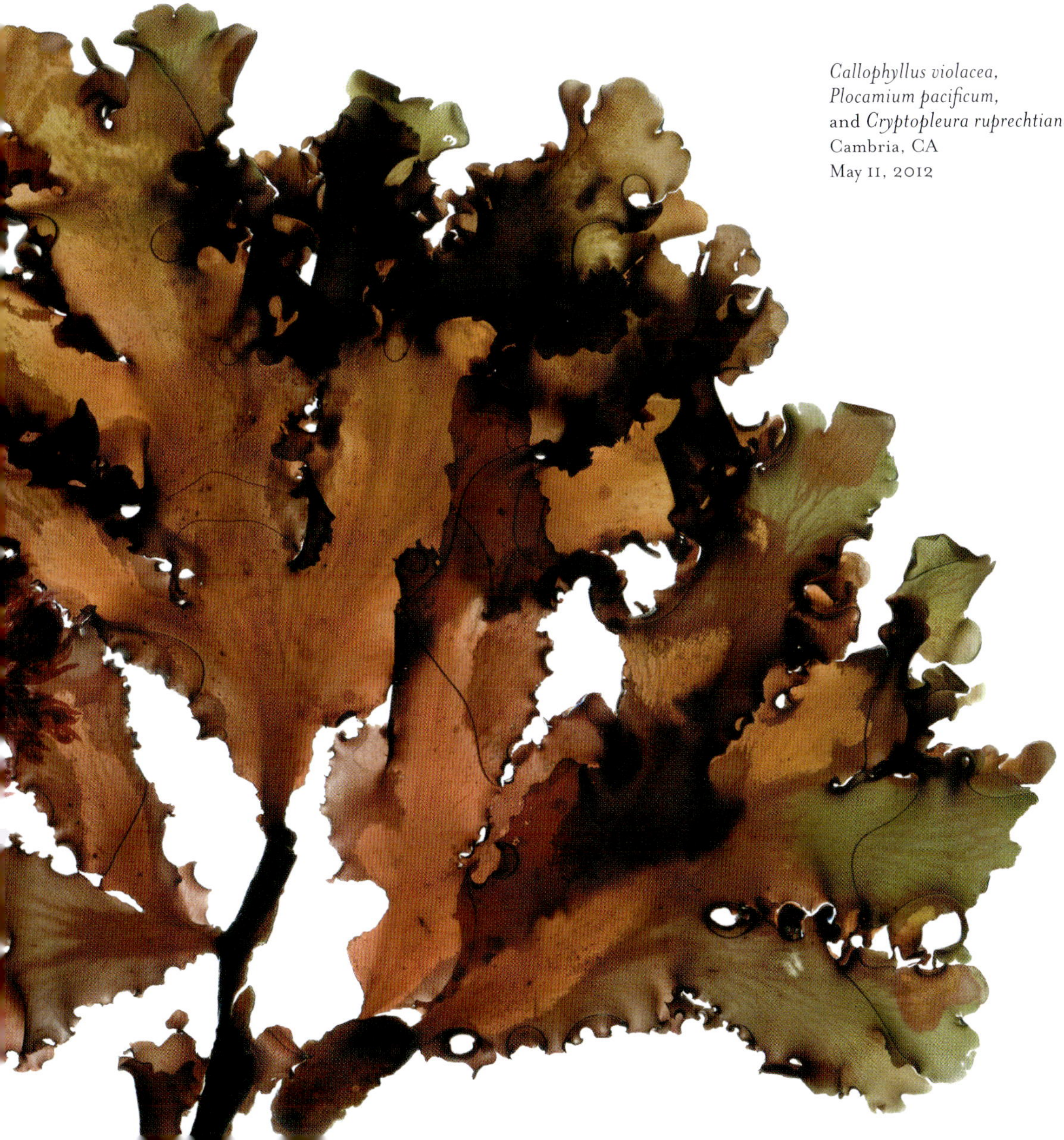

Callophyllus violacea,
Plocamium pacificum,
and *Cryptopleura ruprechtiana*
Cambria, CA
May 11, 2012

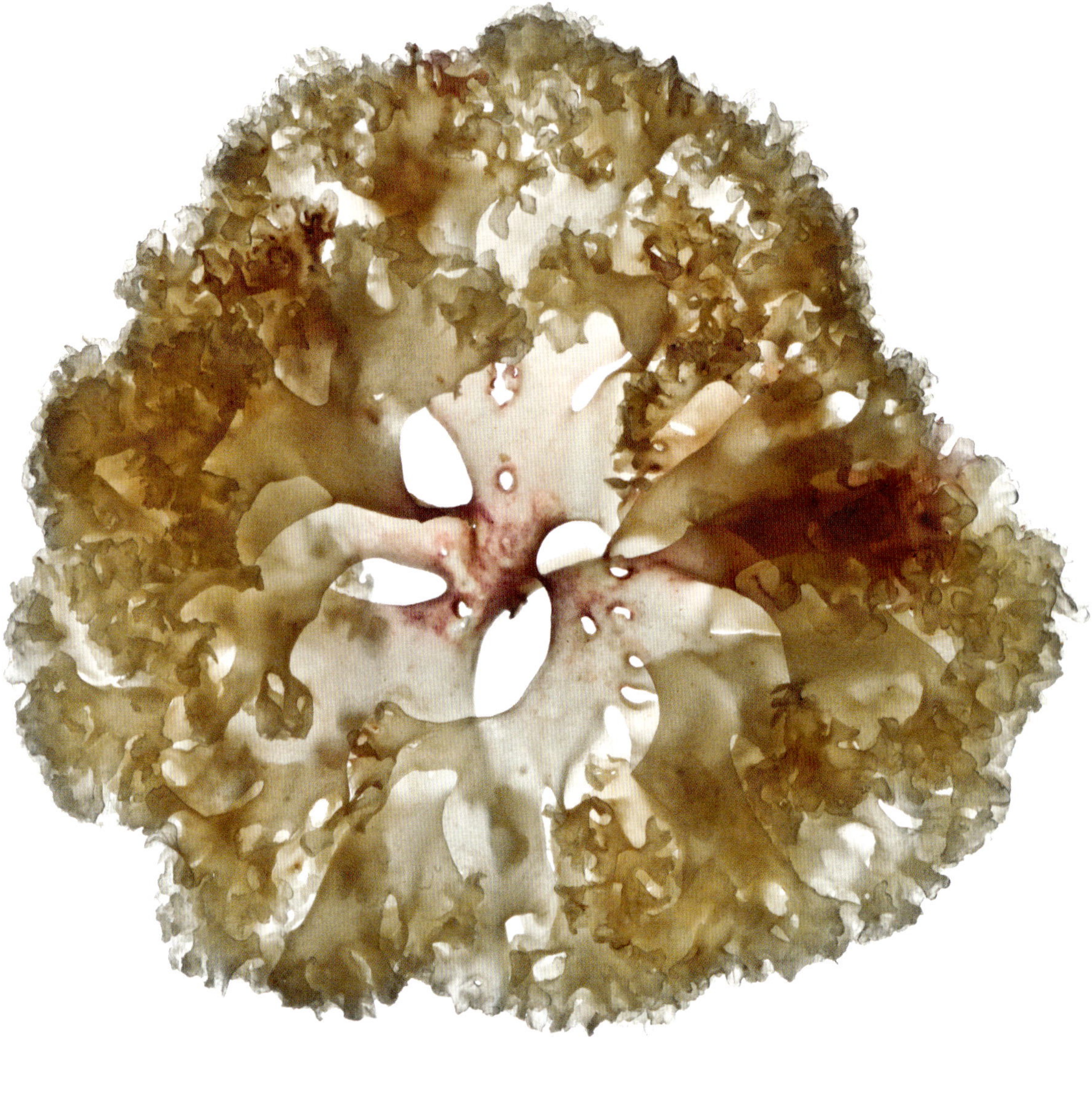

Chondrus crispus

Irish Moss

While some beachcombers might turn up their nose at a slimy piece of seaweed on the beach, they should not. Irish moss is famous for setting the frothy New England fanciness, blancmange, when boiled in milk, and what keeps seaweeds flexible and slippery is also what keeps ice cream, lipstick, and shaving cream smooth. There are three gelling or emulsifying agents that come from seaweed: alginate, carrageenan, and agar. Alginate comes from the alginic acid in the cell walls of kelps and other brown seaweeds. Carrageenan is a cell-wall phycocolloid found in a few specific species of red seaweed, especially *Chondrus crispus*. Agar and agarose, a more highly refined agar, are produced from a variety of red seaweeds, and are best known as the inert, gelatinous growing medium, rich in iodine and trace minerals, filling the petri dishes and DNA-sequencing rigs of university, hospital, and biotech labs around the world.

Marine algae also makes great fertilizer. It has the remarkable ability to concentrate minerals and trace elements from the sea into the soil, thus providing a potent source of nitrogen and potassium for vegetable cultivation. For centuries, storm-tossed seaweeds were gathered and worked into the shallow soils of the west coast areas of Ireland and Scotland, transforming poor soils into a richer mix, the health of the ocean filtering through the roots of every potato and cabbage grown.

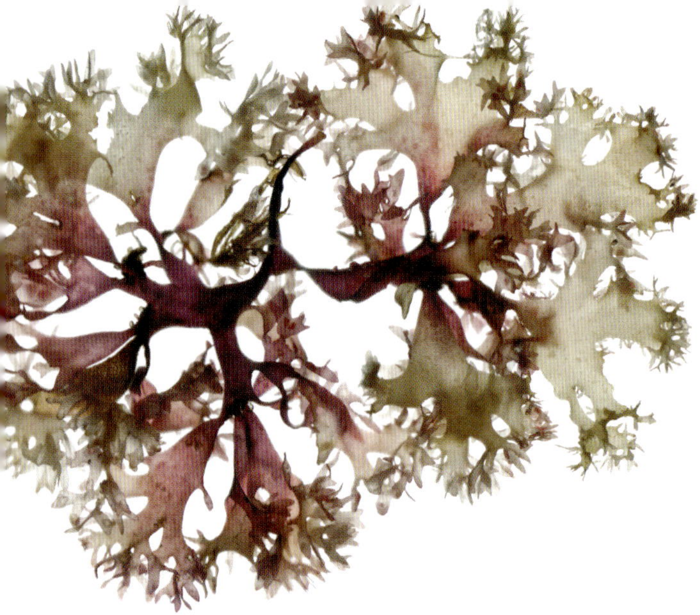

page 126, left, and opposite:
Chondrus crispus
IRISH MOSS
Brimstone Island, Penobscot Bay, ME
July 24, 2011

The Pudding Boys: How We Eat Algae

There is no signage, no visible activity, and no clue as to what goes on inside the seaweed factory in Rockland, Maine. Nor is there the identifying stench of years past, as the factory apparently modernized many years ago. The under-the-radar nature of this facility is like the seaweed industry as a whole: No one seems to know the important role seaweed plays in the goods we use every day. Our contemporary American diet is largely dependent upon seaweed derivatives, beginning in 1940 when Krim-ko, a small dairy company from Chicago, started making chocolate milk and could not keep the cocoa from settling to the bottom of the glass. Krim-ko set up a factory near Boston to manufacture a water extract of Irish moss, which, as an additive, kept the

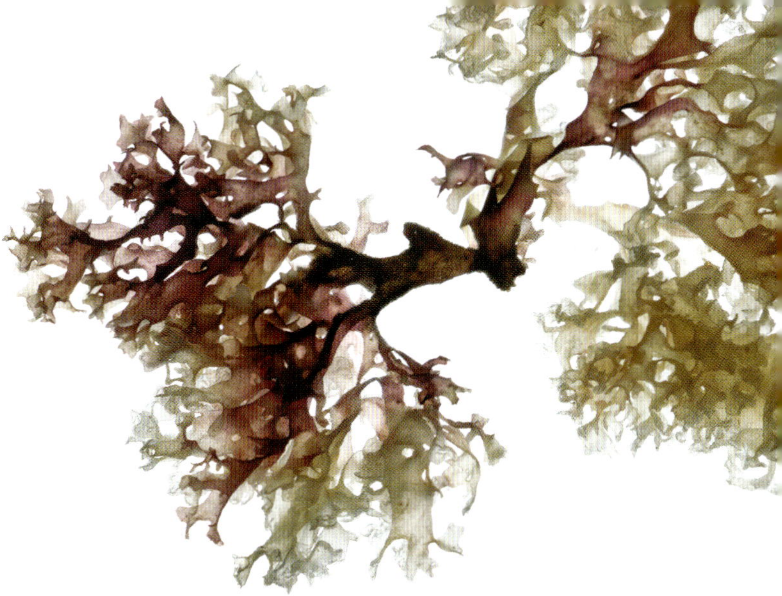

chocolate suspended in the milk. It was also used as the gelling agent in junket, and thus the "pudding boys," those chemical engineers who worked with seaweed for industry giants such as Kraft, Unilever, and Merck, went to work producing the carrageenan and alginate extracts that ensure that the products we use daily function as we expect them to—that the ingredients in toothpaste are bound together to be squeezed out of the tube; that ice cream stays creamy, not crystalline, in our mouths; that our boxed cake mixes can sit preserved for months on the cupboard shelf; or that textile dye is made the perfect consistency for excellent printing. Since the 1950s the manufacture of carrageenan, alginate, and agar from seaweed has been very big business. Anything that needs thickening, stabilizing, gelling, or smoothing uses carrageenan likely produced in the Rockland factory.

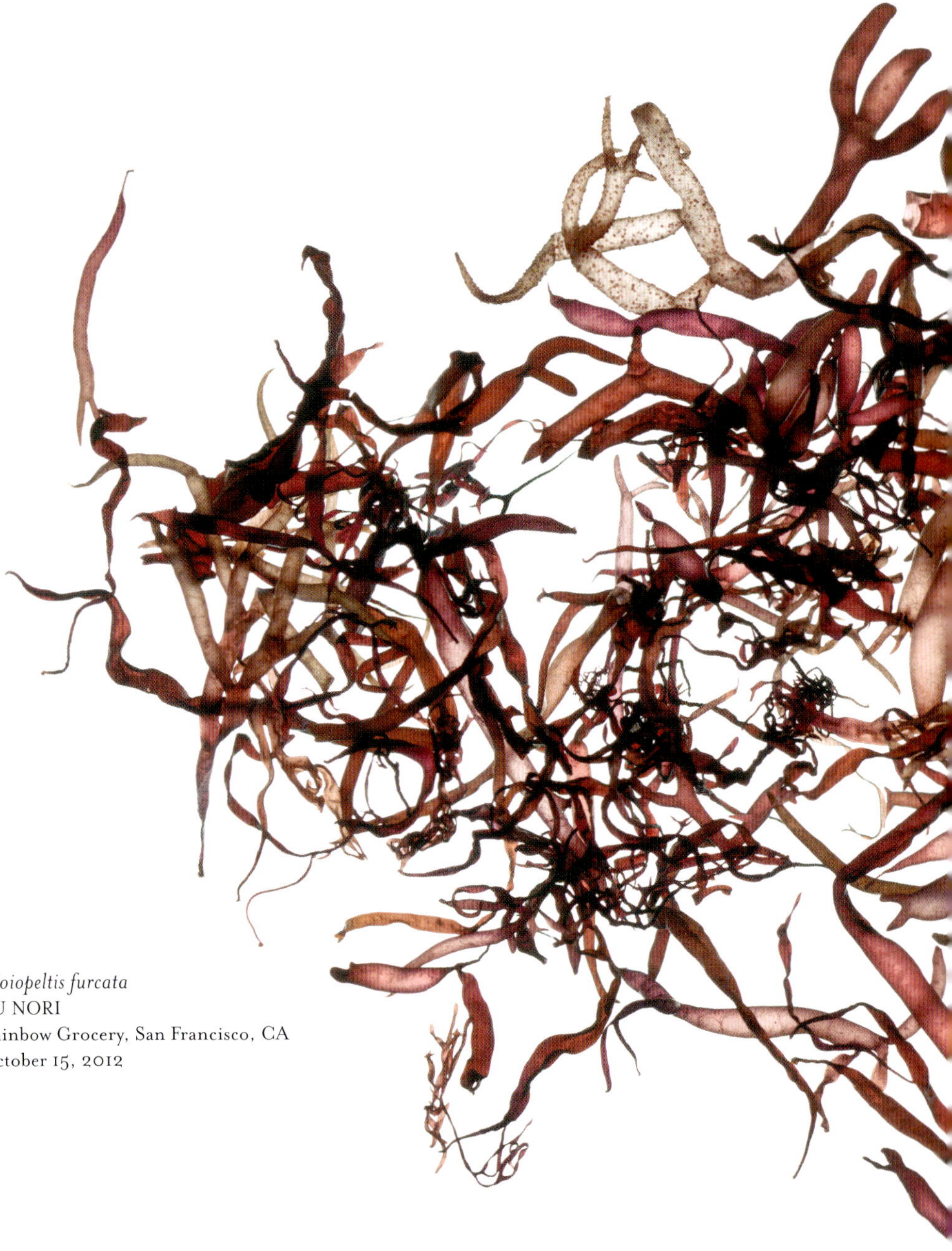

Gloiopeltis furcata
FU NORI
Rainbow Grocery, San Francisco, CA
October 15, 2012

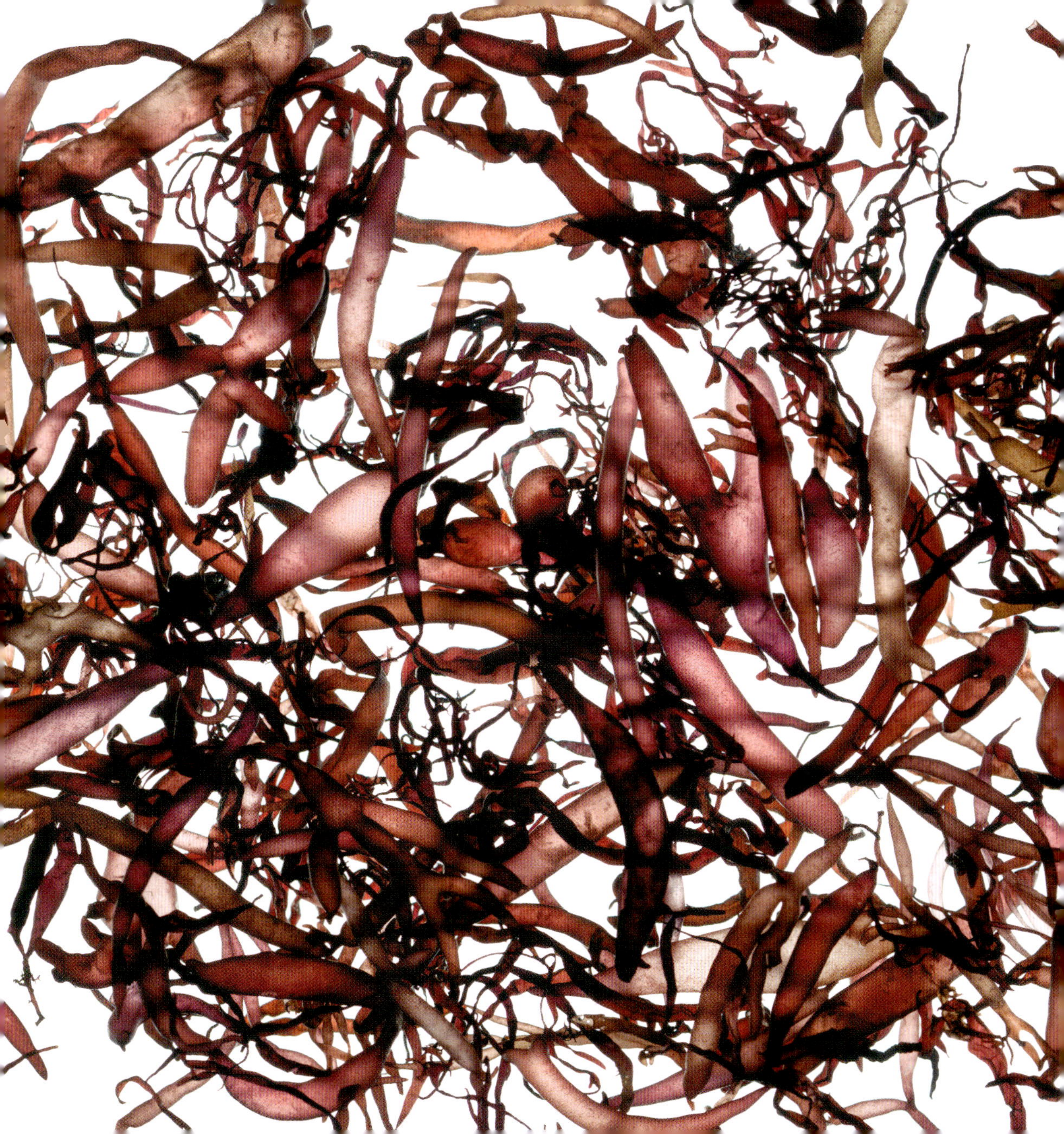

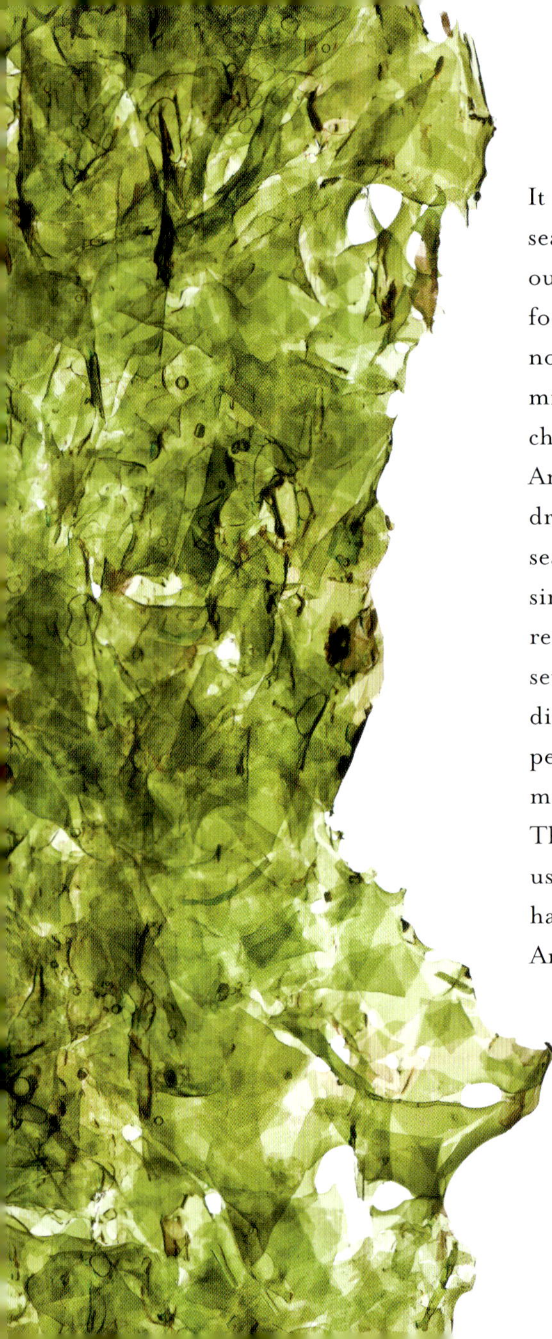

It is profound that the "American way" of using seaweed, one of the greatest dietary resources on our planet, has led to the dominance of processed foods in our culture. The pudding boys were not interested in the abundance of vitamins and minerals in seaweed, only the nondigestible characteristics needed for smoothing and gelling. And so we have Velveeta cheese, creamy salad dressing, and sliced bread that won't dry out. But seaweed has been supporting the human species since the very beginning. In 1975 the archaeological remains of a twelve-thousand-year-old human settlement at Monte Verde in southern Chile was discovered. Among the artifacts preserved in the peat bogs were the clear remains of nine species of marine algae from distant beaches and estuaries. These seaweed relics, confirmed to have been used as food and medicine by the ancient people, have stirred intense debate as to how the earliest Americans came to inhabit the continents.

left and opposite:
Trader Joe's
Roasted Seaweed Snack
Palo Alto, CA
September 27, 2010

It was accepted for years that the earliest humans arrived via the Bering Strait land bridge and then slowly populated the southern Americas as hunter-gatherers. The Monte Verde site, however, predates the glacier melt throughout Canada, when overland routes would have been impassable. It is now postulated that the kelp beds along the west coasts of North and South America created a nutrition highway along which the first humans traveled either by boat or along the shore, eating the abundant shellfish and seaweed there. Rowan Jacobsen, in his small book, *The Living Shore*, makes a compelling case that the oysters, clams, seaweeds, crabs, and fish from the shallow ocean estuaries and beaches of the time (many miles out from today's shoreline) provided the fatty acids (important omega-3s), iodine, and other minerals essential for human brain development. He points out that the complex human brain required a very specific mix of nutrients to develop as it did—nutrients found only in shellfish, fish, and seaweed. Iodine, in particular, gave our evolving brain the boost it needed to create language and fully realized societies.

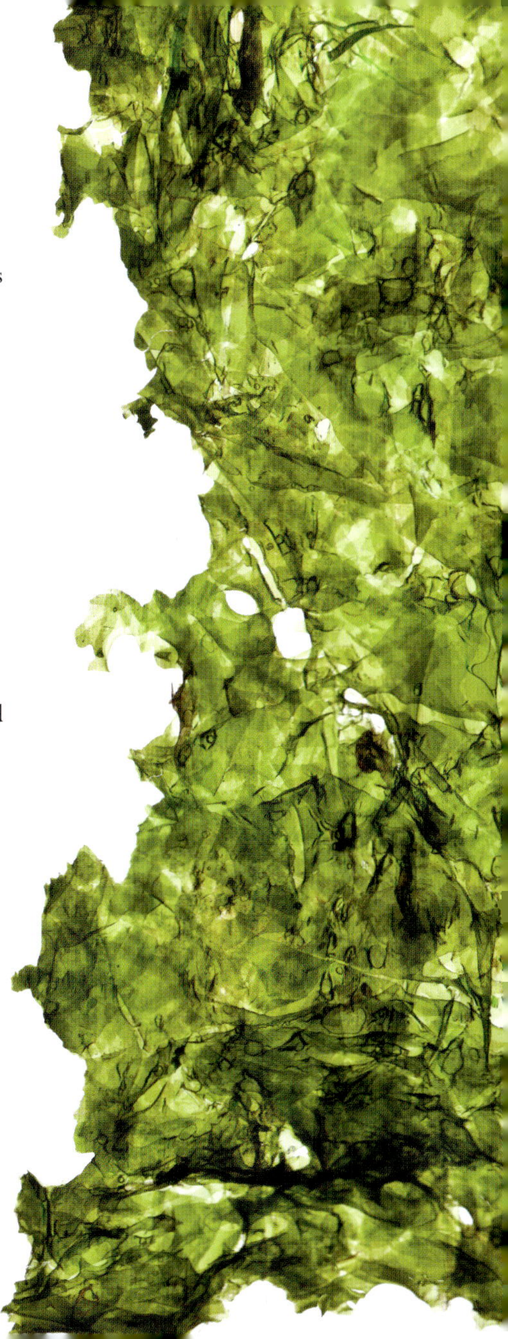

Exploration

Postels and Ruprecht

The hand-colored lithograph that introduces the Postels and Ruprecht portfolio *Illustrationes Algarum* shows a pair of Russian navy sailors on the rocky shore of what was likely present-day Alaska, c. 1830. One has his arms laden with bulky kelp, while the other, holding tight to a sapling to keep from slipping, pulls a long *Laminaria* up from the water world onto the dry land to which the soldiers are clearly limited. This terrestrial world, painstakingly rendered with tree trunks and moss, is, however, relegated to the top third of the lithograph. The majority of the image, clearly delineated by the surface of the water, depicts the realm of the seaweeds beneath the tide. Colored in greens, golds, and reds are masses of *Nereocystis*,

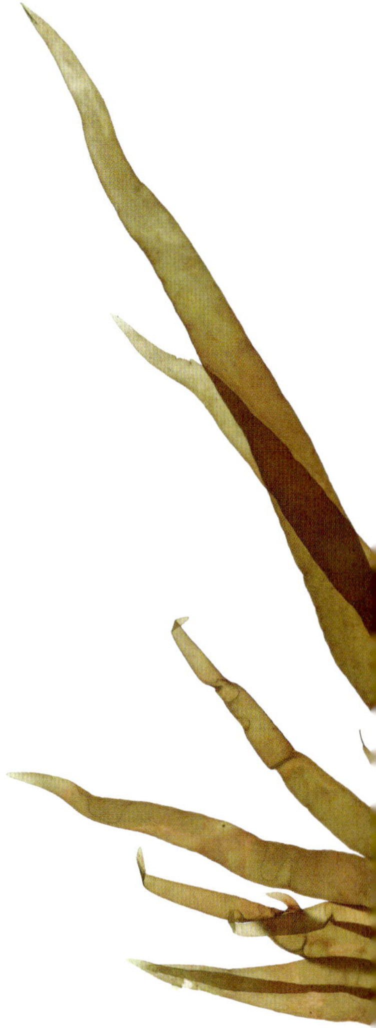

Prionitis sternbergii
Cambria, CA
May 12, 2012

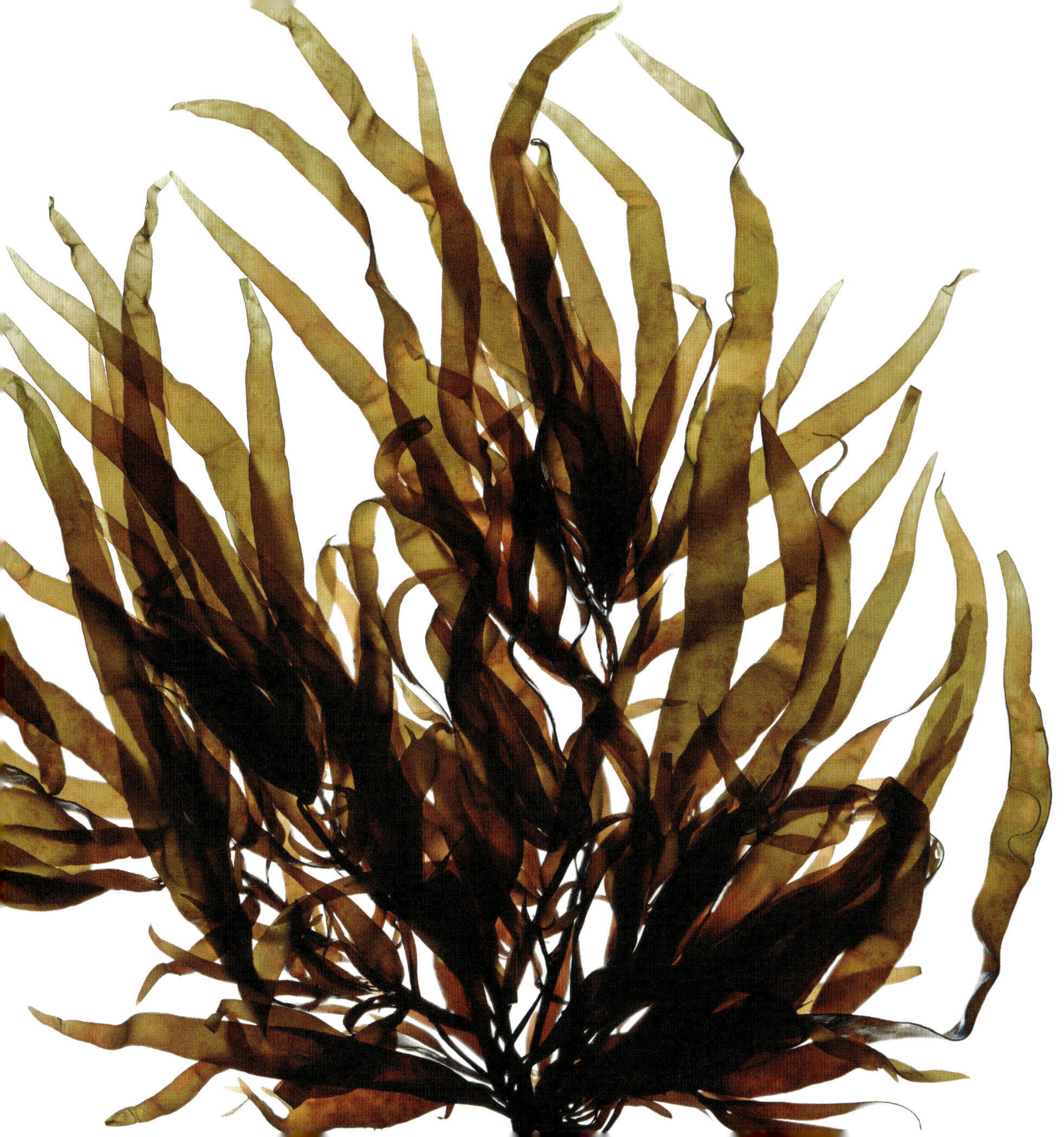

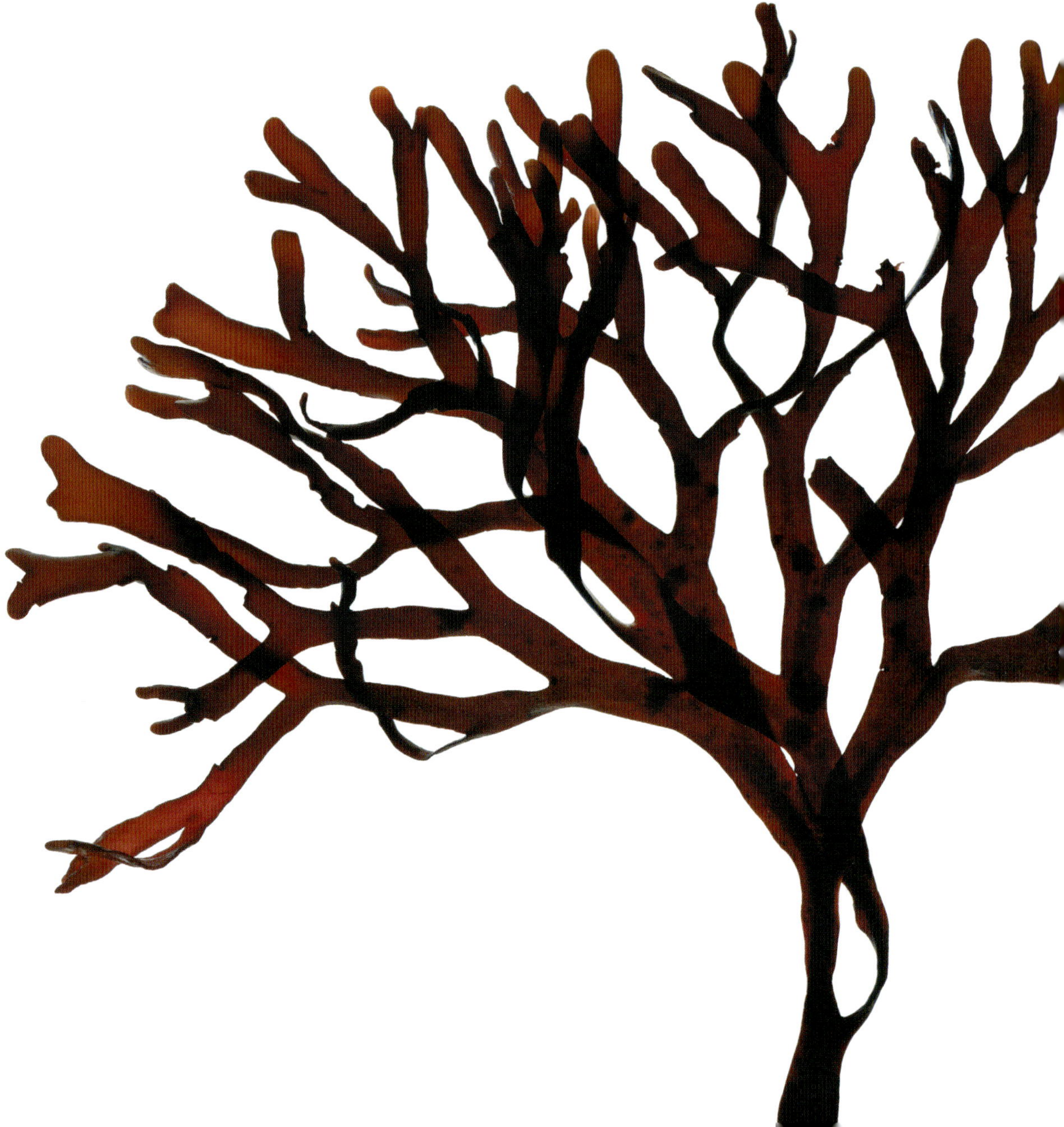

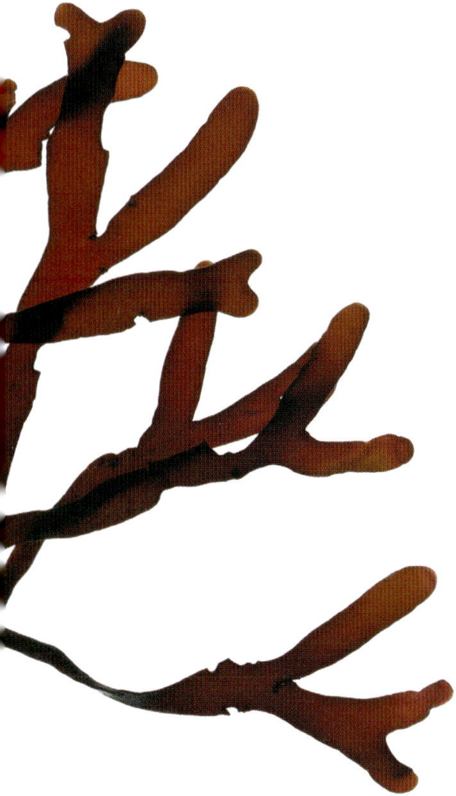

Fredericqia chiton
(formerly *Gymnogongrus chiton*)
Cambria, CA
May 13, 2012

Macrocystis, *Alaria*, and *Mazzaella*, bent with the current, their holdfasts connected to a rocky bottom. Clearly the soldiers cannot see this world right below them. Neither can we. It takes a steadfast sense of exploration, a willingness to put on boots and wade out into slippery terrain, or to pick up what might initially seem repellent when walking the beach, to learn about this secret life of seaweed. If we love the beach and all it is trying to teach us about our connection to the oceans, it is worth the effort.

Afterword

Seaweed is most emphatically of the ocean until the tide recedes and leaves it clinging to its rocks, a marker of the transition from one realm to another. It regains its fluid composure as the tide rises, revitalized into the array of shapes and forms you see on these pages. This book covers only a minute subset of the thousands of species of marine algae. Most of the specimens here were found as wrack or drift. This is typical for both annuals, where the entire organism loses hold each year (*Nereocystis* and *Postelsia*), and perennials, where the majority of the blades slough off while the holdfast continues producing the next season (*Egregia* and *Macrocystis*). These specimens were brought back to my studio and placed on the scanner either wet or dry. My goal was to make a true portrait of each one, letting the color and form speak as directly as possible, to prompt questions and investigations.

As a beachcomber I have become more attentive to the status of where I am. Fortunately, there are a growing number of marine reserves around the world where the adjacent coast is protected and artifacts cannot be taken unless a permit is obtained. This kind of care should extend to every beach we are on. Seaweed is typically abundant, but the rise in ocean temperatures puts stress on these essential organisms. They deserve our utmost respect. As we explore the intertidal world, we must look carefully and with consideration; seaweed is generous in providing habitat, protecting and nurturing the hundreds of organisms that depend on it to survive the whims of the moon and tide. As always, the beach is a portal into our ocean world and a source of inspiration. We must treat it kindly.

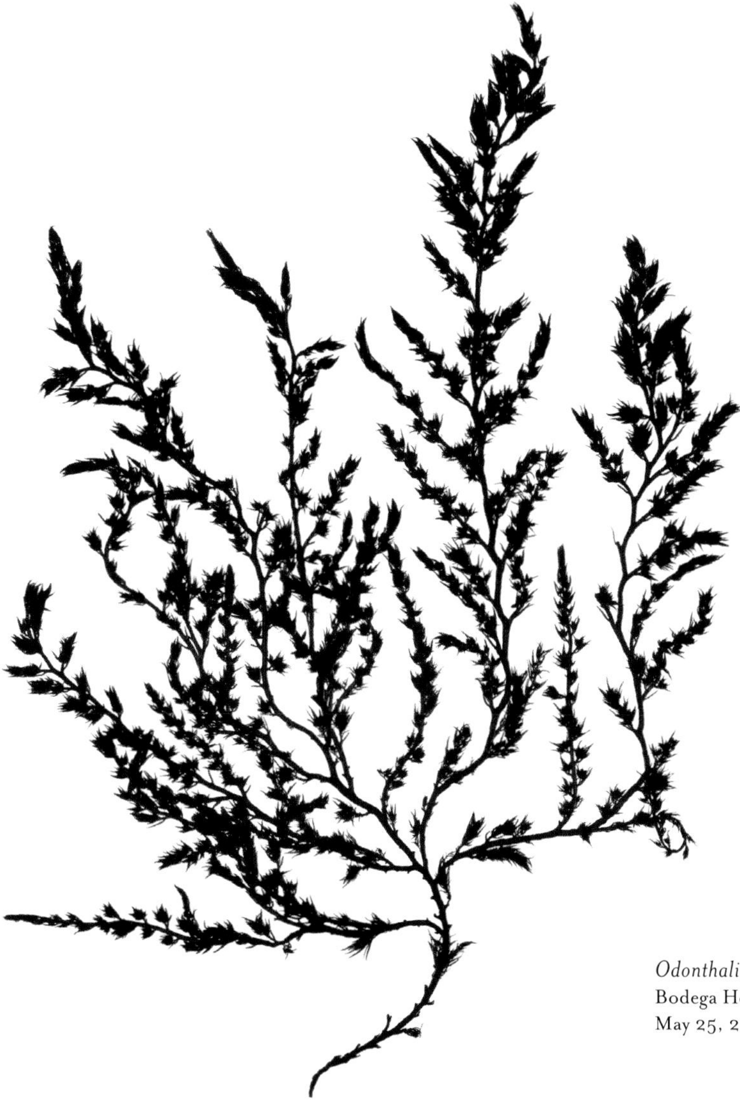

Odonthalia floccosa
Bodega Head, CA
May 25, 2010

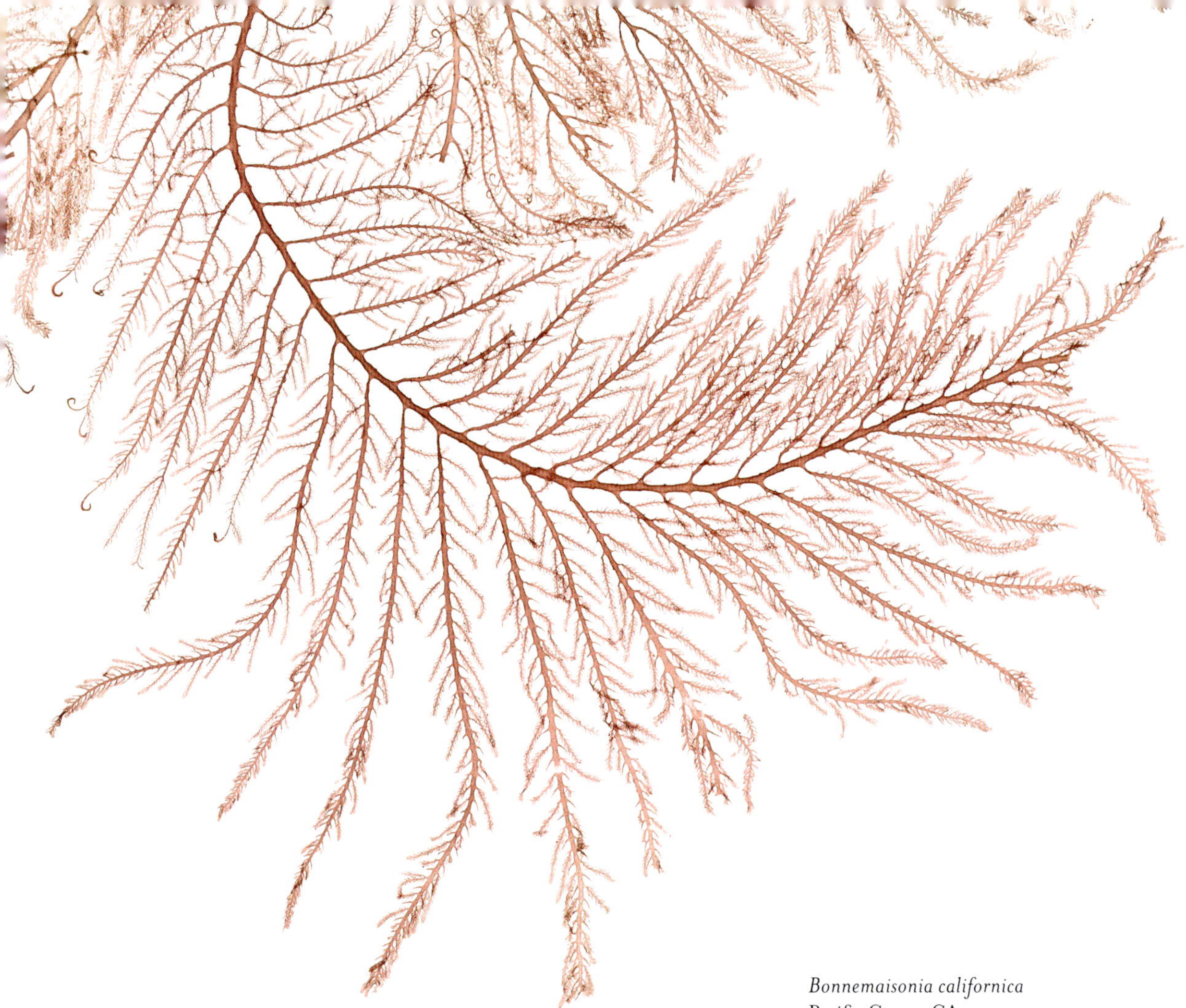

Bonnemaisonia californica
Pacific Grove, CA
c. 1880
Collection: University Herbarium
UC Berkeley, CA

Acknowledgments/Further Reading

My greatest thanks go to the plethora of marine scientists and graduate students who have welcomed an artist into their midst and shared their vast knowledge and love of the seaweeds with me. The Phycological Society of America (PSA) has been especially supportive and I count these remarkable seaweed knowledge-holders as close friends. The PSA has generously donated to the reprinting of this book. Thank you! My current work has moved into ocean advocacy and I thank my partner Marianna Leuschel and the fellow artists in the Above/Below collective for helping combine art and design thinking with a deep understanding of natural history to highlight the extraordinary worlds of kelp and seaweed, emphasizing their resilience in the face of changing oceans.

The resilience of this little book is a testament to a mission that looks to art and design as a way in to a deep understanding of these remarkable, essential, yet under-recognized organisms: the flora of the oceans. Publishing books on seaweed is a leap of faith, so my heartfelt thanks go to Kim Hogeland and the Oregon State University Press for taking a chance on the re-release of this book. My hope is that it continues to inspire young ocean scientists and writers from a variety of backgrounds, as well as artists of all sorts who care about the oceans, from illustrators to quiltmakers to tattoo artists.

For additional reading, there are now many books and cookbooks with great information about seaweed, but Rachel Carson's *The Edge of The Sea* (1955) remains the pinnacle of lyrical prose about the interconnectedness of life in coastal waters. A next step would be to read my book *The Curious World of Seaweed* (2019), which takes a deeper dive into the art and science of ocean flora.

Index of Images

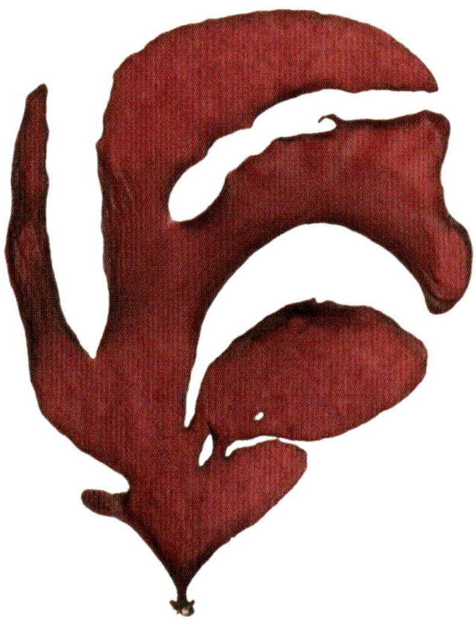

REDS Phylum Rhodophyta

NOTE: Many seaweed genus names are changing due to new research. For up-to-date information on seaweed names,visit www.algaebase.org.

opposite:
Dilsea californica
Bodega Head, CA
May 31, 2010

overleaf:
Macrocystis pyrifera
(sporophyll blades)
Cambria, CA
May 12, 2012

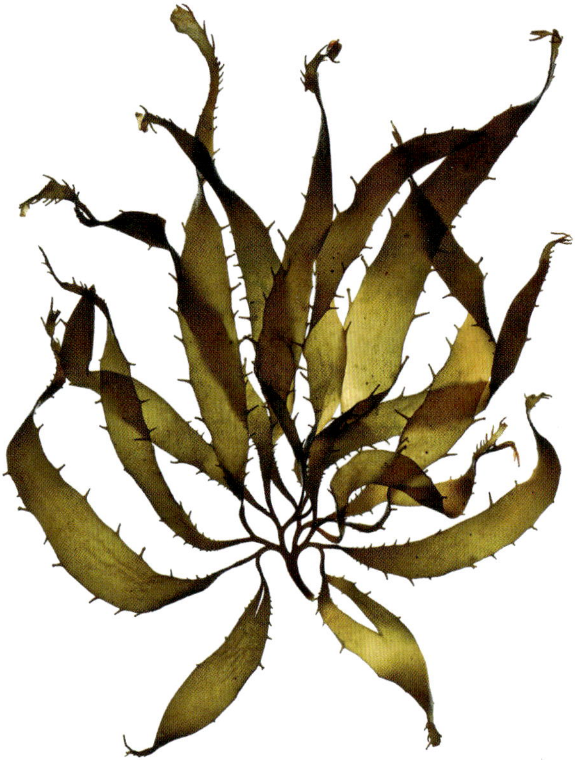